THE LOST SAMURAI SCHOOL

THE LOST SAMURAI SCHOOL

SECRETS OF MUBYŌSHI RYŪ

Antony Cummins

with Mieko Koizumi

BLUE SNAKE BOOKS
BERKELEY, CALIFORNIA

Published by Blue Snake Books, an imprint of North Atlantic Books
Huichin, unceded Ohlone land
aka Berkeley, California

Cover art or photo by unknown.
Cover design by Howie Seversan
Book design by Brad Greene

Printed in the United States of America

The Lost Samurai School: Secrets of Mubyōshi Ryū is sponsored and published by North Atlantic Books, an educational nonprofit based in the unceded Ohlone land Huichin (aka Berkeley, CA) that collaborates with partners to develop cross-cultural perspectives; nurture holistic views of art, science, the humanities, and healing; and seed personal and global transformation by publishing work on the relationship of body, spirit, and nature.

North Atlantic Books' publications are distributed to the US trade and internationally by Penguin Random House Publishers Services. For further information, visit our website at www.northatlanticbooks.com.

PLEASE NOTE: The creators and publishers of this book disclaim any liabilities for loss in connection with following any of the practices, exercises, and advice contained herein. To reduce the chance of injury or any other harm, the reader should consult a professional before undertaking this or any other martial arts, movement, meditative arts, health, or exercise program. The instructions and advice printed in this book are not in any way intended as a substitute for medical, mental, or emotional counseling with a licensed physician or healthcare provider.

Library of Congress Cataloging-in-Publication Data

Names: Cummins, Antony, author; Koizumi, Mieko, author.
Title: The lost samurai school : secrets of Mubyoshi Ryu / Antony Cummins.
Description: Berkeley, California : North Atlantic Books, 2016.
Identifiers: LCCN 2016017044 (print) | LCCN 2016030735 (ebook) |
   ISBN 9781623170875 (paperback) | ISBN 9781623170882 (ebook)
Subjects: LCSH: Swordplay—Japan. | Martial arts—Japan. | Samurai. | BISAC:
   SPORTS & RECREATION / Martial Arts & Self-Defense. | HISTORY / Asia / Japan.
Classification: LCC GV1150.C86 2016 (print) | LCC GV1150 (ebook) |
   DDC 796.80952—dc23
LC record available at https://lccn.loc.gov/2016017044

3 4 5 6 7 8 9 5LP 26 25 24 23 22

To the memory of Niki Shinjūrō and Hagiwara Jūzō, the core founders of Mubyōshi Ryū, who collected these skills together in defense against their enemies. Also to Kaneko Kichibei, who kept the school alive.

CONTENTS

ACKNOWLEDGMENTS

I would like to thank the current grandmaster of Mubyōshi Ryū, Uematsu Yoshiyuki Sensei, for his help and enthusiasm in this project. Also to Joe Swift, his longtime student and core adviser on this venture; without him it would be all the poorer. Also his colleague Kawasaki Yūki. Thanks to Hashimoto Yoshiyuki for his help with acquiring some of the texts. Finally to Yoshie Minami, who supplied many of the translations for this book, especially the *shinobi* teachings and secret scrolls.

AN INTRODUCTION TO THE LOST SCHOOL

MUBYŌSHI RYŪ AT A GLANCE

Mubyōshi Ryū is a samurai warfare school from the Kaga domain from around the time of the fourth lord of Kaga, Maeda Tsunanori (1643–1724), who is sometimes also considered the fifth lord. The school appears to have been established in the mid to late seventeenth century, with some of the earliest scroll transcriptions dated to around the 1670s. The school itself contains a collection of "civilian" samurai skills,[1] concentrating more on personal protection than battlefield warfare, including the arts of the *shinobi* and some esoteric magic. The origins appear to center on a samurai named Hagiwara Jūzō and his colleague Niki Shinjūrō, who as contemporaries appear on nearly all the school scrolls. The name Mubyōshi Ryū (無拍子流), which can also be pronounced as Muhyōshi Ryū, is best translated as "the school with no discernible rhythm" or "the school that has no gap between event and reaction."

無: without
拍子: rhythm
流: school

The name implies that a student of the school will be a samurai who has no identifiable gaps in their skills and defenses, making their offensive and defensive skills complete and whole. Furthermore, as discussed in the schools original scrolls, the name implies that a student of the school shows no delay between an event and the student's reaction. According to the school's introduction within the *Yawara Jo* scroll, *mubyōshi* is the lack of distance between the beat of a hand clapping and the echoing sound it produces. This means that the student is without gap in their ability to react in combat and that no discernible shape can be found in their strategy.

Mubyōshi Ryū is considered to be connected to the school named Shinjin Ryū (深甚流), which infers a connection to the famed swordsman Kusabuka

Jinshirō. Mubyōshi Ryū continued down the centuries, taught in the Kaga domain throughout Japan's Edo Period when the Tokugawa clan ruled the land. Student records show that the school was healthy and thriving until the end of the period of peace and lasted beyond the end of the samurai themselves, which came about with the Meiji Restoration in 1868. It was at this time—just before the fall of the samurai—that a man named Kaneko Kichibei (1795–1858) really pushed the school to probably its highest level of popularity. After this point it began to decline. Some of the school's teachings are now no longer a part of the "living tradition," a percentage of which have been lost forever while some have been preserved through scrolls that remain in multiple collections. The most recent and still current grandmaster of the school is Uematsu Yoshiyuki, who lives and runs his *dōjō* in Nonoichi within the Ishikawa Prefecture—previously the Kaga domain. Mubyōshi Ryū lives on through Uematsu's dedicated efforts, through a traditional dance found in the local area, in various scrolls in library and personal collections, and now within this book. Mubyōshi Ryū, the school that gives a person "no discernible rhythm," is a thrilling and motivating facet of Japanese culture that deserves its place in Japanese history and world recognition to live on alongside its more famous counterparts.

UEMATSU YOSHIYUKI SENSEI

Uematsu Sensei was born in Nagasaki on New Year's Day, 1948. He began his initiation into Zen Buddhism training at the age of nine under his uncle Mori Gohō in Saga, and received tutelage in the martial arts (mostly Okinawan karate) from Mori. He moved to Ishikawa Prefecture at the age of twenty-four to join the Sōjiji Temple in Monzen. He opened the Mushinkan Dōjō shortly thereafter. He continues his martial arts study with Shinkage Ryū *(iaijutsu)* and Mubyōshi Ryū *(jūjutsu),* among others.

Figure 1.1. Uematsu Yoshiyuki, 15th Grandmaster of Mubyōshi Ryū,[2] 11th Grandmaster of Mukaku Ryū

JOE SWIFT

Joe is a native of upstate New York and has lived in Japan since 1994. He has been training in the martial arts since 1985, has been a student of Uematsu Sensei since 1995, and has operated the Tokyo branch of the Mushinkan since 2001. He works as a meteorologist, and in his spare time translates Okinawan karate texts from Japanese to English.

Figure 1.2.
Joe Swift

ANTONY CUMMINS

Antony is an author and historical researcher. He concentrates on investigating and disseminating the history of the Japanese shinobi. Taking on the role of project manager and producer, Antony, with the Historical Ninjutsu Research Team, has translated and published multiple shinobi and samurai manuals, including *The Book of Ninja*, *The Book of Samurai*, *Iga and Koka Ninja Skills*, *The Secret Traditions of the Shinobi*, *True Path of the Ninja*, and *Samurai War Stories*. He has also published his own works on the samurai and shinobi, *In Search of the Ninja* and *Samurai and Ninja*. Antony has appeared in the TV documentaries *Samurai Head Hunters*, *Ninja Shadow Warriors*, *Samurai Warrior Queens*, *The 47 Ronin*, and *Ninja*.

Figure 1.3.
Antony Cummins

SUPPORT ARTISTS

Andrija Dreznjak

Andrija Dreznjak was born in 1985 in Serbia and graduated from the University of Niš after studying Law. Andrija's hobbies include painting, sculpting, and graphic design. He has worked with Antony Cummins on a few projects, including *Secrets of the Ninja*. He lives in Serbia and works as a freelance sculptor, graphic designer, comic book artist, and script writer for graphic novels.

Figure 1.4.
Andrija Dreznjak

3

James Baker

James Baker is a Cuban American multimedia artist from Indiana. He holds a bachelors in media arts and science from the Indiana University School of Informatics and Computing, where he studied new media. He has also studied various martial arts and has always been fascinated by the ninja. Currently James resides in Indianapolis, where he enjoys making alternative media with a DIY ethic.

Figure 1.5.
James Baker

Richard Couck

Richard Couck is a machine builder by trade who lives in metro Detroit and has over fifteen years' experience in modern machining, welding, and traditional blacksmithing, which has given him the ability to recreate many historical items. He enjoys and is constantly on the lookout for new and unusual tools or weapons to create, not only to see how they worked but to gain full understanding of how they could or could not be used. He creates replica items to fully understand the warriors of history and their tools, and has created the replica tools for this book.

Figure 1.6.
Richard Couck

THE DISCOVERY OF THE SCHOOL

Like most good stories, the story of the "rediscovery" of Mubyōshi Ryū has elements of the fairy tale and a series of events that seem almost impossible but which are true. I had previously heard the name Muhyōshi Ryū as a branch of Shinjin Ryū from the *Shinobi Hiten* catalog and included it in my book *In Search of the Ninja,* but no more than its name and a possible connection to the shinobi was understood. During the filming of the documentary *Ninja Shadow Warriors,* Nakashima Atsumi allowed me to photograph small sections of the ninja scroll called *Mizukagami.* Later, while looking for ninja scrolls, I managed to obtain copies of a scroll called *Gokuhiden Shinobi no Sho,* which, as always, came in photocopied format and well printed in monotone gray. The text was in difficult *sōsho*—cursive style—leaving its secrets hidden in the pages with only a slight glimpse given in some characters. Sōsho was the "curse of my life" at that point and needed to be defeated, so to combat this mysterious handwriting style, my team and I contacted a then-defunct group of specialists in Warabi, Saitama Prefecture, in Japan, who had in the past dealt with this type of manuscript. They agreed to reestablish their group and to concentrate on this document. My colleagues Mieko Koizumi and Yoshie Minami joined the group to deepen their understanding also.

Much later, on a snowy winter day, Yoshie and I found ourselves traveling to a semi-famous bookshop a short distance outside Tokyo, trying to find any out-of-print twentieth-century books on the ninja. They had a single copy left, which I purchased. As we discussed my work, the owner of the shop told us that we had timed it just right, and that there was a two-day secondhand book event in Tokyo that was to happen the next weekend, and they had listed a shinobi book that I did not have. So, that weekend, list in hand, Mieko and I made our way to this short event in Tokyo. After some searching and fighting through a mass of old men, we found the book.

Having had quite enough of the jostling and crowded environment, we made our way to the stairs leading up to street level. Below the stairs was a locked glass cabinet filled with old scrolls, documents, and expensive and rare Western books. Looking at the glass, I restrained myself and thought, *No, I have been through a million scrolls, and I never find anything of worth to me in these shops.* Backing away and waiting for Mieko to retrieve her umbrella and bag from the improvised cloak room, I was accosted by a wizened old man, bent over and overzealous. With his hands on my arm, he led me to the cabinet and started to unlock the glass. I protested as much as I could, knowing that there would be nothing I would want to spend the hundreds if not thousands of dollars that these scrolls could fetch. Mieko came to my side to help me refuse the offer, but by that point I was deep in the scrolls. Unrolling one, I saw the flowers of a flower-arrangement scroll; the next had images of arrows and bows, a typical archery scroll.

Figure 1.7. Mieko Koizumi in kimono the day we went to the book festival

5

Mieko began to translate the titles for me: medicine, archery, jūjutsu, and so on, but then I stumbled across a thin but solid roll that looked quite aged.

Opening the scroll the limited amount that the glass area would allow, the cursive style was set against the beautiful paper with an elegant gold-painted background. It had the title torn off along with the first few sentences, leaving it nameless. Opening it as best we could, Mieko started mumbling as she read and then explained that the sentences, while difficult to understand, were very familiar, with words such as *lantern, wind,* and *rain* starting to emerge from the text. Then she said, "Antony, this sentence is from the shinobi scroll we're using at the sōsho club. This is the exact same sentence that we studied last week, I'm sure of it." Looking to the scroll and the price, I thought that there had been some mistake. Scrolls cost hundreds if not a thousands of dollars, but this one said three thousand yen (under $30). I thought there was no possible way that this scroll was so cheap. This price should be understood as cheap on a mythological scale, on the verge of being impossible. Scroll in hand, I went to the counter, and sure enough, they took off a tag, charged me three thousand yen, and put the beautiful object in a rather dull plastic bag. Flabbergasted and excited, I walked out to the waiting Mieko—in a splendid yellow kimono—and we walked to the nearest coffee shop for a cup of tea and a better look.

Sitting in the coffee shop, we opened the scroll on the table and made our way through the contents. Bit by bit and with exclamations of glee, we saw the word *shinobi* and *shinobi no mono* appear. Could it be that I had really bought a real life ninja scroll for the price of a few cheap meals? Making our way to the end, a seal, names, and a date appeared:

Given to Igarashi Kin'emon by Hagiwara Jūzō in the year 1678

It was evident that I had purchased my first shinobi scroll. The seal appeared to be the original seal of the author, and only one year given. I had stumbled on an unknown ninja scroll by an unknown warrior called Hagiwara Jūzō, and it was an original, actually penned in 1678. Taking my scroll to Yoshie—my main translator—she began to search for Hagiwara Jūzō on the Internet. Only a single result came up. A woman named Mizui Mitsuko was continuing the business of her father who had recently died. He had been an avid collector of military manuals, and now she was selling his collection. In her catalog it stated that she owned a manual titled *Mizukagami by Hagiwara Jūzō*. Boarding a train to Tokyo, we arrived at her shop in Takadanobaba and settled down to a cup of tea. She produced the manual—this time in book

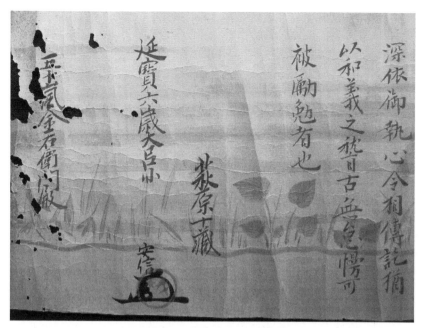

Figure 1.8. The end of the shinobi scroll with the signatures

form—and allowed us time to go through it. Yoshie turned to me and said, "This is the same manual as the scroll you just bought," and with that, my scroll had a name and a place in history. Buying the *Mizukagami* and two more shinobi-related manuals from her, we set off home. Quickly I opened the photos of Nakashima's *Mizukagami* (the scroll that I had taken photos of on the documentary shoot) and we compared his *Mizukagami* to both of mine. It seemed that our original idea, that only two copies of the *Mizukagami* existed, was wrong. One was in Nakashima's collection, and one in an Iga collection, but now there were four. This led me back to the *Shinobi Hiten* catalog and my original quotation about Muhyōshi Ryū in my book *In Search of the Ninja*.

At this point we had the name Hagiwara Jūzō and his School of Muhyōshi Ryū and little else, but it was a start. We found, again recently listed on a website, a scroll called *Yawara Jo*, for sale in Tokyo, with the name Muhyōshi Ryū attached. Ordering via the telephone, we had it sent to us, and again his name was there, Hagiwara Jūzō. The school and an idea of its history was starting to build. The problem was that the *Yawara* scroll was a *mokuroku*, which means that it was a list of skills and not instructions. If only the school still existed, we could turn this useless list into a real book. From here we searched in more detail for the school name and came upon an old and somewhat out-of-date website outlining how the school Muhyōshi Ryū had been passed down and was now in the hands of Uematsu Yoshiyuki. It was not long before I was demanding Mieko get on the phone to him and get me an appointment.

Just before this, I had come across an organization that held and promoted certain martial schools, and in their list I found three scrolls connected to Muhyōshi Ryū: the *Mizukagami*, The *Yawara Jo*, and the *Kaishaku narabini Seppuku Dōtsuki no Shidai*. I asked if I could visit them the next time I was in Japan, being in England at the time, to which I got the very Japanese answer, "It's a possibility." Strangely, however, a short time later the very same scrolls went up on Yahoo Auction, and the comments stated something to the effect of "There is a Western man researching Muhyōshi Ryū, and we do not wish for him to purchase or be given these scrolls." They set the price at around $2,000, which at that time was too much for scrolls that I already had. As it turns out, no one bought this collection of three, and they again went on sale for $1,000, and I bought them through Yoshie. I still don't know if the seller knows that I ended up being the owner against their wishes.

By contacting the local libraries in Kanazawa to try to find more information on the school, we found many more scrolls, more copies of the *Mizukagami*, and even to my great astonishment, "new" versions of this ninja scroll with the oral traditions recorded, and even an additional scroll. Without hesitation we ordered copies of most of them. Packing my bags for a trip to Kanazawa to meet Uematsu Sensei and to visit the library, I headed off. The library was more than accommodating, and we photographed all the scrolls we had not ordered, and found our way to the Dōjō of Muhyōshi Ryū.

By coincidence, Joe Swift, a longtime student of Uematsu Sensei, was at the dōjō, managing to only get there once a year while he teaches in Tokyo. The dōjō focuses on karate and *iaijutsu* sword skills and is where Uematsu keeps the Mubyōshi tradition alive as an undercurrent in the training (it was here that I learned that he called the school Mubyōshi Ryū and not Muhyōshi Ryū). Uematsu Sensei took time to make us welcome and to answer all of my questions, showing us the various publications that we were unaware of and that contained Mubyōshi Ryū information. It was here we first discussed the idea of this book, and later on, Joe Swift kindly offered his help and has become key in the production of this record, the preservation of the skills of Mubyōshi Ryū.

Armed with aid from Uematsu Sensei's dōjō, a list of original Mubyōshi Ryū documents, scattered and scant publications on the school, and hopefully the divine protection and blessing of the long dead Hagiwara Jūzō, we set out to bring this book into reality. This led us to find many manuals and much information on the school that is not complete but intriguing enough to continue. However, the first step was to decipher the beautiful and elegant grass-style writing found in some of the manuals, and to achieve this we turned to the Warabi Sōsho Group.

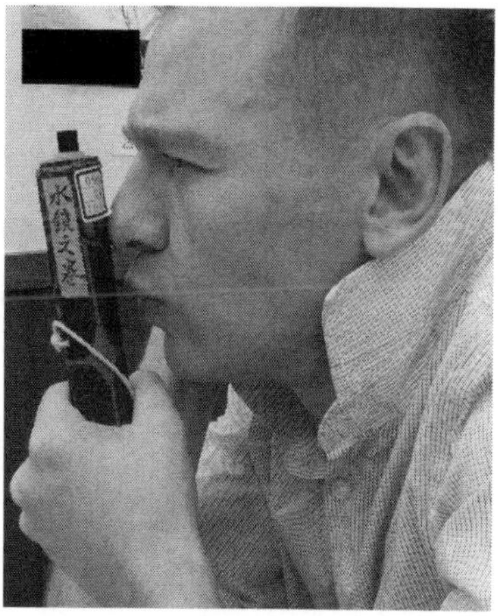

Figure 1.9. The author at Kinsei Shiryōkan-Tamagawa Library with a copy of the **Mizukagami**

WARABI SŌSHO GROUP

Japanese texts can be classified by their writing format in three ways:

Kaisho: block style
Gyōsho: half block, half cursive
Sōsho: cursive

It is a blessed event indeed if a scroll obtained from a library or collection is in block style, as the only difficulty in reading it is unknown vocabulary or context. It is more likely, however, that the text will be in either half cursive or full cursive, which may sound simple but is disastrous for someone not trained in reading it. To combat this and to deal primarily with the *Mizukagami* scroll, I approached the then-defunct sōsho club based in Warabi, Saitama Prefecture. They agreed to reopen the club to work on this scroll and to help bring the teachings within to light for the publication of this book. Their role should not be undervalued, and thanks must be given to them for their superb effort and achievements.

Club Members

Mieko is also a member of the Historical Ninjutsu Research Team and the main partner on this project. She is without doubt the world's most knowledgeable person on the history of the school of Mubyōshi Ryū.

Not pictured is Yoshie Minami, also a member of the Historical Ninjutsu Research Team and the main translator for the schools produced by the team.

Figure 1.10.
Shimizu Takashi

Figure 1.11.
Hatada Tadanori

Figure 1.12.
Mieko Koizumi

A History of Mubyōshi Ryū

The precise origin of the school is unknown, but a logical and educated attempt can be made to ascertain the story behind how the school came into being. It starts with Shinjin Ryū (深甚流), a sword school said to have been founded on the teachings of Kusabuka Jinshirō. The school had reportedly been passed down in the Kaga domain and arrived in the hands of one Niki Shinjūrō. It is here, in the mid-seventeenth century, where the story of Mubyōshi Ryū starts.

It appears that Niki Shinjūrō was not a wholly pleasant character and that some of his deeds may have been unscrupulous. However, before his name is blackened, we have to establish what is known about him. Under the lord of the Kaga domain, Niki Shinjūrō was a surprisingly and relatively high-ranking samurai with the position of *yoriki* (group commander). This position gave him control over a body of men who were not paid for by his income but were loaned to him by the lord, and he held captain's rights over them. It is known that he ran into some trouble or was at least disliked by his school, because in one document (fig. 1.13), his name has a black mark against it. This means that the master, a future master, or a senior in the school disliked his conduct. The mark shows that he was either removed from the school, some internal issue unfolded, or even that his name was scratched off from the list. The facts of this incident have been lost, but what remains is that Niki Shinjūrō is named at the start of most scrolls in Mubyōshi Ryū, and beside his name the samurai named Hagiwara Jūzō can be found.

These two names, Niki Shinjūrō and Hagiwara Jūzō, provided an anchor for the origins of Mubyōshi Ryū and places the establishment of the school

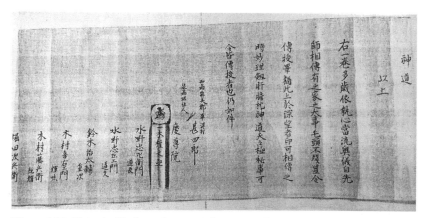

Figure 1.13. Note the black mark next to the name Niki.

at around the mid-seventeenth century. One might automatically place Niki Shinjūrō as the founder of the school because his name appears on most of the documents in the primary position, but the case is not so simple. According to the document *Bishamonden* (translated in full in chapter 7), Hagiwara Jūzō was a samurai who faced trouble from an early age. Having to deal with old family feuds and repercussions from mistakes in his youth, the young Hagiwara Jūzō sought the teachings of masters of the martial arts and warfare to help defend himself, which indirectly led to the creation of his school, presumably Mubyōshi Ryū.

Through investigation it seems more likely that Niki Shinjūrō was a member of Shinjin Ryū and that Hagiwara Jūzō studied that school under him, including other forms, such as grappling and chain weapons. Therefore, it appears that Hagiwara Jūzō was the founder of Mubyōshi Ryū but that he gives Niki Shinjūrō respect through his prime position in the school's list of masters. This, of course, is to display two major points: first that the skills have a lineage that is authentic, and second that this lineage can be traced back to Kusabuka Jinshirō—a famed samurai and sword master.

It is imperative to understand that Shinjin Ryū is primarily a sword school and that Mubyōshi Ryū has a distinctive lack of swordsmanship. This means that Hagiwara Jūzō did not adopt these sword skills—he simply and most likely became and continued to be a student of Shinjin Ryū—and that Mubyōshi Ryū contained all the other elements, such as grappling, rope skills, and quarterstaff work (it does involve a small amount of swordsmanship). In addition to this, Hagiwara Jūzō also added *ninjutsu*—the arts of the ninja—to his curriculum. It made the combination of Shinjin Ryū and Mubyōshi Ryū a solid school for an independent warrior, giving that warrior all the skills he would need to survive in postwar medieval Japan.

Mubyōshi Ryū seems to have been started by one man to defend against his enemies and appears to have thrived and continued, a testament to its effectiveness. Upon observing the gathered collection of Mubyōshi Ryū scrolls, a pattern of names begins to appear, showing a core group of strong members around its origin. As discussed above, the name Niki Shinjūrō always appears first, with Hagiwara Jūzō directly after him, and then followed by others that constantly reappear and should be considered the founding members or first set of masters, with Niki Shinjūrō being the link to the past:

Niki Shinjūrō Masanaga
Hagiwara Jūzō Shigetatsu
Tōmi Gen'nai Nobuna
Kitagawa Kin'emon Sadahide

It seems evident that Hagiwara Jūzō is the founder of the school, under the guidance of Niki Shinjūrō, but also that others core members of the school were training with them or directly after them in succession. The school clearly becomes a standard school for the Kaga domain, and students flock to its banner while it resides in the Keibukan (the main samurai training hall of the Kaga domain) with the other official schools of the area.

MUBYŌSHI RYŪ LINEAGE CHART

From its conception in the mid-seventeenth century through the friendship of Hagiwara Jūzō and Niki Shinjūrō through to the current Grandmaster Uematsu Yoshiyuki, the school has broken off into multiple branches and offshoots, leaving a spiderweb network of lineage trails. Of all these, only one branch school survives to this day and should be considered one strand among a web of others, all of which have now faded.

The following lineage chart was rebuilt by Mieko Koizumi from original scrolls. Before Mieko's efforts, the lineage kept by the current grandmaster was only considered to go back as far as Kaneko Kichibei (profiled in the following section). Furthermore, as Hagiwara Jūzō is taken to be the founder, based on the present information, the current grandmaster is the 15th generation and the only remaining master of the school.

The Mubyōshi Ryū lineage, based on our research:

1. Hagiwara Jūzō Shigetatsu (萩原重蔵茂辰)
2. Tōmi Gen'nai Nobuna (東美源内宣名)
3. Shimano Zenzaemon Naokata (嶋野善左衛門直賢)
4. Nagai Kagami Katayoshi (永井各務方叔)
5. Tsuchikawa Kakuemon Takayoshi (土川覚右衛門貴好)
6. Nanbu Shōzō Atsuyoshi (南部庄藏篤慶)
7. Nanbu Shōsuke Atsukuni (南部庄助篤圀)
8. Kaneko Kichibei Masatake (金子吉平正武)
9. Yamazaki Sōsuke (山崎惣助)
10. Michiseya Jinshichi (道清屋甚七)
11. Sono Kōsuke (曽野幸助)
12. Kishii Kiyozō (岸井清藏)
13. Nishimura Yosabei (西村興三兵衛)
14. Nishimura Seitarō (西村清太郎)
15. Uematsu Yoshiyuki (上松義幸)

Japanese names have multiple possible readings. The above transliterations are considered correct, but other readings are possible.

A MUBYŌSHI RYŪ WHO'S WHO

The constant use of Japanese names and terms can become tiresome, especially without context. The following list has been created to give a quick overview of the names found within the school, including the surrounding arts that are connected. Over the centuries, Mubyōshi Ryū has had hundreds if not thousands of students, but this list gives insight into the names found on the school scrolls and inferred history.

Kusabuka Jinshirō (草深甚四郎)

- a Sengoku Period warrior, dates unknown, known to be an expert swordsman
- in legend had a sword and spear fight with Tsukahara Bokuden (塚原卜伝), with Bokuden being the victor in sword, and the spear match being a draw
- said to have founded Shinjin Ryū, which was the basis of Niki Shinjūrō's knowledge, some of which found its way into Mubyōshi Ryū
- only in the school history through association

Niki Shinjūrō Masanaga (二木新十郎政長)

- held the position of yoriki (captain of men) within the Kaga domain
- studied Shinjin Ryū under a man named Keison-in
- taught Shinjin Ryū to Mizuno Chūzaemon and Hagiwara Jūzō
- appears to have been expelled from Shinjin Ryū
- his teachings form the foundations for Mubyōshi Ryū

Hagiwara Jūzō Shigetatsu (萩原重蔵茂辰)

- considered the founder of Mubyōshi Ryū and to have taken most of his teachings from Niki Shinjūrō
- appears to have written the shinobi scroll *Mizukagami,* or collected the teachings from elsewhere and complied them
- was instructor to Tōmi Gen'nai
- considered to be Mubyōshi Ryū's key figure
- most likely studied Shinjin Ryū under Niki Shinjūrō

Tōmi Gen'nai Nobuna (東美源内宣名)

- ?–1715
- a *rōnin* in Kaga
- taught Shinjin Ryū and Mubyōshi Ryū

Ikegami Yōsuke Hisamasu (池上用助久益)

- taught *kumiuchi* (grappling) in the Keibukan, the official school of the Kaga domain
- transcribed a version of the *Mizukagami* scroll

Yanase Kihei Yoshitomo (柳瀬喜兵衛義知)

- taught Shinsō Ryū in the Keibukan

Morita Kohei (森田小兵衛)

- his ancestor studied under Tōmi Gen'nai (profiled above)

Mizuno Jūzō Mitsutoyo (水野重蔵光豊)

- studied both Mubyōshi Ryū and Sodeoka Ryū Bō jutsu (quarterstaff)
- wrote the document *Kaimokusho,* which lists the school's entire curriculum, including all the scroll titles and the list of oral traditions

Kaneko Kichibei Masatake (金子吉兵衛正武)

- 1795–1858
- prolific martial artist, especially jūjutsu, *kodachi* (shortsword), and magic
- his father was a public servant, serving as a rice storage manager
- he was *ashigaru* (foot solider) in Komatsu Castle; lived in Komatsu City
- was given a bonus by Maeda Nariyasu
- built his own dōjō with the dimensions of 3.5 by 7 *ken* [21 by 42 feet], situated next to his house, which was built between 1818 and 1830 in Sono Machi, in Komatsu City, near Raishōji Temple
- four legends associated with him: (1) crossing a river on a straw mat; (2) performing the skill of disappearing beneath *tatami* mats and reappearing elsewhere to escape, done at Raishōji Temple; (3) having the ability to travel great distances at speed; (4) curing people of malaria and toothache; people used to use powder taken from his gravestone near Raishōji Temple to use as medicine

- two graves exist for him, one in Komatsu City public cemetery and one near Raishōji Temple

Yamazaki Sōsuke (山崎惣助)

- owned a dōjō in Komatsu City, land still owned by the family, though the dōjō has been destroyed

Michiseya Jinshichi (道清屋甚七)

- student of Kaneko Kichibei Masatake

Sono Kōsuke (曽野幸助)

- student of Kaneko Kichibei Masatake

Kishii Kiyozō (岸井清藏)

- student to Kaneko Kichibei Masatake

Machida Hanbei Hisasada (町田半兵衛久定)

- 1832–1909?
- studied Mubyōshi Ryū, Toda Ryū, Shizuka Ryū, Asaka Ryū, Yamaguchi Ryū, and Mizuno Ichi Ten Ryū
- established Hanbei Ryū lion dancing troupe, based on the above schools

Nishimura Yosabei (西村興三兵衛)

- taught Mubyōshi Ryū at the Keibukan around 1854
- taught Shintō Ryū In-jutsu (in-jutsu is an unidentified art)
- studied Toda Kongō Ryū

Nishimura Seitarō (西村清太郎)

- 1869–1919
- born in Nakabayashi in 1869 into a family of farmers
- studied swordsmanship, grappling, quarterstaff, halberd, sickle and chain, iron weapons, and more from Machida Hanbei when he was seventeen
- built a dōjō in Nakabayashi in 1901 and had over two hundred students from the Meiji period into the Taishō Period
- organized a local kendō association and helped local development

- students built a monument next to his dōjō in 1919
- established a lion dance in the Nakabayashi area performed on festival days in front of his monument

Ōta Nabejirō (大田鍋次郎)

- studied Mubyōshi Ryū from Kaneko Kichibei's student, Shimomura Fuyuzō; studied Issō Ryū from Matsumoto Koredayū Takahisa; said to have combined Mubyōshi Ryū and Issō Ryū and formed Issō Mubyōshi Ryū, teaching at the Keibukan around 1854

Uematsu Yoshiyuki (上松義幸)

- current grandmaster of Mubyōshi Ryū
- inherited mainly the jūjutsu sections of the school and some weapon skills
- current grandmaster of Mukaku Ryū

The Current Grandmaster

A selection of the traditions from the school have been passed on to its current master, Uematsu Sensei, who runs the school to this day. Mubyōshi Ryū entered into the Uematsu family traditions in the twentieth century, and it must be made absolutely clear that Uematsu Sensei does not claim to have inherited the shinobi tradition; he is the inheritor of the jūjutsu side only with some other smaller aspects. However, the Uematsu family has long held their own military tradition, called Mukaku Ryū, a samurai school that focuses on *chū-kodachi* (shortswords) and *shuriken* (throwing blades). In an effort to preserve the maximum amount of skills, both Mubyōshi Ryū and the Uematsu family traditions of Mukaku Ryū have been recorded here, but they were never historically connected. Any student wishing to train in either of these schools is welcome to attend the dōjō in Japan.

3

KEIBUKAN, THE DŌJŌ OF KAGA PROVINCE

Kaga was the name of the domain in which Hagiwara, Niki, and others served in the mid to late seventeenth century. They would have trained and taught privately, of course, taking on personal students, continuing their school. It would not have been known to them that in 1792 the 10th lord of the Kaga domain, Lord Maeda Harunaga (前田治脩), who is sometimes considered the 11th, established two domain schools, the Meirindō and the Keibukan, adjacent to each other.

- The Keibukan (経武館) taught the military and martial aspects of samurai education.
- The Meirindō (明倫堂) school taught the literacy and scholarly side of samurai education.

Mubyōshi Ryū became a staple samurai school within this establishment, and while it had both versatile and varied skills within its curriculum, the school became one of the official jūjutsu (grappling) schools of the Keibukan. Students studied Mubyōshi Ryū alongside other schools of martial arts. Clearly, the school became popular in this time period. Listings and blood oaths taken show that vast numbers of students joined its ranks.

The school moved its physical location during its existence:

- 1792–1819: near the Kenrokuen Garden's plum grove and Kanazawa Shrine
- 1819–1822: the Okumura family house site, today the Kanazawa Medical Center
- 1822–1868 or 1870: around the Ishikawa Museum of Modern Literature

The school closed its gates in 1868 or 1870 and merged with the newly founded Western military school, the Sōyūkan (壮猶館).

JAPANESE LITERATURE ON MUBYŌSHI RYŪ

Although there are a few publications that briefly discuss the school, the main Japanese book that deals with Shinjin Ryū and Mubyōshi Ryū is pictured in figure 3.1.

> **Title:** *Kensei Kusabuka Jinshirō*
>   (剣聖草深甚四郎)
> **Year of publication:** 1990
> **Author:** Kensei Kusabuka Jinshirō
>   Editing Committee
> **Publisher:** Kawakita-machi
>   town office

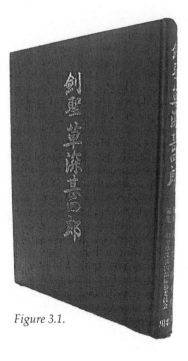

Figure 3.1.

4

TRAINING IN JAPAN TODAY

The last Mubyōshi Ryū dōjō is called Mushinkan Sō Honbu Dōjō, located in the town of Ōgigaoka in Nonoichi City, Ishikawa Prefecture. It is under the guidance of grandmaster Uematsu. Uematsu Sensei welcomes students from around the world and cordially invites anyone who wishes to become an earnest student of his school to his dōjō.

Any prospective student should first contact the dōjō through the information below or through currently active social media. Upon verifying the availability of Uematsu Sensei or one of his students, prospective students are encouraged to make the trip to Japan to enjoy the ancient teachings of the school. All lessons are given in Japanese, and a grasp of the Japanese language will aid in comprehension. However, as martial skills are physical in nature, don't let a lack of Japanese language ability stop you from making such a journey. Following is a full set of travel instructions to help students find their way from Tokyo or Osaka to the dōjō.

Mushinkan Sō Honbu Dōjō
36-6 Ōgigaoka
Nonoichi City, Ishikawa Prefecture
921-8812 Japan
Phone +81 (76) 246-4759
English-speaking contact: Joe Swift, info@tokyo-mushinkan.com
無心館総本部道場
館長　上松義幸
〒921-8812
石川県野々市市扇が丘36-6
Tel. 076-246-4759

Figure 4.1. Uematsu Sensei (left) and Joe Swift

TRAVEL INSTRUCTIONS

Remember that your final destination is Magae Station. If you are having trouble, show the characters for the station name (馬替) to a train station staff member.

Train 1

Buy a ticket to Kanazawa Station.

- From Tokyo Station, take the Hokuriku Shinkansen to Kanazawa.
- From Osaka Station, take the Thunderbird Express (pronounced "sandābādo") to Kanazawa.

Train 2

Buy a ticket to Nishi Kanazawa Station.

From Kanazawa Station, take the Hokuriku-honsen Line to Nishi Kanazawa Station, the first stop from Kanazawa.

Train 3

To change train stations, leave by the East Gate exit and follow the signs for Shin-nishi Kanazawa Station. Look for the sign (fig. 4.2) as you get to the East Gate, and follow the directions for the Hokutetsu Ishikawa Line.

It is a short walk, about a hundred yards, between the two stations. Note that the East Gate has two ways to exit.

At the time of publication, you don't buy a ticket at the station. Instead, board the train and pay the conductor as you disembark at your stop. On the return journey, you have to take the small ticket given by the machine at each door as you board.

Figure 4.2.

Shin-nishi Kanazawa Station is a very small local station.

Go through the entrance, cross the track, and take the Hokutetsu Ishikawa Line.

Your train will be on the far side, farthest from the small station building. Take the train on the farthest track (fig. 4.6).

Figure 4.3.

Figure 4.4. Shin-nishi Kanazawa Station

Figure 4.5.

Figure 4.6.

Get off at Magae Station—the dōjō is at this station. It is the fourth stop:

- Oshino
- Nonoichi
- Nonoichi Kōdai Mae
- Magae (the dōjō station)

Figure 4.7. Sign at Magae Station

23

Pay at the machine as you get off the train (have some change ready).

Figure 4.8.

Getting to the Dōjō

Cross the track and position yourself looking along the train line with the tracks to the left.

Walk along the road with the tracks to the left (fig. 4.10).

Figure 4.9.   *Figure 4.10.*

Get to the end of the road and cross the bridge.

As you get off the bridge, turn right and walk down the road with the stream to your right (fig. 4.12).

Figure 4.11.   *Figure 4.12.*

You will come to a building and bend in the road. Follow the bend left.

Follow the road down. The dōjō is just behind the building at left in figure 4.14.

The dōjō is on the left.

Figure 4.13.

Figure 4.14.

Figure 4.15.

As you are expected, knock and wait for an answer. If no answer comes, knock until you get one, as no one may have heard you. If not, call out "Uematsu Sensei." If you are expected and still there is no answer, politely enter slowly while announcing your presence.

Figure 4.16. The dōjō entrance

Figure 4.17. Name plates at the dōjō entrance

When you are making the return journey, remember that the train station you depart from is very small. Make sure to board the train going in the correct direction, as shown in figure 4.18.

Figure 4.18.

DŌJŌ RULES

The following rules are found in the main dōjō and apply to all students of any art within the Mushinkan organization:

- Do not maintain an evil mind.
- Respect your superiors.
- Respect the gods and Buddha and retain that mind set; do not be conceited in the level of your own ability.
- Know yourself and be positive; train every morning and every evening.
- Even in combat, the way of the mind should be the same as normal times.

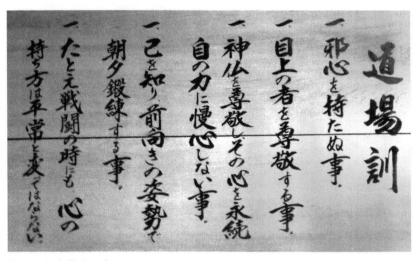

Figure 4.19. Dōjō rules

5

THE MUBYŌSHI RYŪ CURRICULUM

Without doubt, much of Mubyōshi Ryū and the teachings of its founders have been lost, leading to an abstract feeling when trying to envision the school as a whole. However, inside the Ishida Tarō collection currently in the Amagasaki Municipal Archives (尼崎市立地域研究史料館) is a scroll named within its internals as *Mubyōshi Ryū Kaimokusho*. In the collection, however, the scroll is listed under the title *Mubyōshi Ryū Heihō Hidensho* (The secret military skills of Mubyōshi Ryū). This scroll was written by Mizuno Jūzō Mitsutoyo with the aim of compiling a complete list of the skills and elements of the school. Therefore, this scroll is considered a treasure in discovering the history of Mubyōshi Ryū because it gives a step-by-step account of the school's contents and the levels within the teachings.

*Figure 5.1. The Ishida Tarō collection of scrolls, including **Mubyōshi Ryū Kaimokusho**, now in the Amagasaki Municipal Archives* (尼崎市立地域研究史料館蔵石田太郎氏文書)

*Figure 5.2. The **Mubyōshi Ryū Kaimokusho** of the Ishida Tarō collection*

A paraphrasing of the scroll is given below for ease, but note that in the original writing the skills for each section were listed with their titles. Here they have been removed, and in their place the number of skills has been given. This scroll includes not only the skill lists of physical abilities, such a grappling and chain weapons, but also a list of the oral traditions *(kuden)* alongside a catalog of the scrolls that make up the school's body of work. The oral traditions list is given in full in chapter 16.

The list of scrolls are those that were in the school at the time of writing in 1786. It is noteworthy that many of the oral traditions from the kuden list appear in later scrolls like *Mizukagami Kuden no Oboe* and *Mizukagami Shinsatsu*, both of which were written well after the founder and are clearly collections of the school's oral traditions—they have been translated in full in this book, which means that some of the oral traditions have been recorded. Therefore, allow the following lists to give a clearer overview of the ways of this medieval school. Be aware that some sections do not have direct English translations, as without context, there is too much potential for error.

The prologue and epilogue of the *Kaimokusho* scroll have not been translated in full, but the following is an overview of their contents.

THE PROLOGUE

The prologue includes a description of the origin and principles of the universe and the superiority of human beings to other living creatures. It states that only human beings are of perfect existence, representing heaven and earth, thus there should be nothing humans are not capable of. Samurai should learn multiple arts and principles, but all should be based on command of their bodies and limbs and freedom of movement.

Intellectual knowledge is essential for samurai, but first they have to train themselves to move freely to take advantage of the knowledge in actual fighting.

The school Mubyōshi Ryū has accumulated a number of scrolls that incorporate various skills, and they have been copied into this one scroll, which is named *Kaimokusho*. This is done to transmit these skills to the students of future generations.

It discusses the concept of studying principle over skills and techniques, and states that while many other schools study the concept of rhythm and no-rhythm, without knowing the truest of principles (that is, free movement over technique), a student will never reach achievement. Also, the teaching of no-sword will not work if you learn with an inappropriate teacher.

In Mubyōshi Ryū, you should not try to gain victory but instead concentrate on not being defeated. After focusing and training on this principle, a student will reach the truth of fighting. The difference between this school of Mubyōshi Ryū and others is this:

If you give priority to learning forms, your movement will stagnate. In training you should always train to attain free movement. Without it, you will get nowhere. If you keep training hard all the time throughout your life, you will defeat those who are not as good as you, but it does not allow you to win over your master because there are countless teachings to learn. However, constant training will surely lead to improvement, year by year and day by day.

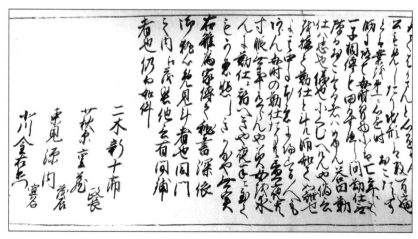

*Figure 5.3. The epilogue to the **Kaimokusho** scroll*
(尼崎市立地域研究史料館蔵石田太郎氏文書)

THE EPILOGUE

The main duty of teachers is to inherit their predecessor's teachings and pass them on to their students in order to transmit the skills for generations. Teachers, if asked a lot of questions by students, should answer as much as possible, but there are hints on how to deal with the differing types of students.

- Those students who ask a lot of questions but who are not eager to train should not be given secrets.
- To those who train hard, you should give answers to all their questions. Teachings and training are both indispensable.
- *Shūshin* (enthusiasm) consists of donating gold and silver and treasures, thus do not hesitate to transmit anything to them as offering treasured items shows their seriousness.
- Those who are poor. If they are enthusiastic and dedicated to follow their teacher, you should transmit teachings. Money does not matter in this situation.
- Those who always train hard and learn from the teacher should be allowed to have *isshisōden* (full transmission) after seven years of hard training.
- Those who are busy with their official duties. Remember that official duties are priorities, but if you find they are lying and are only making excuses, do not chastise them. They may realize themselves some day and return to the correct way.

This is the end of the epilogue to the *Kaimokusho* scroll.

The following is the complete list of skills and scrolls found in the *Kaimokusho* scroll. The skill names have been removed and their number inserted. This constitutes the bulk of Mubyōshi Ryū's teachings.

SECTION OF SKILLS (業之部, WAZA NO BU)

[The following skills are those which are used in Mubyōshi Ryū.]

Mubyōshi Ryū Part One (無拍子流前, mubyōshi ryū mae)
20 skills
Mubyōshi Ryū Part Two (無拍子流裏, mubyōshi ryū ura)
20 skills
Mubyōshi Ryū Basic Level (無拍子流真, mubyōshi ryū shin)
20 skills

Mubyōshi Ryū Mastery Level (無拍子流草, mubyōshi ryū sō)
20 skills

Mubyōshi Ryū Applications (無拍子流行, mubyōshi ryū gyō)
20 skills

Mubyōshi Ryū Grappling (無拍子流立合, mubyōshi ryū tachiai)
15 skills

[Tachiai is normally associated with standing skills, but that may not be the case here.]

Mubyōshi Ryū Grappling Lower Part (無拍子流真, mubyōshi ryū shin)
15 skills

Mubyōshi Ryū grappling Higher Level (無拍子流奥, mubyōshi ryū oku)
15 ways

Middle Level (中通, nakadōri)
12 skills

The Scroll of Reflecting on the Mind (心鑑之巻, shinkan no maki)
33 articles

Jūjutsu skills (外之物勝負之巻, tonomono shōbu no maki)
33 articles

[Read as *sotonomono shōki no maki* in this lineage of Mubyōshi Ryū]

Sword Striking and Jūjutsu (組討太刀打之巻, kumiuchi tachiuchi no maki)
23 skills
[Skills missing]

The Scroll of Mounted Combat (馬上組討之巻, bajō kumiuchi no maki)
23 skills
[Skills missing]

抜身 (nukimi)
25 articles
[Skills missing]

Important Ways of Jūjutsu (腰廻り要法, koshimawari yōhō)
12 skills
[Skills missing]

Sodeoka Ryū Quarterstaff (袖岡流棒, sodeoka Ryū bō)
15 skills

Chain and Weight Part One (前乳切木, mae chigiriki)
9 skills
[Skills missing; some chain and weight skills still exist in the school.]

Truncheon Part One (前霞, mae kasumi)

9 skills

[Skills missing]

The Scroll of Rope (縄之巻, nawa no maki)

12 skills

[Skills missing]

The Scroll of Tools (道具巻, dōgu [no] maki)

11 tools

Chain and Weight and No-Sword (無刀乳切木, mutō chigiriki)

7 skills

[Skills missing]

Deeper Skills of the Chain and Weight (奥乳切木, oku chigiriki)

3 skills

[Skills missing]

Deeper Skills of the Truncheon (奥霞, oku kasumi)

4 skills

[Skills missing]

Quarterstaff Scroll (踏返巻, fumikaeshi [no] maki)

7 skills

[Skills missing; this is stated as oral tradition only.]

Sodeoka Ryū Quarterstaff (袖岡流棒免, sodeoka ryū bō men)

7 skills plus 2 skills

[Skills may have changed, but a version is recorded in this book.]

Distance in Combat between Swords (相寸離劔之次第, aisun riken no shidai)

[Missing]

Some skills have been omitted from the above. (外数手業有之畧ス, hoka kazu tewaza ari kore ryakusu)

List of Mubyōshi Ryū Oral Traditions (無拍子流口傳之部, mubyōshi ryū kuden no bu)

158 skills

[Some of these skills are passed down within this book in the magical texts and shinobi scrolls. The full list is found in chapter 16.]

THE VARIOUS SCROLLS AND WRITINGS OF MUBYŌSHI RYŪ (諸巻書物之部, SHO KAN SHOMOTSU NO BU)

[The following is considered a complete list of Mubyōshi Ryū scrolls at the time it was written. Some scrolls that have been added to this book, such as the *Mizukagami Kuden no Oboe*, were written later and therefore do not appear in this list. Others have been added by other masters.]

Antony Cummins says: Some of the following translations have been simplified because of problems with seated and standing combat, and have been translated as jūjutsu skills. For full translations of the titles see the list in appendix D.

Jūjutsu Skills (居捕巻, idori [no] maki)

[Skills appear in this book. Read as *iho no maki* in this lineage of Mubyōshi Ryū]

Jūjutsu Skills (立合之巻, tachiai no maki)

[Skills appear in this book.]

The Scroll of Chain and Weight (乳切木巻, chigiriki [no] maki)

[Missing]

The Scroll of Reflecting on the Mind (心鑑之巻, shinkan no maki)

[Scroll translated in this book.]

Jūjutsu Skills (勝負之巻, shōbu no maki)

[Skills appear in this book.]

The Scroll of Grappling (組討巻, kumiuchi [no] maki)

[Skills missing]

The Scroll of Sword Striking (太刀討巻, tachiuchi [no] maki)

[Skills missing]

Mounted Riding Scroll (馬上之巻, bajō no maki)

[Skills missing]

The Rope Skills Scroll (縄之巻, nawa no maki)

[Skills missing]

The Scroll of Tools (道具巻, dōgu [no] maki)

[Tools appear in this book, but some skills with the tools are not recorded.]

Yawara Jo Tradition (流儀和序, ryūgi yawara jo)

[Short introduction for the school's combat system, translated in this book]

付り追伽

[Missing; unknown scroll and reading]

The Water-Mirror Scroll (水鏡巻, mizukagami [no] maki)

[Skills of the shinobi, translated in this book]

毘沙門傳 (bishamonden)

[Possibly missing; foundation version to the following scroll. The following scroll appears to be extracts from this scroll, but it is unknown how big or comprehensive the original is. Clearly it is of great importance to the school.]

Teachings from the Deity Bishamonden (毘沙門傳抜書, bishamonden nukigaki)

[Translated in this book]

武用鑑 (buyō kagami)

[Missing]

笞動劔 (katsudō ken)

[Missing and unknown]

The Correct Mind of the Warrior (武士真直, bushi shinchoku)

[Missing]

The Scroll for Assisting in Ritual Suicide (介錯巻, kaishaku [no] maki)

[Skills appear in this book.]

The Scroll of the Star Hagun (破軍巻, hagun [no] maki)

[Skills appear in this book.]

The Nine Spell Ritual (九字, kuji)

[Skills appear in this book.]

The Ten Spell Ritual (十字, jūji)

[Skills appear in this book.]

Protection Scroll (護身法, goshinpō)

[Skills appear in this book.]

The Scroll of the Immovable Mind (不動心巻, fudōshin no maki)

[Missing]

免之巻 (men no maki)

[Missing]

同哥巻 (dōka [no] maki)

[Most likely this scroll's title has a transcription error or uses other characters. The reading *dōka* can be read as "poems about the arts." This could be *The Scroll of Poems* (歌之巻, uta no maki), which has been translated in this book.]

The Scroll of the Quarterstaff (棒之巻, bō no maki)

[Missing]

鳴劒巻 (meiken [no] maki)

[Missing]

玉鍼巻 (tama hari [no] maki)

[Missing]

櫃之巻 (hisagi no maki)

[Missing; possibly *The Scroll of the Altar* (壇之巻)]

Battle Fan Scroll (軍扇巻, gunsen [no] maki)

[Missing]

踏返巻 (fumikaeshi [no] maki)

[Missing]

Expelling the Spirit of the Fox Scroll (狐落巻, kitsune otoshi [no] maki)

[Missing]

There are thirty-three scrolls listed above which make up the teachings of the school. (以上三拾三巻)

List of Deep Secrets (極秘傳授之部, gokuhi denju no bu)

41 articles

一子相傳之部不書之 (isshisōden no bu kore ni kakazaru)

[It is unknown which are recorded in this book and which are not.]

Teachings on Resourcefulness (指南知謀之部, shinan chibō no bu)

[Missing]

Here ends the Mubyōshi Ryū *Kaimokusho* scroll, which has given a wide-ranging overview of the school of Mubyōshi Ryū.

6

THE INHERITED TRADITION

When Hagiwara Jūzō founded the school under the guidance and instruction of Niki Shinjūrō, the school would have been considered a comprehensive combat school, including but not confined to:

- sword quick draw
- hand-to-hand fighting
- projectile weapons
- rope skills
- chain and sickle
- quarterstaff
- the arts of the shinobi
- defensive magic
- mounted warfare
- martial philosophy
- secret traditions

When the school became an official school taught at the Keibukan dōjō, it is listed as a jūjutsu, kumiuchi, and taijutsu school, all of which are unarmed combat skills. This raises the question, how many of the traditions of Mubyōshi Ryū were passed on? If the school was registered as only teaching hand-to-hand combat, where did the other skills go, and for how long were the traditions passed on? The current grandmaster, Uematsu Sensei, is the inheritor of the unarmed combat tradition. The skills of the *kusarigama* (sickle and chain) are the result of his research, and the *Mubyōshi Ryū Shinobi Arts* and other scrolls were collected and presented by me, Mieko Koizumi, and Yoshie Minami. Through the multiple transcriptions and scrolls, we know that many of the skills continued to be passed on even into the nineteenth century, but the fact that a selection of them is no longer passed on shows that a concentration on unarmed fighting skills has led to a loss of sections of the school.

ADAPTING JŪJUTSU TO THE MODERN DAY

For an aficionado of jūjutsu, the images in this book may contain stances that appear peculiar and that resemble more of a karate attitude. For those who are not familiar, traditional jūjutsu often begins with a raised hand and, for want of a better word, a chopping motion, giving the iconic and wrongly titled "judo chop" its fame. Japanese martial arts start with this rigid chopping action, and *kata* (forms) are used to defend against them.

Karate, on the other hand, is not Japanese and was introduced from the Okinawan islands in the early twentieth century. The current grandmaster of Mubyōshi Ryū is also a teacher of traditional karate and decided that he would adopt a more karate-like attitude to the traditional jūjutsu. This may be horrific for some traditionalists, who may disagree with his intention (me included). However, know that the stances in this book are based on a karate attack and a jūjutsu response. Those who wish to return the skills to a more traditional slant may adopt the classic jūjutsu-style attack, a transition that will offer little difficulty.

That being said, lurking like a dragon at the rear of a cold cave is an argument that is at the forefront of my mind. It has to be understood that over the hundreds of years that traditional schools have existed, stagnation, dogma, and simplification have crept into their techniques, and what may once have been a very dynamic, versatile, and effective skill may in some

Figure 6.1. Karate and jūjutsu opening stances. There are multiple versions of both karate and jūjutsu stances, and this image represents the basic differences. Each traditional school has its own version.

schools have become a theater show of its original form. Kata may have lost the "middle elements," the connecting flow between each position where body manipulation would have originally been found. It is my opinion that the world of Japanese martial arts needs a complete overhaul, and the skills need to be stripped back to their original incarnation. Keep this in mind as you study old schools.

TO SIT OR NOT TO SIT, THAT IS THE QUESTION

The question of sitting or standing to execute a martial technique has long been a factor that never "sits" well with me. In both swordsmanship and grappling, adopting a seated position is sometimes used. Most people jump to the conclusion that such skills were performed when samurai sat together, but this is not as straightforward as it appears. There are often hierarchical seating positions to consider, the tradition of taking the longsword off the waist, the retaining of the shortsword in the sash, and the distance between the seated people—which could be some distance away. In addition, it appears that in some schools, skills that were once displayed and practiced from a standing position moved to be practiced while seated. This has led to schools of many arts using skills only when seated but which may have been established as standing combat.

I would like to suggest that the reader and any neophyte of the skills in this book keep in mind that most of these skills should be studied from a standing position, but that they can also be attempted while sitting. Retain this mind while remembering that it is the principle of the application that should be studied, not the detail. Some of the skills in the book change between both, but always remember that most skills would have started from a standing position. The argument behind this and its answer have yet to be satisfied, and a journey into discovering the truth behind "to sit or not to sit" is well outside of the scope of this work. Even though the argument cannot be settled, it is best to understand and consider these factors:

- All skills were originally developed to tackle unexpected situations, fast and unplanned.
- Most likely, the predominant number of skills were performed standing.
- Some skills were developed and originally used from a seated position.
- A samurai would not sit down with his *katana* in his belt, except in some cases. He may retain it at the waist while being present in ritual suicide

or when arresting others, thus some skills may have been developed for those situations.

- At some point in the Edo Period—the period of peace and the last era of the samurai—traditional standing drills moved from being performed upright to being done from the floor in a seated position.
- It is important to note that this move from standing to seated has caused an immense complication in understanding what was originally intended as a sitting skill or a standing one.
- While Edo Period manuals—such as those found in Mubyōshi Ryū—state that a skill is done from a seated position, this may be a reflection of the trend to move to a seated position and may not have been the original way it was practiced, even though the schools' scrolls themselves say so.
- This issue causes problems with the names of some scrolls, as some are considered to mean standing skills and some mean sitting skills. See the scroll list in appendix D.

In conclusion, understand that at present there is no definite way to establish those skills that should be performed seated and those that should be performed standing. Instead, apply yourself to understanding the concept of each skill from both positions.

Figure 6.2.

PRESSURE POINTS AND VITAL STRIKING AREAS

Striking vital points is a cornerstone of Japanese martial arts. Figure 6.3 shows the vital striking points on the human body and is studied in the main dōjō itself. These can be found in many arts.

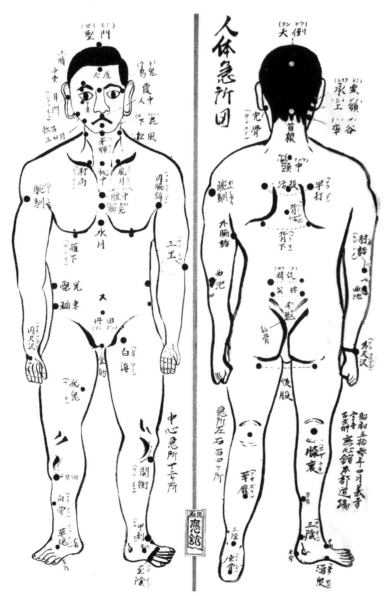

Figure 6.3.

7

THE ORIGINS OF THE SCHOOL

Like most martial schools in Japan, the establishment of a new martial system requires not only a blessing by a god or gods but also a divine spark of ignition. A common yet powerful element of a samurai school is a direct connection between the founding master and a god, normally set against the backdrop of the founder undergoing an extended period of training. His efforts subsequently allow him to receive divine inspiration and wisdom from a deity, who, personified, visits the swordsman and endows him with its blessing.

In the case of Mubyōshi Ryū, the god in question is Bishamonten (sometimes called Bishamon), who, after appearing as a dragon, and also being represented by the star Polaris, gives his protection to Yoshitsune. Yoshitsune is an immense figure in Japanese history, and multiple schools claim to be descended from him. Yoshitsune lived hundreds of years before Mubyōshi Ryū, in the twelfth century, and therefore his name is used to imply a distant connection.

The school's origin story then takes a more realistic slant and describes how Hagiwara Jūzō, hot-tempered in his youth and faced with ancient family feuds, killed an enemy, which led to nine years of vengeance attacks and open fighting with his enemies. Such a situation led him to pray for the protection of Marishiten, a deity of warriors, and to Bishamon, but also to take a more practical approach. Visiting many schools, Hagiwara Jūzō sought the teachings of masters of their arts, learning all he could from them and going on to develop his own school. He even came to understand *shinobi no jutsu* (the arts of the shinobi).

Our window into the origin story comes from a scroll titled *Bishamonden (The Traditions of Bishamon)*. Observe that even though Hagiwara Jūzō is clearly the originator of the school in the text, we see that the position of pride—the top slot—is given to Niki Shinjūrō, helping to connect the school back to Shinjin Ryū. Note that it is only through the following story in this scroll alone that Hagiwara Jūzō is considered the main founder. Without it, all evidence points to Niki Shinjūrō. The name "Shigetatsu" in the story is Hagiwara Jūzō's familiar name, as he would be known to those close to him.

THE TRADITIONS OF BISHAMON (毘沙門伝, BISHAMONDEN)

In the early days of his training in martial ways (武道), Minamoto no Yoshitsune had a very important wish, and commenced a thousand-day prayer ritual to Bishamon in Kurama (鞍馬). With this he made every effort to fulfill his desires, enduring every hardship. One night in a dream, a divine dragon of one *jō* (ten feet) in length appeared from the direction of the western sea. It said to him that he would give this writing to him and that he, the dragon, was the deity of Polaris, the North Star. After this meeting, the dragon ascended to heaven. Yoshitsune woke up in tears, gratified with such a dream, and worshipped the north. Afterward he gave this writing the title *Bishamonden (The Traditions of Bishamon)*. Yoshitsune respected this for the remainder of his life and thought it supreme to all his military skills (兵法). As a result, he never failed and was never defeated during his lifetime. He recorded the teachings in a single scroll and kept them in the temple Bishamon-do in Kurama.

Long after this time, the scroll was transmitted to the Hōjō clan, and they prospered for a few generations. In the end, however, they forgot about the past and paid the scroll no attention, and as a result they were punished and defeated, which brought the clan to ruin. A descendent took notice of this scroll and donated it to Atsuta shrine. A spy *(kanja)* for Lord Nobunaga, whose name is Kobayashi Oboro, heard of this scroll and reported its existence to him discreetly. Nobunaga took interest in the writing and had Kasadera Shinzaemon bring it to him so he could observe it. We do not know what he thought of it, but he changed the title of the scroll from *Bishamonden* to *Tsukiyoden* (月夜伝), which means "tradition of the moonlit night." After this, it became a tradition passed down in the Kobayashi clan. It has wondrous articles within its many points and holds the subtleties of the gods. Among them are five core disciplines to adhere to:

1. The Precept against Unnecessary Killing—an Oral Tradition
   (殺生戒　口伝)
2. The Precept Against Adultery—an Oral Tradition
   (邪淫戒　口伝)

3. The Need to Retain a Strong Mind, to Protect the Clan, Day or Night, Maintain Your Energy, and Act Flexibly—an Oral Tradition (心強持テ其家ヲ守昼夜加勢機働事　口伝)

4. To Stamp Down with Both Feet Any Vicious Thoughts That Rise from Within; This Will Dispel Any External Disaster—an Oral Tradition (心従発悪念ヲ両足仁踏テ外ヨリ来災難ヲ払事　口伝)

5. To Know the Will and Benefits of Heaven and Earth and Be Devoted to Loyalty and Fidelity for the Sake of Righteousness (天地之思ヲ知テ儀ノ為仁忠孝ヲ励事)

Those who follow these above five points will fulfill the will of the Gods of War.

By having respect for the gods, you can increase your spirit and have a higher level of virtue. Evidence for this can be seen by the example of [Hagiwara Jūzō[1]] Shigetatsu, who obtained divine protection thirty-two times in martial situations, seven of which his life was in true danger. Miraculously he survived, a feat that was due to a vow to Marishiten that had been given, including a promise to be punished if he should fail [in the above precepts]—let it be known that he never failed a single time. This is not because he fought with prowess by himself or because he had mastered all the various martial skills; it was due to the protection brought through the traditions of Bishamon.

Also, Yoshitsune, when he was at a travel lodge in Akasaka, killed thirteen people. They were Kumasaka Chōhan and his men, and this was not an achievement of man but due to this very tradition. When [Hagiwara Jūzō] Shigetatsu was young, he unexpectedly had to kill someone, and because of this he was targeted, day and night, for nine years. In order to kill the enemy, he devoted himself to training in the martial ways (武芸) and sought various schools and asked for many teachers to instruct him. There were numerous troubles due to blood feuds that started when his ancestor had killed their enemy in warfare. In those troubles there were times when he barely escaped. Due to the actions of the many enemies and without intending to do so, [the martial skills] he learned became the skills of his own school.

A wish [to develop these skills] arose from within, and he quickly identified elements from the deepest secrets of various schools, together with their theories. Furthermore, he divided them into those which were *in* and those which were *yō* and devised a method of training that lasted for seventy-two days; this he implemented [into his school]. Be it in the day or at night, no matter how good a master is that you fight with, this way [of training] ensures advantage and victory. This is through divine intervention.

The tradition of Yoshitsune says: "If you are determined in the martial arts and wish to acquire such divine protection through an oath, you should be like the moon reflecting upon the water." The transitory nature of combat is like passing back and forth before a bow that has been drawn. Although you may fear the stronger elements of other schools, our tradition is just like a wondrous medicine that has been transmitted in a family that is not familiar with the healing path, for it cures serious disease without them knowing why.[2]

Due to your earnest request, I fully and discreetly transmit to you the essential principles of the *bushi* that are useful and wondrous for each person to study.

The Deep Secrets of the Bishamon Tradition (毘沙門傳極意, Bishamonden Gokui)

Chant the following three times when you see this scroll:

Tenka taihei kokudo an'on / On anichiya sowaka

(天下泰平國土安穏　ヲンアニチヤソワカ)

(*Universal peace will enter the whole world, and safety will rest within our country.*)

[The following is a set of skill titles. On the whole, their context and meaning have been lost.]

The form of the shadow of flying birds (飛鳥之翔影之躰)

The mirror-like mind that reflects [the enemy mind] as water reflects the moon (鏡心水月之移)

The posture of the limitless gate (無極鳥居[3]之構)

The surge of dropping rocks and stones[4] (巖石落)

Submerging dragon and the many petal chrysanthemum[5]—also the cluster of clouds (潜竜八重菊附村雲)

The principle of the three gods (三神之大事)

The golden pole (鉾結鴈) [and cutting edge] of the Yuikarigane crest[6] (also written as *spear*; 金軸結鴈)

The principle of Tōhachi Bishamon (刀八毘沙門之大事)

The art of grass hiding (草隠之事)

The furious energy of lions and the attack of the tiger (獅子分身虎乱入)
The golden mean of Ryōtō Marumono (両当丸物之中梨)
The golden mean of living, killing, and death (活殺死之中梨)

The twelve points above are deep secrets; however, because of your many years of training, I will transmit them to you. You should have these principles in mind, for they are the golden rules of combat. Uncountable words cannot reveal them.

Niki Shinjūrō Masanaga
Hagiwara Jūzō Shigetatsu
Tōmi Gen'nai Nobuna
Kitagawa Kin'emon Sadahide
Kishimoto Genshichi Sadanobu
Sawamura Matsuemon Tadanawa

Transcribed in Bunka 5 [1808], a *tsuchinoe* year and a Year of the Dragon, on a lucky day in the fifth month, by Takakuwa Chōzaemon Yoshimasa

[Another version of this scroll was found in the Kinsei Shiryōkan collection in the Tamagawa library and is dated 1698. It is signed only by Hagiwara Jūzō and has only nine points, two of which differ.]:

The principle of the three types of dagger (懐劔三品之大事)
The curtain of mist—supplementary to this is the shinobi-ball[7]
  (霞之幕附忍玉)

8

THE MARTIAL ARTS
OF MUBYŌSHI RYŪ

Uematsu Sensei primarily inherited a jūjutsu school with a small array of weapons skills. While other skills, such as esoteric magic and the arts of the shinobi, are a part of the school, without doubt the school is truly focused on hand-to-hand combat, and personal protection is the main emphasis, no matter which form it takes. Mysteriously, there appears to be a distinct lack of swordsmanship in Mubyōshi Ryū, leading to the conclusion that Hagiwara Jūzō studied and continued to be a part of another sword school, most likely Shinjin Ryū, alongside his colleagues Niki Shinjūrō and Tōmi Gen'nai. Even with the lack of swordsmanship—only a small amount is present— the teachings contain many captivating skills, including grappling, striking, hand-thrown arrows and bullets, truncheons, chains and weights, hidden blades, and canes, among other elements. These skills are found in the school's primary scroll, the *Yawara Jo*.

The *Yawara* scroll is simply titled *Yawara Jo*, meaning "an introduction to grappling skills." Note that the word *jūjutsu* is not used at this time. It contains most of the school's hand-to-hand combat skills. It is difficult to determine whether the author meant that the whole scroll was an introduction to fighting, or that the scroll was called *Yawara* and the first paragraph at the start was the introduction. Either way, the scroll outlines the skills and opens with a short introduction on the philosophy of fighting. This introduction is based on an understanding of Chinese culture, and a direct translation loses the originally intended basic meaning, which was given to an audience with such an education. Therefore, it was decided here that an overview and outline should be provided in its place.

The introduction within the scroll teaches that within music and sound there is no gap between the cause of the sound and the audible sound itself. For example, a clap of the hands initiates a sound, and this comes after the clap. However, the gap between the clap and the sound reaching the ears of

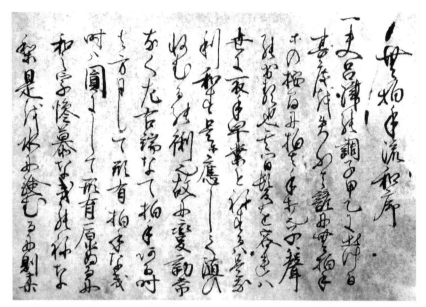

*Figure 8.1. The original introduction from the **Yawara** scroll (Cummins Collection)*

those nearby is not discernible—a person cannot see the space between the clap and the sound. Because the person listening to the clap cannot find the space between the clap and the sound, this gap or process cannot be identified, and the observer cannot manipulate or comprehend it. In addition, the introduction states that the art of combat should have no understandable form, no discernible rhythm. If given shape, such as a square or construct of angles, it can be identified, but instead it should remain circular and without an assembled form, allowing the enemy no time to plan or respond.

Furthermore, a combat master should understand the concepts of hard, flexible, soft, and strong. Hard or rigid is the opposite of flexible and yielding, while softness and gentleness are in opposition to strength. A practitioner of Mubyōshi Ryū must know when to be strong, when to have rigidity, when to be gentle, and when to apply flexibility. Combat is won through an understanding of this.

Lastly, the manual states that hand-to-hand combat should be like an arrow or iron needle, hidden in silk cloth, masking the danger so that the enemy has no ability to predict or comprehend where the attack will come from. Thus, taking the basics of this introduction, a student of Mubyōshi Ryū should know that they have to adapt between the four elements of hardness, flexibility, strength, and gentleness to be without rigid form and not to allow the enemy to predict his movements—in essence to achieve a state of *mubyōshi,* to have no discernible rhythm.

Antony Cummins says: Be careful not to let this be confusing. Physical form in martial arts is there to develop proper movement, but a fight is not undertaken in pure form. Form develops good standing and correct skills, but actual combat is fast, "dirty," and abstract. The idea is to hide the form internally. Consider form to be the basic steps of a child learning to walk, and the highest level is the freedom of athletes in peak condition. They have studied the form of their sport but act purely on their training and move in a way that is necessary for the situation. They don't stick to form in the middle of a game or competition. Formulaic martial arts should be considered in this way.

In addition, some of the names used by Uematsu Sensei in the following list of scrolls are not the same as the common readings; these variations are included.

The Combat Skills of Mubyōshi Ryū
(無拍子流和序, Mubyōshi Ryū Yawara Jo)
Iho no Maki (居捕之巻)

KURUMAGAESHI (車返)

KAKEHASHI (掛橋)

UKIFUNE (浮舟)

HANEGARAMI (羽搦), SITTING

HANEGARAMI (羽搦), STANDING

BYŌBUGAESHI (屏風返)

SANGETSU (山月)

MATSUKAZE (松風)

KUTSUGAESHI (沓返)

TAKIOTOSHI (瀧落)

OMOKAGE (面影)

JUNPO (順捕)

GYAKUHO (逆捕)

HANEGAESHI (羽返)

SUIKYŌ (水鏡)

IKADA (筏)

NAMIMAKURA (浪枕)

TOKOGAESHI (床返)

YUMEMAKURA (夢枕)

Tachiai no Maki (立合之巻)
KORAN (虎乱)

SASEN (左旋)

OIKAKEHO (追掛捕)

ENPI (燕廻)

TSUMATEHO (妻手捕)

KITEKI (扃擲)

HIKIUKEOTOSHI (引請落)

YŪHIKIGAESHI (誘引返)

USHI (右被), INSIDE

RŌRYŪ (瀧流)

MUSUBIITO (結絲)

BUTTŌ (佛倒)

GANSEKIOTOSHI (岸石落)

岸
岩石
落

NEHO (寝捕)

HŌGAI (鋒外)

TOWAKI (戸脇)

HASSOKUTŌ (八足倒)

MARUMI (丸身)

HISSHI SANDAN CHŪ (必死三段中)

SANKAKU KORE NAKA (三角之中)

NUKIGUCHI (抜口)

IKIAIDAORE (行合倒)

HOGAESHI (捕返)

MUNEGARAMI (胸搦)

HIKIOTOSHI (引落)

TEKI NI KORE KASA (敵二之笠)

SŌMUBŌSŌ (雙六忘艸)

KUSARIDAMA KENYŌ (鎖玉遣様)

鎖長サ　柄長四尺三寸　二尺一寸六分（乳切木）

TSUKI NIN SHIHO (突忍死捕)

CHISAI CHŌTAN (地際長短)

DAIHACHIDOME (臺鉢留)

臺鉢留

KOSHIHIKI TSURIAI (腰引釣合)

KARI SHINAJINA (狩品々)

FUTARIMUSUBI (二人結)

OMOMI (重身)

FURIMI (振身)

SUTEMI (捨身)

YORIMI (倚身)

MAKUBISHIN (慕廻身)

The Scroll of Tools (道具之巻, Dōgu no Maki)
Mist (truncheon; 霞, kasumi)

- The length of this is one *shaku*, one *sun*, and five *bu* [13.72 inches].
- The shaft should have sixteen sides.
- [Attach] a rope of six *sun* [7.16 inches] with a ring.

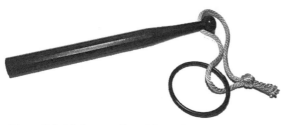

Figure 8.3. Modern replica of the tool

Figure 8.2. Mist

Chain and Ball (鎖玉, kusari-dama[1])

- The chain is three shaku five sun [3 feet, 6 inches] long.
- The ball weight is thirty to thirty-five *momme* [4–4.6 ounces].
- The chain should be of the *sunoko* style.

Figure 8.4. Chain and ball

Figure 8.5. Sickle and ball

Sickle and Ball (鎌玉, kama-dama)

- The sickle is five sun [6 inches] long.
- The chain is three shaku five sun [3 feet, 6 inches] long.
- The ball weighs thirty to thirty-five momme [4–4.6 ounces].
- The length of the handle is one shaku and eight sun [21.5 inches].

The Tool of Ten Uses (十德, jittoku)

- The handle fits into your fist.
- Inside is a rope ring with three chains four sun [4.8 inches] in length.[2]
- The length of the drill is one sun two bu [1.4 inches] long.

Antony Cummins says: this is an enigmatic tool. It seems to be a drill or spike inside a housing. The middle point above shows that it stores more internally, yet it is not described in detail.

Figure 8.6. Tool of ten uses

Figure 8.7. Use of the arrow-shooting cylinder

Arrow-Shooting Cylinder
(筒打矢, tsutsu uchiya)

- The cylinder is one shaku two sun [14.3 inches] in length.
- The arrow is of iron and the flights are made of leather.

Figure 8.8. Modern replica of the arrow-shooting cylinder

Figure 8.9. Ball-shooting cylinder

Ball-Shooting Cylinder (筒打玉, tsutsu uchi dama)

- The cylinder is one shaku [12 inches] long.
- The ball should fit inside the cylinder.

Beginning and End (阿吽, a un)

- It should weigh fifty to seventy momme [6.6–9.3 ounces].
- It should be wrapped with leather.

*Figure 8.10.
Beginning and end*

Figure 8.11. Capturing with a Musket

Capturing with a Musket[3]
(生捕鉄砲, ikedori teppō)

- This has a bamboo bullet.

Staff with Chain and Weight
(乳切木, chigiriki)

The Holy Symbol (卍字, manji)

[Unknown tool in the shape of a swastika]

- This is eight sun (9.5 inches).
- The handle is made of copper and is one shaku [12 inches] long.

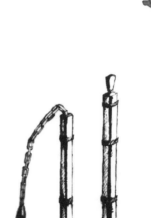

Figure 8.12. Staff with chain and weight   *Figure 8.13. Holy symbol*

THE CHAIN AND SICKLE SCROLL OF MUBYŌSHI RYŪ (無拍子流鎖鎌免許, MUBYŌSHI RYŪ KUSARIGAMA MENKYO)

The Art of the Weight (分銅之事, fundō no koto)

This chain and weight should be thrown at the enemy, and then he should be cut down with the sickle while you pull him toward you.

- The chain [bottom of the weapon at right] should be seven shaku [7 feet].
- The handle for this weapon is one shaku five sun [18 inches] long.

- The chain [top on the weapon at left] should be three shaku five sun [3 feet, 6 inches].
- The handle for this weapon is one shaku eight sun [21.5 inches].
- The blade should be five sun [6 inches].

[The chain in figure 8.14 and the reconstruction is shorter than stated in the original scroll.]

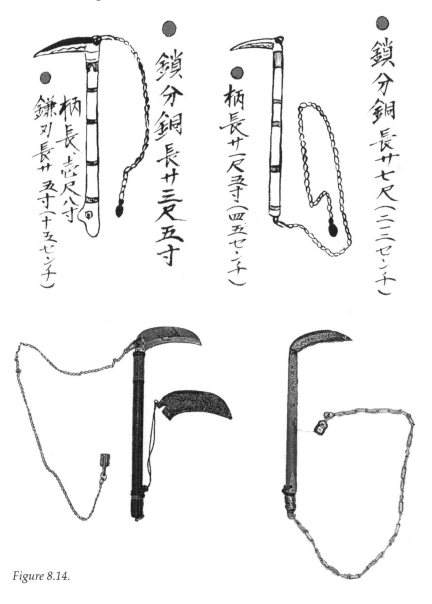

Figure 8.14.

Figure 8.15. *The Windmill above the Head* (頭上風車法, *zujō fūsha hō*)

Figure 8.16. *The Way of the Windmill at the Side* (横風車法, *yoko fūsha hō*)

Figure 8.17. *The Figure-Eight Windmill* (八字風車法, *hachiji fūsha hō*)

The Way of the Falling Flower (落花之事, rakka no koto)

When you attach the chain to the back of the blade, swing the chain over the head or body of the enemy.

Various Ways of Capturing (狩品々, kari shinajina)

[Title for the following five skills]

Figure 8.18. *The Posture of Looking at the Eye* (青眼之構, *seigan no kamae*)

Figure 8.19. The Face
(面影, *omokage*)

Figure 8.20. Catching the Sword
(太刀搦, *tachigarami*)

Figure 8.21. *Capturing the Leg and Pulling Down* (足搦倒, *ashigarami taoshi*)

Figure 8.22. *Capturing the Neck and Bringing Down* (首搦落, *kubigarami otoshi*)

The Art of the Chain and Weight (分銅鎖之事, fundō kusari no koto)

[The following are types of these.]

- Chain and Weight (万力鎖, manrikigusari)
- Truncheon with Chain (鎖十手, kusari jitte)
- Ball with Chain (玉鎖, tamagusari)
- Sleeve Chain (袖鎖, sodegusari)
- Chain inside the Kimono (懐鎖, futokorogusari)

Various Shapes (様々形之事, samazama katachi no koto)

[This is a title for the next six points.]

- The hook is for grappling.
- It has four prongs.
- The whole length is eight shaku [8 feet].
- The whole length is two shaku four sun [2 feet, 5 inches].
- The whole length is two shaku eight sun [2 feet, 9 inches].
- The chain length is two shaku and two sun [2 feet, 2 inches].

Figure 8.23. The Dragon-Snake Chain (鎖竜蛇, kusari ryūda)

Figure 8.24. Kiraku Ryū Bell Shaped Weight (氣楽流鈴型分銅, kiraku ryū suzu-gata fundō)

Figure 8.25. Toda Ryū Style with Square Ends and Rounded Corners (戸田流撫四角柱型, toda ryū nade shikakuchū-gata)

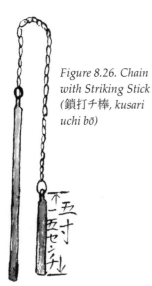

Figure 8.26. Chain with Striking Stick (鎖打チ棒, kusari uchi bō)

Figure 8.27. Long Chain and Weights (長分銅鎖, naga fundō kusari)

Figure 8.28. The Flying Stick (棍飛, bō tōbi)

- The right side end is five sun [6 inches].
- The left side is one shaku two sun [14.3 inches].
- The whole length is six shaku [6 feet].
- The whole length is four shaku [4 feet].
- The weight is the same as a playing piece from the *shōgi* game.

間具利身 (Magurishin)

[This is the title for the following five skills.]

Antony Cummins says: For Circling to the Right, move to the opposite side to figure 8.30.

Figure 8.29. The Tiger at War (虎乱之構, koran no kamae)

Figure 8.30. Circling to the Right (右旋, *usen*) and Circling to the Left (左旋, *sasen*)

Figure 8.31. Pulling and Throwing Down (引請落, *hikiuke otoshi*)

Figure 8.32. Catching the Left Hand
(弓手捕, *yumiteho*)

Antony Cummins says: The left hand is captured while it holds the sword, as shown in the traditional illustration at the top of figure 8.32.

The above are the skills of Mubyōshi Ryū Kusarigama-jutsu.

Praise Bishamonten.

Illustrated and recorded on paper by the current grandmaster in 2012.

THE QUARTERSTAFF SKILLS OF SODEOKA RYŪ (袖岡流, SODEOKA RYŪ BŌJUTSU)

Antony Cummins says: Sodeoka Ryū was originally taught as a part of Mubyōshi Ryū. It left Grandmaster Uematsu's lineage, and to return it to the school, Grandmaster Uematsu studied under one of his own students who had studied this style externally, allowing it to be reintroduced. There are differences in the names used in the two versions, however. The version presented here and the original names found in the Mubyōshi Ryū scroll, *Yawara,* differ, which implies some changes have occurred over time, or that this version is a variant. Therefore, it is unknown how close the following images are to the skills collected by Hagiwara Jūzō.

SEIGAN (正眼)

DOKKO (独古)

INJI (隠持)

INJI CHŪDAN
(隠持 中段)

TANBŌ (短棒)

HANE GAESHI (羽返)

KOSHIGURUMA (腰車)

KOHŌ (虎法)

133

NAMIGAESHI (波返)

FŪYŌ (風揚)

FUMIKAESHI (踏返)

SASHIAI (指合)

HIEN（飛燕）

TACHIGARI (太刀狩)

RYŌKIDACHI TANBŌ (両木太刀 短棒)

THE SIXTEEN POEMS
OF MUBYŌSHI RYŪ

Found within the school's teachings are sixteen poems concerning philosophy of mind. Below are all sixteen poems in English translation, original form, and simplified Japanese form. The poems contain the names Niki Shinjūrō and Hagiwara Jūzō, among others, dating them to at least the latter half of the seventeenth century.

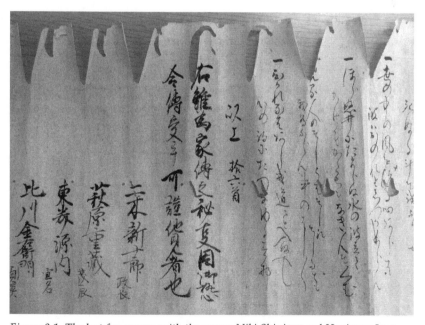

Figure 9.1. The last few poems, with the names Niki Shinjūrō and Hagiwara Jūzō beside them (金沢市立玉川図書館近世史料館所蔵)

THE SCROLL OF POEMS (歌之巻, UTA NO MAKI)

1.

Being lulled by the thought that you have tomorrow, you waste another
day idle.
Original: 明日も阿り登おもふ心尓者可羅れてけふもむなしく暮ぬる哉
Simplified: 明日もありと思う心にはかられて今日もむなしく暮れぬるかな

2.

Thinking that you will avoid inactivity tomorrow will actually encour-
age idleness.
Original: 明日よりハ阿多に月日をおくらし登おもひし可もとけふも暮し川
Simplified: 明日よりはあだに月日を送らじと思いしかもと今日も暮らしつ

3.

Always think your life is only formed of today, as yesterday is gone and
tomorrow is never known.
Original: 世の中はけふ斗とそいつと阿れきのふハ過川阿春ハ知られ須
Simplified: 世の中は今日ばかりとぞいつとあれ昨日は過ぎつ明日は知られず

4.

Going up a river to seek its source, you will only find dew drops on a
thorny bush and drips among the grass.[1]
Original: 山川の其水上を尋れ者蕀の雫苺の志多耳
Simplified: 山川の其水上を尋ぬれば蕀の雫苺の下に

5.

People may forget the words or skills that they have been taught and
have to relearn them once more.
Original: なら飛請し其ことわさをいつとなく王春れて後に学ひぬる人
Simplified: 習い請けし其ことわざをいつとなく忘れて後に学びぬる人

6.

If the mind is pure like crystal-clear water, how could it be possible that
it would not reflect the moon?
Original: 世の中能心の水乃清可らハ(す)なと可ハ月のうつらさらまし
Simplified: 世の中の心の水の清からば(ず)などかは月の映らざらまし

7.

Thin green willow leaves go with the water stream, like flowing threads.[2]

Original: 行水の流尓志たふ青柳の糸引王可る是なれや

Simplified: 行く水の流れにしたう青柳の糸引きわかる是なれや

8.

The thought of calming your mind is itself a movement of the mind.
  Thus, do not try to calm yourself, and do not slacken. Do not slacken
  and do not budge.[3]

Original: 治るとおもふ心の動なりおさめ春たら春たら春ゆるか須

Simplified: 治ると思う心の動なりおさめずたらずたらずゆるがず

9.

Be like a mirror, particularly where there is nothing. When the enemy
  moves, he will reflect within it.

Original: 一物もなき所こそ鏡なれ動可は敵のかけうつ春なり

Simplified: 一物もなき所こそ鏡なれ動かば敵の影映すなり

10.

Try not to concentrate on moving in a direction. Instead, retain the
  thought of a seed and defeat the teachings the enemy has in mind.

Original: 行登たにおもハぬものを種として敵のおしへ尓か川者かりなり

Simplified: 行くとだに思わぬものを種として敵の教えにかつばかりなり

11.

Trying to decide between good or evil inherently establishes doubt. If
  you pursue evil, goodness and evil will emerge.[4]

Original: 善悪とおもふ心もまよひなり悪をたよりて出るせん阿く

Simplified: 善悪と思う心も迷いなり悪をたよりて出る善悪

12.

Of all the lies that flow from people's minds, the only real truth is to
  enter into death.

Original: 世の中能人の心の偽耳死ぬる斗そ誠なりけり

Simplified: 世の中の人の心の偽りに死ぬるばかりぞ誠なりけり

13.

By having an intent to calm the wind of the world, it follows that the wave will naturally settle.

Original: 世の中の風を治る心阿ら者波ハおのれと志つ可為らん

Simplified: 世の中の風を治める心あらば波はおのれと静かならん

14.

Attempting to deal with an opponent who has no shadow or shape is like trying to draw water that has not gathered in a well that has not been dug.

Original: ほらぬ井尓たまらぬ水の波立てかけもか多ちもなき人そくむ

Simplified: 掘らぬ井にたまらぬ水の波立ちて影も形もなき人ぞくむ

15.

Let others slander you as they like, and in the face of such slander, simply discover things that will be useful for you.

Original: 見累人のそしら者そしれそしるとも我為ならん事の者し[者し]

Simplified: 見る人のそしらばそしれそしるとも我為ならん事のはしばし

16.

If tempted, you may fall into evil ways. Do not give loose rein to the horse of your mind.

Original: 飛可れな者阿し幾道ニも入ぬへし心の駒尓たつなゆる春那

Simplified: ひかれなば悪しき道にも入らぬべし心の駒に手綱ゆるすな

The end of The Sixteen Poems (以上　拾六首)

THE SCROLL OF THE MIND

Within the *Yawara* document, which is the main scroll of Mubyōshi Ryū, is a subscroll titled *Shinkan no Maki* (心鑑之巻),[1] which translates as *The Scroll of Reflecting on the Mind* or *The Scroll that is a Model for the Mind*. It is a document that crosses into the boundary of philosophical reflections on the physical realm of combat, an area that is possibly the most problematic in the world of samurai literature. The concept of "the sword and the brush" is a foundation of samurai life, and a samurai must be both capably violent as well as philosophically competent, an attitude that produces documents aimed at capturing the ungraspable—that is, trained combat response.

Capturing the visual or the physical is a problem encountered in all writings and in all cultures. A picture or demonstration supersedes volumes of work in a fraction of a moment. That being said, a samurai has to instill his followers with respect for him in both combat and mental prowess. This leaves stacks of documents in which samurai describe in detail the concepts behind physical combat in the most drawn-out and religiously overtoned ways. Allegories, metaphors, and comparisons are given to aid the reader to grasp the physical or even the mental attitude behind the physical. Some of these consist of elements that existed in the time of the samurai but which are lost to us. For example, "the moon reflecting on the water" is a constant in samurai literature, and one interpretation is the idea that the water is a representation of the mind while the moon is the external world. If the water is in tumult, then the reflection of the moon is scattered and distorted, the same way a person who is in emotional distress or panic finds reality around them distorted. If the water is calm, it will reflect the truth of a situation. If the mind is calm and neutral, a human will perceive that which is around them correctly, allowing the enemy to be observed with accuracy. This is only one explanation for this term. Another example used in this scroll is "the fifteenth day of the month," meaning the full moon. It means a person is in full preparation, and likewise, "the moon coming over the mountain" means a person approaching a state of preparation.

These examples show that the samurai tried to capture the impossible on paper and also added complex analogies to decorate and illustrate it. This type of writing proliferates in Japanese martial literature, and Mubyōshi Ryū is no exception. The *Shinkan no Maki* is their exercise in this form of teaching. This creates a series of issues. Without the transmission of the full teachings, the current state of the school does not hold the key to unlock much of this scroll, which means that there are no people trained in the applications of these concepts as they have been written. That has left a tremendous barrier for me and my translation partner, Mieko, to cross. Without initiation into this scroll or a foundation in the school, we have had to interpret the document. Most translations are a fine line between literal meaning and interpretation, and a translator balances in the middle. For this document, however, we have walked the path more on the side of interpretation. Thus, consider the following translation to be heavily influenced by our own ideas on the original text and that some of that text has been edited out to avoid confusion. We have endeavored to represent the ideas of this scroll as closely as we can to the original writing but in our own words.

THE SCROLL OF REFLECTING ON THE MIND
(心鑑之巻, SHINKAN NO MAKI)

This scroll is a model for your mind, and therefore is called *Shinkan no Maki, The Scroll of Reflecting on the Mind* [or *An Example of the Correct Mind*]. The following list is a model for your mental state [for combat]. People should perceive these teachings through their intellect and with internal feeling, but know that it is difficult to describe such things with words. This is *shinkan* (心鑑), the model for the mind.

Antony Cummins says: The character 鑑 can mean "reflection" or it can mean "model," as in a good example to follow.

1. There are three ways to perceive[2] [the enemy]:
- Perception of the mind (心ノ請)
- Perception of the eyes (眼ノ請)
- Perception of form (形ノ請)

Perception of the mind is speculating about the enemy's mind before you advance upon him.

Perception of the eye is to speculate about the enemy's mind by looking at how the enemy's eyes are used. Also, you should try not to let the enemy know what you are thinking in your own mind by the look of your own eyes.

Perception of form should be conducted in the same way as the above.

When you master the perception of the mind and of the eye, you will be able to achieve perception of the form automatically. Therefore, [perception of the form] derives from the two points of the mind and of the eye—this is a deep secret.

There should be three ways of perception [of the enemy]: the perception of the mind, the perception of the eye, and the perception of the form. When you attack the enemy, to consider what the enemy is going to do next is perception of the mind. But after this, the perception of the eyes and of form may delay your movement. Therefore, sometimes you should not overly speculate about the enemy. Ordinary people should not try to estimate as described above when fighting.

Antony Cummins says: It is good to consider what the enemy will do, but there is a level where this type of thinking will put you one step behind. Therefore, make sure this is not used too much.

2. The art of deciding when to die for duty (義二当リ死ヲ定ル事, gi ni atari shi wo sadamuru koto)

I will teach you how to die in the name of justice *(gi)* for a samurai. Reckless courage is useless. Do not let shame remain after you die. Teachings say that to devote your life to your lord in front of your lord's horse on the battlefield is considered duty (gi). In the case that is not during battle, duty (gi) is [to perform] when you receive an order from the lord. When there is a duty that gives reason to die, then it is your duty to die. This is a samurai's real intention. Also, since old times they say samurai are always prepared to die in the name of justice. To always keep death in mind is a samurai rule.

Know that originally, loyalty *(chūkō)* is born out of justice (gi). If something lacks justice, it will not prevail. Also know that there is a distinction between constructed justice (設ル義) and natural justice (自然ノ義). These two can look similar to each other.

Sometimes you will come across various [difficult] situations, where you have to ignore judging what is good or bad, or you have to engage in something negative to guard your lord even if the lord might blame you for your actions. A samurai's strong will is also justice (gi). Think deeply about various meanings of justice.

3. The art of *kenmon*—estimating distance between you and the enemy (敵二立居間門ノ事, teki ni tachii kenmon no koto)

Antony Cummins says: Kenmon is the gap between a sword hitting and a sword just missing. It is that "magic inch" of being cut or not cut, and is the essence of timing.

Original text: This is about kenmon, the distance between a standing person and a sitting person or two standing people. The standard kenmon is six shaku [6 feet]. Tradition says that a standing person has space to stretch; a sitting person does not have space for this. The standard kenmon of both [standing and seated] is six shaku. That is, the enemy's sword is three shaku [3 feet] long and your own sword is three shaku long. A standing person can move freely, and a sitting person cannot move so freely. It is the difference between having to stretch out or not. There are deep teachings about kenmon, thus sweeping statements cannot be made, and it is difficult to describe. There are various situations in this matter, for example with shortswords, without swords, and so on. Estimating kenmon in your mind depends on the enemy's distance, his timing, and his position. [Understanding kenmon is the same as] the knowledge of the god Dainichi [Nyorai], which concerns heaven and the sky, positive and negative, the sun and the moon, water and fire, substantial and insubstantial, movement and quiet. These are all perceived naturally in your mind [and there is a gap (kenmon) between each of the pairs described here]. Understand them internally.

Also consider long or short tools, wide or narrow spaces, and where it is difficult to observe the distance.

Improve kenmon of mind over kenmon of skill. For example, if you try getting your body close to the enemy's body, the distance tends to be too close. If you try keeping six shaku distance, it is difficult to measure such a distance. If you relax your mind, improvement will come. Think of this during normal practice. It is difficult to say exactly which measurements are best.

4. The art of fighting at the instant the enemy moves (敵ノ変二勝負可仕事, teki no hen ni shōbu shibeki koto)

This means to fight at the moment the enemy is unguarded. But this change of movement is not a change that you have initiated. There is change that is expected and unexpected, both of which are natural occurrences. When fighting, do not miss this moment of change. Victory and defeat are unknown. According to the way of the samurai, samurai should not discuss victory or defeat. Consider *shin* (the mind) and *kan* (the mirror). There are many oral traditions.

Fighting when the enemy moves is difficult to describe with words. Prepare yourself and attack the enemy when the enemy changes his movement. Even if the enemy is weak, it is still dangerous to fight without preparing yourself for an attack. According the way of the samurai, even if you lose the fight, sometimes there is no shame because victory and defeat are due to the chances of war. This is called "the samurai on the correct path."

5. The art of in-between, balance, and the three rhythms (中リ釣合三拍子ノ事, atari tsuriai san-byōshi no koto)

Atari (中リ) means to beat a time as with music (呂律), which is written in the introduction [to our school]. Think of the musical concepts of 律 *(ritsu)* and 呂 *(ryo)* and also 甲 *(kō)* and 乙 *(otsu)* [these are opposites, they are yin and yang]. The middle part between them is atari—that is, the space between. The oral tradition here is to change three beats to one.

This atari means the middle of a thing and represents a balanced center of mind. Do not observe the beginning, the middle, and the end as three beats, because balance and the middle are a single point. Anytime you fight, remember that a unified rhythm is important.

A rhythm of three will beat three times, but mubyōshi [the word that our school is founded on] means "without rhythm" and is to beat a single time. For example, when you throw [ashes or powder] into the enemy's eyes first and then attempt to capture him after that, you are delayed [by a beat], and the skill is divided into two movements [to throw and to capture]. So consider capture before you throw. It looks like you are doing two separate things, but you are doing it with a single mind. Get a feeling for this.

6. The art of knowing two states: right order and reverse order (順逆二ツノ裡ヲ可知事, jun gyaku futatsu no ri wo shiru beki koto)

Goodness [or advantage] changes into evilness [or disadvantage] depending on the time, the place, and the position. Also, evilness changes into goodness depending on the time, the place, and the position. Right order and reversed order are like this. You should try to not mistake the degree of change [in this situation]. There is oral tradition for this.

1. Correctness inside of correctness is correct.
2. Incorrectness inside of incorrectness is incorrect.
3. Incorrectness inside of correctness is incorrect.
4. Correctness inside of incorrectness is correct.

You should know this reason behind everything. For example, the four seasons come in their right order. The wind is cold in the cold season, but if the wind is warm, it is out of the natural order. When traveling and something unexpected happens, it is outside the expected order. In the case of fighting, when you [rightly] consider yourself good, then the enemy may attack as you expected. This is correctness inside of correct [and is a truthful situation]. If the enemy attacks you in an unexpected way, it is incorrectness [and you have misread your own abilities]. Correctness and incorrectness exist in the same place.

When unexpected things happen, you should not be confused but follow the situation. Just be calm. It is essential to administer your mind.

Antony Cummins says: Something that is truly good is always good. The reverse is that something that is truly bad is always bad. To try to hide something of malice inside goodness is still malice in truth, but to hide something good in something that is considered bad still has a core foundation of goodness. Remember, correctness and incorrectness come from intent, and what is good for one situation may not be good for another.

7. The art of observing the point of the fifteenth night of a lunar month (十五夜ノ目附ノ事, jūgoya no metsuke no koto)

This is the concept of "seven, five, and three." If you add the numbers in each line [as shown in figure 10.1], they all add up to fifteen. Also, oral tradition says it is like the rising full moon of the fifteenth night of the lunar month [which means the point of full preparedness].

This teaching—seven, five, and three (七五三, shichi go san)—comes from Shinto thought.

3	7	5
7	5	3
5	3	7

Figure 10.1.

The example of the rising moon is essential when you face the enemy. It is essential to capture the boundary between the moon rising above and not rising above the top of the mountain. When the moon is already away from the top of the mountain [and is full in the sky], there is no weakness to be observed [because it is in a state of fullness]. If [the enemy] does not change [his movement], they are perfectly prepared. You cannot capture a perfectly prepared enemy.

The fifteenth night means "completion" [or "fullness," as the moon is full]. It can be the case that both you and the enemy are in a state of full preparation. It is a secret in fighting to nip the enemy in the bud [before they are prepared].

Know that there is morning, daytime, and evening in a single day. People initiate in the morning, act vigorously in the daytime, and return home in the evening. So attack before the fifteenth night [before he is at his full capacity] or the time when [the enemy] is weak after he has passed the point of "fullness." Also, if you have overconfidence in your own perfect preparation, it may sometimes bring defeat. Therefore keep the thought of fullness as an idea in mind [but do not concentrate on it]. People who are well encamped will not fight, and people who fight well should not die.

Antony Cummins says: The fifteenth day is the height of the full moon. It is a night when monsters walk openly, and all is at its positive height. Here the scroll is telling us that when an enemy is in a fully guarded, well defended, and prepared position, it is useless to attack, like trying to batter down a strong and fortified wall. Therefore it is before and after this height that you should attack. From a practical point of view, this is when the enemy is going through a change in his movement.

8. The art of the position of the moon on the water
(水月ノ位ノ事, suigetsu no kurai no koto)

Pour water into a lidded bowl, and the moon will light the lid. If you open the lid even a little, the moon reflects a little on the water. If you open it widely, the moon reflects fully on the water. Also, there is a tradition about the coming together of the wave and the moon.

When the moon reflects on the water, it follows the wave. [The reflection] always moves in accordance. When the wave is breaking, the reflection of the moon on the water also breaks apart. When the wave becomes calm, the reflection of the moon on the water returns to its original condition. Understand this in your mind. This concept teaches that you need to move according to the situation. This is a skill you should consider and use.

When the enemy attacks, you should observe his "seat" [the hips or lower part] and not his face. This is the principle of position. Consider where the moon reflects on the water: it is where the enemy's movement appears with haste in your vision. This happens when you fight and are not in full defense. When you look at a single point, you will see movement around it [meaning the use of peripheral vision to observe the whole]. There is deep tradition about this article.

When the water moves, the moon on the water moves as well. If the water is clear, the moon reflects on the water. If the water becomes muddy, the moon does not reflect on the water. This is called *sumashi no kurai*—the position of clarity.

Antony Cummins says: The latter parts of this teaching are concerned with observing the opponent with a wide view and not a direct view. Concentrating on the hips of the opponent will allow you to see his movement, however looking at him directly will give the impression of haste and speed. Remember that broader vision is better than direct looking, so it does not matter if you are looking at the face or the lower body; the aim is to observe the whole situation by using a full field of vision instead of a direct and single point.

9. The art of creating distance with long weapons
(長ハ継ト云事, nagaki wa tsugu to iu koto)

This constitutes knowledge for using long tools. In the case that the enemy attacks you up close, if you have a long tool, there is no way to use it [as it should be used]. So you should create distance. Also, this is a teaching for when the enemy wears a shortsword *(wakizashi)* and you have a longsword (katana). Remember, longer tools may have a lot of disadvantages. Also, there is an oral tradition about distance in this art.

It is a mistake to try to make distance when you are already close and inside the enemy's kenmon (the space where he can cut you), because you are too close to reach the enemy with a long weapon. Therefore, when you try to go close to the enemy, if you are actually out of reach, make sure to push yourself that extra bit toward enemy and attack.

Make distance with long tools [such as spears] and get in close when you have a shorter tool. Consider this point. You should fully understand distance and timing between you and the enemy. Consider distance and rhythm, and from that you will better understand your position for a skill you are to use.

This constitutes the knowledge for using long tools. Also, to estimate whether the distance is long or short in your mind is more important than if the tool is long or short itself. Consider this deeply.

10. The art of getting in close with a short tool (短ハ切ト云事, mijikaki wa kiru to iu koto)

When you have a shortsword (wakizashi), it is essential to step toward the enemy suddenly and cut him before he is fully prepared. Kenmon (the art of distance) is of primary concern in this scroll, so keep it in mind when you cut with a short tool. *Mutōdori* (capturing without a sword) is also connected to this. [Matsumoto Koredayū] Takahisa says there are cases where you may be without your swords but the enemy may have such tools [and thus, understand the situation from both sides].

Consider this and understand:

- timing an attack
- moving in close
- making distance
- capturing without a sword

You should create distance with a long tool and get in closer with a short tool, but also the enemy can do likewise. To put it another way, when the enemy has a long tool, he will try to create more distance from you. You can find it is a disadvantage if you only consider these teachings from your own point of view, so consider that the enemy will do the same. When the enemy has a short tool, the enemy will try to attack and get in close. You can find it is a disadvantage if you only concentrate on creating distance with a longer tool [remember to consider his actions and not to be rigid with your own]. Consider both long and short tools. The mind is the foundation, skill rests on your spirit, and the art rests on your skill, so do not fall into laziness.

11. The art of pushing a cart up a high mountain (高山ニ車ヲ推ト云事, takayama ni kuruma wo osu to iu koto)

If you become careless during a fight with the enemy, you will be pushed back, and the result will be the same as in the following situation:

If you become careless when you climb a mountain pushing a cart upward, you will be pushed back by the cart. In order not to be pushed back, you need to go carefully. Practice and think things through diligently both day and night. Capture the enemy by "killing" your body and keeping your mind alive. People who try to gain victory ninety percent into the task will become careless. This feeling is like pushing a cart up a high mountain. If you have won a victory, do not become careless, and if you lose, never surrender [your mind to doubt]. Do not become distracted.[3] Also, in order to perform in the arts well, you should practice diligently both day and night. If you are careless, the cart will roll downhill, even if you think that you have stopped the cart on flat ground.

12. The art of sticking to the circle and moving into the circle (輪ニ付輪ニ移ト云事, wa ni tsuku wa ni utsuru to iu koto)

This skill is to plunge into the place where the enemy's drawn sword reaches. It is called "sticking to the circle." To dodge at the place where the enemy's sword nearly cuts you [but will in fact miss] and then attack him—this is called "moving into the circle." This is the same in standing and sitting combat. The first point is called "sticking to the circle" because you estimate the circle when the enemy lifts up and cuts for an attack. Make sure to understand the arc of the enemy's sword, and dodge it at the moment that the enemy's sword nearly cuts you. How to attack is passed down along with this skill.

When you fight with the enemy, your spirit competes with the enemy's spirit. This is like a set of wheels. So it is essential in fighting to comprehend the circle and move into the border of the circle where he has become careless. Always practice finding the place to infiltrate the circle and contemplate your improvement.

Antony Cummins says: the original text talks heavily about "sticking to," but in English the essence can be hidden. Overall the teaching is to understand the enemy sword arc, to know where to break through that boundary, and to dash into the circle's center to gain victory. This teaching breaks down into two points. Staying just outside the enemy's cutting arc, and infiltrating his cutting arc at the correct place.

13. The art of receiving (請身ノ事, ukemi no koto)

When the enemy attacks you, create distance and capture the enemy, measuring the timing in your mind. The feeling is like a floating boat on the water that follows the wave or like a bird of the water follows the water itself. "Receiving" is a little different from "making distance." *Ukemi* contains an unconventional way for the mind. Also the skill of *oikakeho* has this feeling of ukemi (see the "Tachiai no Maki" section in chapter 8). This is an important principle in jūjutsu.

Antony Cummins says: Receiving is different from blocking. Blocking is to directly stop the opponent. Receiving is to meld with him and to take control. Furthermore, receiving is also different from creating space. The creation of space is to move outside the enemy's threat range, while to receive is to bring in the enemy attack and manipulate it.

14. The art of capturing the enemy by forcing him to be seated (立ヲ去テ座ヲ可捕事, tachi wo sarite za wo toru beki koto)

When a standing enemy attacks you, you should think he will attack with standing skills. You should pretend not to fight with him and stay seated. In this case, you say, "Please have a seat. I understand that I cannot gain victory, even if I stand," or say something to make the enemy become angry. At this point, move and capture him at the instant of the change of his movement.

For example, when you observe the enemy wanting to attack with a standing skill, force him to have a seat and capture him at the good time for you to make the capture. Keep patient even if it takes a long time. When you are seated, the enemy will attack vigorously with a standing skill, but remember you can still fight from a sitting position. Trying to stand up is wrong if the enemy is already standing [nearby].

15. The art of capturing the enemy by forcing him to stand (座ヲ去テ立ヲ可捕事, za wo sarite tachi wo toru beki koto)

This is reverse of the above article. When a seated enemy attacks you, force him to become angry by saying something to make him lose his concentration. If the enemy stands up as you are talking, capture him on the border of him moving from seated to standing. A sitting person always attacks with a sitting skill, so it is essential to think about this and get him to move where it is inconvenient for him to use his skills.

It is difficult to capture an enemy who is seated and well guarded. Let an enemy stand up with resourcefulness and capture him in the moment he moves from seated to standing. When you cannot be patient during an argument, keep calm and say, "We should not argue here." Or, if there are many people, you should ask people to reconcile your argument so that a fight will not start. Consider this well and observe. [In conclusion: if the enemy leaves his seat, it makes his mind change. When his mind changes, victory is already on your side.]

16. The art of taking away spirit and capturing "before" or "after" (気ヲ去テ前後ヲ可捕事, ki wo sarite zengo wo toru beki koto)

Opening (序, jo): fill your mind [with victory].

Middle (破, ha): take away the enemy's spirit.

End (急, kyū): follow your enemy's [mind, intent, movement] and capture him.

There is a teaching in which you should take away the enemy's perfectly prepared spirit and then capture the enemy "before" [that is, the moment he starts to change movement] or "after" [by following the situation]. When the enemy obeys your spirit, you will be able to freely do anything you wish. To capture the enemy at the start of his change of movement is known as "before."

You can bring about victory, even if the enemy has seventy percent advantage while you only have thirty percent advantage during a spoken quarrel [so take heart; you can reverse a bad situation]. In such a case, digress from the subject and speak to the enemy about what is unexpected. Do this to kill the enemy's fighting spirit. It may sound vulgar to a samurai, but it is possible to perform such things when upholding duty for your lord.

When fighting, take away the enemy's sharp spirit and then fight with him. If the enemy takes the initiative first, let him attack you freely and take the initiative later. This is to take away the enemy's spirit.

Also, when the enemy thinks that you will attack from the west and pays attention to the west, attack from the east. "Before" and "after" are about taking the initiative [or not taking it]. You should break the enemy's spirit. There is an old episode about Kamiizumi Ise no Kami in which he captured a prisoner on his travels. He disguised himself as a monk and he gave grilled rice [to his opponent]. You should capture in unexpected ways like this.

17. The art of capturing weakness, not strength (強ヲ去テ弱ヲ可取事, kyō wo sarite jaku wo toru beki koto)

When the enemy's right hand is too hard to capture, suddenly you should take the enemy in a weaker direction, be it forward or backward or elsewhere. For example, if the enemy tries to go around behind you when using the skill of the *Mizukagami* (水鑑; see chapter 14), hit the enemy's nose to knock him down and backward with one beat.

Things have two sides. When you prepare the front, your back is not prepared. Left and right, front and back, all are the same as this. This is the knowledge of capturing the enemy off guard. If the enemy has strength in his right hand, usually he has weakness in his left hand. This weakness is also applicable to you. So do not put too much confidence in your own abilities. Just perceive the enemy's points of weakness.

Antony Cummins says: While in motion, the human body has strong and weak points. If more strength is put into one hand, the opposite one is weaker. This is the same for all parts of the body. When an enemy is pushing against you, pull; when they are pulling, push, and so on.

18. The art of capturing strength, not weakness (弱ヲ去テ強ヲ可取事, jaku wo sarite kyō wo toru beki koto)

When an enemy shows that he is not going to draw his sword and pretends to be weak, you induce anger in him and capture or dash yourself against the enemy to utilize his weakness (as show in the principle above). When the enemy becomes angry, he will draw his sword. Understand both weakness and strength and their balance. This teaches you the substantial and the insubstantial (虚実, kyojitsu). For example, when it is difficult to capture a weak point, capture the enemy's approaching strength with power. This is also the mind of capturing someone off guard. Strength has change, weakness has change, and truth has change. Remember the concept of opening, middle, and end (序破急, jo ha kyū).

A person who does not fight with people and lacks the spirit to fight may be like a dead body, so that his movement cannot be guessed [and he only takes up a defense]. In this case, it is difficult to capture him. Therefore, hit the enemy on his side to give him the spirit to fight, then capture him by using [his reaction]. You should discover the points where the enemy is off guard. In short, capture him after pushing and making his real intentions appear.

19. The art of capturing the body, not the sword (劔ヲ去テ躰ヲ取ヘキ事, ken wo sarite tai wo toru beki koto)

When you try to capture an enemy who prepares to draw a sword from a sitting position, go into the enemy's sword striking distance. When the enemy draws the sword, dodge and seize the enemy's right wrist with your right hand. Take the hand you have seized to his right side and push him down. This is capturing the body, not the enemy's sword.

There are two teachings here: to capture the body, not the sword, and to capture the sword, not the body. These teachings make the arts limitless. You can either capture the body or the sword, but this will depend on enemy's movement. If you concentrate only on capturing the body, but the distance is too far from the enemy, there may be nothing you can do. In such a case, you should capture the sword [as with article 20]. When you capture the enemy's body, which is the base of his movement, you always have victory.

20. The art of capturing the sword, not the body (躰ヲ去テ劔ヲ取ヘキ事, tai wo sarite ken wo toru beki koto)

This is the opposite teaching of the above.

When you try to capture an enemy who prepares to draw a sword from a sitting position [and you are standing], move into the enemy's threat range, and when he draws the sword and tries to cut, lift your right leg high, in a semi-hopping motion, to dodge his sword. Interlock your thumbs with your hands out (palms down), then push the back of his sword to the ground. This is to capture the sword, not the body. The feeling is similar to the above article.

When the enemy is coming to attack with a sword, a spear, and so on, you should have some tool to prevent the enemy from using his tools. Here, to capture the enemy sword is to cut the enemy's dominant arm off quickly—do this in a desperate fight.

21. The art of knowing eight people and of fangs (牙八人ト可知事, kiba hachi nin to shiru beki koto)

Oral tradition says, even if an enemy has pinned you down, bite the enemy's nose or wrist with your fangs (teeth), so that the enemy will die. You should use any part of your body when the enemy holds you down and you cannot do anything with your sword. *Kiba hachi nin* in the title means to have the spirit of attacking eight people. Also, when you hold the enemy down and there is no way to use the sword or shortsword, you should bite through his wrist with your teeth.

You should always know that a cornered rat will bite a cat. Even if you bite through dozens of people's wrists, it is same as "to bite eight people with your teeth" [eight is just a nominal term]. You should be fully guarded against even a single enemy. We say "eight people," but it does not actually mean eight. It means there are many enemies, and you stand alone. It is good to hurt an enemy, even if just a little. You should do it with your hands, legs, mouth, and so on. This is called kiba hachi nin because it means fighting against eight people with one mouth. For example, you should hurt the enemy any way you can, even by biting. If you have many enemies, do not be surprised by the number. When there are many enemies and you are alone, if you are defeated, such a defeat is not your shame. Just move on and fight. The opposite of this, if the enemy is alone and you have many people, be aware that a cornered rat will bite a cat.

22. The art of capturing with rope (搦ノ事, karame no koto)

These skills are in our scroll called *Nawa no Maki*.

The way of arresting is to capture the enemy: [when the enemy is on the ground after a grapple], kick the enemy's face with the right foot, hit him, and then move onto his back quickly. Step between the enemy's arms and twist his arms behind his back. Put his right hand on your knees. With this, the enemy will be extremely hard-pressed. Keep your hands empty. When you capture the enemy's left hand as well as the right hand, keep both your left and right hands empty. Take a rope from inside your kimono and put the enemy in bonds in any way that you wish. When you capture in this way, if you stand up, stepping on an enemy's large biceps, usually the arms will break. You should mount the enemy's back as if you are horseback riding.

These skills are transmitted in the *Nawa no Maki*.

Antony Cummins says: The skills in this scroll have not been recorded. Only their titles remain, and thus the details for these versions are lost or may be found in other schools. However, it does say that generals should be bound in white rope or a type of rope called *kaino-o*.

23. The art of the insubstantial becoming substantial and of substantial becoming insubstantial (虚則実実則虚ト成ル事, kyo sunawachi jitsu jitsu sunawachi kyo to naru koto)

Do not change [between substantial and insubstantial when you capture the enemy]. When you judge the enemy's action, if you find it is difficult to capture him, you should not use the insubstantial but move to the place where you can capture with the substantial. When the enemy uses insubstantial, if you attack the enemy with substantial, the enemy will also change and attack with that which is substantial. Thus, capture at the moment his true intentions appear. Or, when the enemy is substantial, capture him after making him move to insubstantial. You do not have to use the insubstantial because his insubstantial state will appear when you change the person's mind-set with words.

Unlike military tactics, you do not have to use the insubstantial on purpose. If you use that which is insubstantial against an enemy who is a master, he will attack your lie. It is wrong to use such deception on purpose.

When the enemy attacks you with a sword and you do not have a sword, you should fight earnestly, whatever happens. If the enemy and you fight each other sword against sword, and if the enemy is weaker than you, you should not think, "I will never be injured [because he is weak]." Remember, even if you are injured but still gain victory, your eagerness was strong because your substantial mind made it so.

24. The art of the formation of the moving cart and knowledge of four seasons (車懸リ四季ノ心得ノ事, kurumagakari shiki no kokoroe no koto)

This means to advance when you attack an enemy. But it does not mean just to advance directly. You should have both a mind to attack and also to have the ability to wait for the enemy's attack. It is like a wheel that advances and returns. A cart has four wheels. If it had six wheels, the cart would not turn around. So compare the movement of the cart to the four seasons; the beginning of summer falls in the fourth month of the year [based on the Chinese calendar], but it is not hot yet. The beginning of winter falls in the tenth month of year, but yet it is not so cold [meaning that movement flows with natural rhythm and speed]. This is the same as an accelerating cart. Practice for a few decades [to improve], just as the four seasons come and go each year.

In the case of using skills, when you capture an enemy, you should approach with the mind of attack, but wait for the enemy's attack, and then advance like four seasons or wheels on the ground [meaning with the correct flow and rhythm]. With physical skills, it means to move steadily without futility of movement. When you pull a cart on the flat ground, it moves slowly, but if a cart goes down even a small slope, it will increase speed as if it was an arrow. Practice and think of this in usual practice so as to do it well and smoothly.

25. The art of receiving and distance (敵ヲ請テ身ヲスカス事, teki wo ukete mi wo sukasu koto)

This is to understand the situation and distance and is connected to article 12. This is a way for fighting well. Tradition says that when you fight with an enemy, if the enemy's kenmon (distance) is good for you to dodge, you should and then capture the enemy at the moment he changes his movement. Swordsmanship is the same. When you enter in close, jump in and capture. If you misjudge the dodge, the situation will become worse. Be careful not to engage with distance creation in a dangerous place. When the enemy comes at you from above, strongly, you should move outside the enemy's attack range, letting the enemy swing [his sword] completely. In such a case, the enemy stretches [out his arms with the sword]. At this point, give him a little distance, and he will rush to come in close [at which point you can overcome him]. Sometimes you should defend when the enemy thinks you will not, and sometimes you should not defend when the enemy thinks you will. This is to receive the enemy.

26. The art of placing your body up close to the enemy to capture (敵ヲ捕ニハ身ヲ附ル事, teki wo toru niwa mi wo tsukeru koto)

When you try to capture an enemy, even if you are swung around by him, you should cling to the enemy by all means and dash yourself against him so as to make the capture.

If you are at a distance from the enemy, you cannot capture him. It is essential not to be at a distance from the enemy's body. Also consider atari (see article 5). Never fight to capture an enemy. If you are swung around by the enemy, you should follow him. Sooner or later, you can find atari (that moment in the center) and capture the enemy after following his movement.

Antony Cummins says: Do not struggle with an opponent. Even if he is trying to throw you around, move with it until you find the gap and the point where you can capture him. There will be a moment when you can manipulate his movement and thus ride out his attemps at controlling you.

27. The art of projectiles and the curtain in the field (飛剣野中ノ幕ノ事, hiken nonaka no maku no koto)

When an enemy is shooting arrows toward you, make a shield by placing your jacket on the end of your scabbard. If done like this, it will not hit you. If it does hit you, you will not get injured as severely because the arrow's power is reduced. Also, in case of shuriken (throwing blades), it is same as the above.

To hold your sword in the posture of *sha* (捨ノ構, the posture of abandonment) is an important rule. Keep low. The posture without spirit is called posture of sha.

When moving toward the enemy with a bow or musket, hang your *haori* jacket or the like on the top of a three-shaku [3-foot] bamboo pole or a fan and use it as a shield.

28. The art of capturing by understanding the middle point (左右前後 引合中ヲ折テ可捕事, sayū zengo hikiai naka wo orite toru beki koto)

You should not use all one hundred percent of your advantage; instead you should utilize eighty or ninety percent and leave nearly twenty percent unused. Try to maintain at least ninety percent control of the combat to ensure victory.

On the human body there is the left and the right, the front and the back. Always maintain a central posture. Consider that there is always an opposite to your direction and inclination of the body. Keep inside the middle area [that is, do not overexert to either side].

Antony Cummins says: This section has been simplified and heavily edited. The original is extremely indulgent in its explanation. However, the core teaching here is that there is a natural effort or power within a combat, that you should not go "all in" with one hundred percent but instead understand the fluctuation in this power between the two combatants, and that by taking control of ninety percent of this power will lead to victory. Also, while a fighter has to move, never overreach, but maintain a good footing inside the middle of your own balance.

29. The art of the four judgements against an enemy (敵ニ四ツノ目 利有ル事, teki ni yottsu no mekiki aru koto)

The four:

- flexibility (柔, jū)
- rigidity (剛, gō)
- strength (強, kyō)
- weakness (弱, jaku)

It is good for a skill to be flexible (jū).
Rigidity (gō) is overbold, therefore it is negative.
Strength (kyō) is brave, which is good.
Weakness (jaku) is totally different from flexibility. Do not use weakness.

[The four steps:]

First: You should enter in close or make distance.
Second: Observe if the enemy cuts or does not cut.
Third: Observe if the enemy parries with the sword or not.
Fourth: Observe if the enemy stabs with sword or not.

These four articles are secrets for victory. You should observe them carefully. Estimate the enemy's weapon: if it is a weapon for stabbing, if it is a weapon for slashing, if it is weapon for shooting, or a weapon for striking blows.

[Weapon strengths:]
- Musket: 100 percent
- Bow: 70 percent
- Sword: 50 percent
- Striking weapon: 30 percent

These are flexible (柔), hard (剛), strong (強), and weak (弱). Have an estimation of them.

30. The art of capturing with powder and impromptu tools (薬捕附道具ヲ密ス事, kusuri dori tsuketari dōgu wo misu koto)

Remove the contents of an egg [without breaking it]. Grind Japanese pepper *(sanshō)*, pepper *(koshō)*, or red pepper *(nanban)* and insert them into the egg. Cover the opening with paper. Throw this into the enemy's face. There are various powers that can be used.

Capture the enemy by throwing any appropriate tool around you. Capture the enemy directly after hitting him with the object.

Also, remove the contents of an egg [without breaking it]. Grind pepper and insert it into the egg. Cover the opening with paper and put it in your sleeve to carry. Throw this between the enemy's eyes and nose. It makes a person move into a kind of fit. Also, in case of emergency, pour boiling water or tea into a bowl and break tobacco in it. Bring this and throw it into the enemy's face; it will help blind him.

The only point is distracting the enemy's attention. You should throw this when the enemy cuts you, and then move in on him.

31. The art of capturing with ruses and the way of speaking to people (方便捕言葉掛様之事, hōben dori kotoba kakeyō no koto)

When a thief infiltrates a house on a dark night, if you call people's names, such as "Mr. (insert any name from any place)" around the house here and there, the thief will not wish to infiltrate, because he thinks there are many people in the house. Also, you can speak to the enemy directly to ensnare [his mind]. Also if you call people's names (as the above), it makes a person's insubstantial *chi* disappear [and he will lose heart]. In old times, a samurai from Kōshū and sword master called Kamiizumi Ise no Kami [who founded Shinkage Ryū] traveled through the country to perfect his skill in the martial arts. A murderer shut himself up, holding a young child hostage in an inn. Ise no Kami used a ruse in his appearance [by dressing as a monk] to capture the murderer. [Another trick is to] call a close friend [of the murderer] to talk to him from outside, or get him to enter from another entrance [at this point, infiltration can be achieved]. Even if you enter where the murderer has shut himself away, and it is difficult to fight with him, use words to encourage a settlement.

32. The art of knowing two things: (1) consciousness and the mind and (2) of using peripheral vision (心ニテ眼ヲツカヒ意心ノ二ヲ知事, kokoro nite me wo tsukai i kokoro no futatsu wo shiru koto)

This means that you should not lose an understanding of the enemy's lower body, even if you look at the enemy's face. Consciousness and the mind are found in the six sense organs [the eyes, ears, nose, tongue, body, and mind] and also the six conscious states [which are functions of the six sense organs: seeing, hearing, smelling, tasting, touching, and reasoning]. There is only one mind, and attention is managed within and managed by the mind. Even if you focus your attention upward, you should keep your eyes on low things through the mind. If you do not keep your eyes on [a low position] with your peripheral focus, you cannot truly observe the whole. There is deep oral tradition for this. It is essential not to take your eyes off the enemy.

Usually other people's eyes show what they think. When the mind is focused only on one side, know that the insubstantial [and therefore weakness] is present on the other side. So you should pay attention to the upper, middle, lower, left, right, front, and backward, and remove that which is insubstantial. It is the same as the example *Suijō no Koroshi* [水上胡芦子, a quote from the text *Fudōchi Shinmyō Roku* (不動智神妙録) by the priest Takuan, which talks about a gourd that floats on water and the idea that it will move away from you if you try to strike it.]

The following is the secret of the skill. If you observe with the mind, everything appears in the eyes. When you observe, do not look at the enemy with only your eyes. When you think you are going to take something on your right side, you should look at it with your peripheral focus. This is the "great eye." Then take what you wish [so that the enemy does not know your intentions]. When you take something, the principle of mind is first; the principle of eyes is second. When you enter a room that has a lot of people, observe people's eyes. When you pass someone, observe his eyes first. In reverse, do not show your mind through your own eyes. If you have anger in your mind, your eyes become sharp. Eyes are the mirror of the soul.

33. The art of the order of execution (手討ノ次第ノ事, teuchi no shidai no koto)

Execution (手討, teuchi) is to put people to death with the sword and not to kill oneself. This can also be the death of those who are not fellow retainers.

After you kill the retainer with your sword, never tell others that is was your exploit. If you say so, people will think that you are telling tales. Be careful: when people talk, they will use your name, and the story will change as it moves and is retold. Remember, what has been said cannot be unsaid. If you learn all of the articles [in this scroll] without laziness, you can put others to death by the sword without making mistakes. Thus this article is written here at the end of this scroll. If you do not fail to perform *teuchi* executions, you will gain victory [in other combat].

To perform teuchi is quite an unexpected thing. Teuchi itself is fighting. If you fail at it, it is your shame. If you cut the target down well, then make sure to maintain a calm mind [afterward]. People have said for a long time, a person who has failed in teuchi will often be killed by the object of his vengeance. Therefore, such an order hold's every family's dignity.

This article was written at the end of this scroll about the arts of fighting. With this in mind, you should not abandon your good name. Fully train yourself in the martial arts. Martial arts training is not only done by traveling [on martial pilgrimages], but also it is found through the teachings of this scroll. Become familiar with skillful people, abandon evil, and follow good ways. There are two things you should aim toward, and they are loyalty and filial piety.

11

LION DANCE

Figure 11.1.

A Lion Dance is a troupe of dancers united together under a patterned cloth with a snarling wooden head of a fantasy lion in the lead position. Normally seen around Chinese New Year, they snake their way toward an audience, snapping wooden jaws in mock attack. However, in Kanazawa, the Kaga domain and the home of Mubyōshi Ryū, the Lion Dance has a different format. Here, the lion faces down one or two opponents who are crowned with a splendid flowing white or black wig.

Figure 11.2. Performers from the Honmachi 1-Chōme Seinenkai Lion Dance group

The fighters face down the lion, and after a prolonged battle, they slay the beast, to claps from the audience. The images are of Hijikata Ryū, taken in Tokyo in 2014 by the author, and from the Nakabayashi Lion Dance Preservation Society.

Figure 11.3. The music troupe that accompanies the dance

Figure 11.4. Two fighters face down the lion.

Figure 11.5. The lion prepares to attack.

Figure 11.6. A fighter prepares to face the lion.

The origin of this form of Lion Dance is unknown. It is claimed that it goes back to the Ikkō Ikki Uprising in the fifteenth and sixteenth centuries, but this is unsubstantiated and much of our information on the performance is based in the nineteenth century. This Lion Dance appears to be prevalent in Kanazawa, but the Kanazawa council takes an active involvement in maintaining this tradition, and there are about forty Lion Dance groups in the area. Each troupe claims ancestry to a specific samurai school or collection of schools, Mubyōshi Ryū being one of them. This means that the skills of Hagiwara Jūzō and Mubyōshi Ryū can be found mixed into the dance along with other schools.

One of the main Lion Dance troupes connected with Mubyōshi Ryū is Hanbei Ryū. This school was established by Machida Hanbei, who taught in and around the 1850s. He is thought to have taught people, including farmers, at his home dōjō. He taught the schools of:

- Mubyōshi Ryū
- Toda Ryū (stick and chain weapons)
- Shizuka Ryū (halberd)
- Asaka Ryū (quick draw)
- Yamaguchi Ryū (hand-to-hand combat and quarterstaff)
- Yamaguchi Ryū (swordsmanship)
- Mizuno Ichi Ten Ryū (swordsmanship)

The home dōjō of Nishimura Seitarō, a student of Machida Hanbei, has now been replaced by a modern house, but the descendants still live there, and a monument to Nishimura Seitarō has been erected on the grounds for his lifetime contribution.

There is no record of which skills from which school were included in the Lion Dance. All that is known is which school each Lion Dance is associated with. The current grandmaster of Mubyōshi Ryū, Uematsu Sensei, studied from the Nishimura Seitarō line, who taught the Lion Dance in his dōjō in Nakabayashi, Nonoichi City. Nishimura Seitarō studied from the Machida Hanbei line. The current troupe leader for the Machida Hanbei line of Lion Dancing is Mukōda Seiichi (向田誠市). In 2014 I brought both the Lion Dance group and Mubyōshi Ryū back together after being separated for possibly nearly one hundred years. This extremely successful meeting, which can be difficult in Japan, was attended by the leaders of Mubyōshi Ryū, the Machida Hanbei Lion Dance Troupe, and Shinjin Ryū, the sword school studied by Hagiwara Jūzō and Niki Shinjūrō.

Figure 11.7. The monument to Nishimura Seitarō

Figure 11.8. The original site of Nishimura Seitarō's dōjō, where Mubyōshi Ryū was taught along with the Lion Dance; now the modern family home

Figure 11.9. Mukōda and Nishizaki displaying sections of the dance skill; at bottom right, Koizumi Mieko

Figure 11.10. Mukōda Seiichi (left) with group member Nishizaki Mikio at Nakabayashi Kasuga Shrine, the home of the dance troupe

Figure 11.11. Mukōda Seiichi with the troupe's lion head, which is over one hundred years old

Figure 11.12.

It is difficult to discover just how much of the Lion Dance represents the skill sets found in Mubyōshi Ryū, but it is satisfying to know that the thread of Hagiwara Jūzō's skills can be traced from his construction of a "revenge school" through to its inclusion in symbolic combat. Furthermore, the little-known tradition of Japanese martial Lion Dance needs both highlighting and recording. The dances almost died out after World War II and were only saved by a conscious effort. While their existence has been recorded here, the dance itself and its traditions are kept by only a handful of people.

12

SHINJIN RYŪ

Figure 12.1. Jōtō Masato performing Shinjin Ryū kata, seen on the right

It is evident that much of Mubyōshi Ryū was influenced or indeed taken from the samurai school known as Shinjin Ryū. If not for a small group of people, the sword work of Shinjin Ryū would be lost. During the later twentieth century, there was a move to actively continue and practice the kata of the school. Like Mubyōshi Ryū, most of the school is lost, but many of its scrolls were recorded in the *Kensei Kusabuka Jinshirō* book, and its sword kata are now performed annually. It must be understood that to know Mubyōshi Ryū, a foundation in and understanding of Shinjin Ryū is recommended.

The following is a message from Kōichi Ueda, the leading conservationist of Shinjin Ryū:

> The Kendō Association in the town of Kawakita had its beginnings in Kawakita Village where, in 1967, they started the organization Shinjin Kai (深甚会). It was founded in honor of the medieval warrior Kusabuka Jinshirō, who founded Shinjin Ryū. It was founded as a platform to transmit his teachings to future generations. People young and old

who have studied kendō practice and involve themselves in the annual Kusabuka Jinshirō Memorial Service Kendō Match (草深甚四郎慰霊剣道大会), established in 1936 and now affiliated with the Kawakita-machi Sports Association.

Lots of people became interested in our kendō events, and our matches became quite large, with participants numbering over six hundred, from children to adults. Many come to Kawakita each year to join us. Because of the large number of people and the difficulty in organizing the event, our association consulted with the town and created the new organization of Kusabuka Jinshirō Kenshō Kai (草深甚四郎顕彰会) in 1992 with the aim of maintaining Kusabuka Jinshiro's historical identity for all time. Each year with the support of the town, many great kendō athletes take part, and in 2015 we had our sixty-ninth match.

In addition to these standard matches, we also demonstrate the ancient kata of Shinjin Ryū (深甚流) to over six hundred spectators, which is something I consider to be a wonderful moment. We use a specific form of *fukuroshinai* (a bamboo sword covered with leather), and the skills of this school are based on stabbing. Since 1974 we have transmitted the kata of Shinjin Ryū and also teach kendō to children at our kendō dōjō, named Kawakita-machi Shōnen Shinbukan (川北町少年深武館).

We hope that they keep practicing and teaching kendō and also Shinjin Ryū to maintain it for the future, and therefore we would like to invite anyone from the world over to come and study Shinjin Ryū with us, or to attend our annual kendō competition.

—Kōichi Ueda

Figure 12.2.

13

THE ART OF SEPPUKU

Ritual suicide in Japan has a long and varied history. Various names are attributed to it and different forms appear in various locations and times. A vast number of manuals and instructions on *seppuku*, the samurai art of suicide, come from the Edo Period, when social movement was restricted and landholdings were under the direct control of an overlord. This tight control stopped a samurai from fleeing to another province or to simply hole up in defense in his own territory. This was the age of the samurai in the castle town, where punishment would find its way to his extended family if the correct response was not given to a demand of suicide.

The term *suicide* is a subjective one. To a samurai, it can be argued that seppuku is not at all suicide but "death as a warrior." The essential aim of seppuku is to withhold the power of victory from the enemy and to retain command of his own life, even if the result is his death. In essence, a samurai will die by his own hand before the enemy has a chance to bind and kill him. Therefore, while seppuku became forced suicide or execution by your own hand, the underlying purpose is retaining the image of control over your own death. It is impossible to know just how many samurai welcomed death by their own hand and how many were reluctant to follow such a command. The following scroll is the collected teachings of Mubyōshi Ryū on ritual suicide.

MANNERS FOR ASSISTING WITH SEPPUKU (介錯幷切腹胴附之次第, KAISHAKU NARABINI SEPPUKU DŌTSUKI NO SHIDAI)

When you serve as a messenger or inspector at the time of someone committing seppuku, you may sometimes have a drink of sake. In such a case, no meal or side dish should be served. The compliments to be given should not overstated.[1] Concerning the side dish prepared for the man committing seppuku, there should be three pieces of *tsukemono* (pickled vegetables), which should be placed in a triangle on a *kannakake* (shaved wooden tray), which in turn should be placed on a wooden tray called a *tateoshiki*. To pour the sake, do not wrap the neck of the serving vessel, and pour it with the left hand, which is the opposite way [to the normal method]. Also, pour sake so that it will circle around in the opposite direction in the sake cup, and pour it until it is full.

For other people who join him in partaking of the sake, it should be served [in the normal way] and not in this opposite fashion. For other people, everything should be done in the normal way.

For the floor covering for the ritual of seppuku, spread out thin straw mats from the front to rear with the fold [of the straw mat pointing] north.

The proper wakizashi shortsword to be used by the person committing seppuku should be nine sun, five bu [11.3 inches] in length. The assistant should use a katana. The above is known as *daishō no kokoroe*.

The wakizashi [tang and lower part of the blade] should be wrapped with *sugihara* paper in the opposite direction [to normal]. The paper should be folded and should be doubled over at the end [of the tang] and fastened by tying a twisted paper string around it. Leave about two or three sun [2–4 inches] of the blade exposed and place the wakizashi on the stand with the point of the blade toward the person performing seppuku. The [stand and blade] should be carried by an observer.[2]

The water for the condemned's last moments should be given by a master-monk, and then the stand [with the wakizashi on it] should be placed down in position, at which point the condemned should take the wakizashi in his hand and commit seppuku.

The second[3] should stay at the left side of the victim about six shaku [6 feet] away, wearing his long and shortswords, kneeing down with his right knee up. It is essential to observe the "feel" of the condemned man. If the person performing seppuku feels some regret and attempts an attack, without

Figure 13.1.

any delay you should take hold of your wakizashi, draw up your left leg, and from a crouched position, jump and kill him immediately. Do this the moment he takes up the wakizashi [with ill intent].

On the other hand, if he seems to be determined in [the suicide], strike him when he slits his belly and when his body [returns to] a straighter position.

In case you fail to behead him [with a single blow], you should have detailed arrangements with another so that aid

Figure 13.2.

will come from him.[4] You should not attempt a second cut, but instead move over immediately. That being said, a second cut may be attempted depending on the situation.

How to decapitate from the direction of the throat after you have failed to behead him: alter the grip on your sword, and with the blade upward, and then quickly cut the throat [until the head comes] off.

When you assist during seppuku [and behead the condemned], you should first calm yourself and step forward with your right foot close to the left hip of the man performing seppuku. Stretch your big toe upward, keeping your line of sight between his earlobes [and your big toe]. Aim and target the base of his hairline, keep a stable posture, lower your center, and tense the forearm. The moment when chi arises, make the cut.[5]

The proper way to perform this is for the head not to be cut off completely but to remain connected [to the body] by the skin of the neck. However, cutting the head off completely in one blow will suffice [if you cannot retain the flap of skin].

Figure 13.3.

If the person is reluctant to commit seppuku but is forced to do so, you should move closer to his right side and position yourself at a very close distance, [crouched] with your right knee raised and your wakizashi shortsword resting on your left hand. If he turns against you and attempts an attack, you should immediately stab and kill him. If everything is normal, behead him in the normal way [as described earlier].

Figure 13.4.

Figure 13.5.

Figure 13.6.

When dealing with the ritual seppuku of a young boy, the second should have him hold a folded fan and simulate a cut of the belly but without telling him that he is going to commit actual seppuku. Instruct him to try various positions of the neck, and when all is settled and correct, behead the boy.

The appropriate time to behead someone is as follows:

1. When he makes the first stab with the wakizashi [into his abdomen]
2. When he makes a straight cut across his stomach
3. When he makes a cross cut[6]

All depends on the situation, and depending on that situation, behead him when his neck is straight. It is essential to judge the situation correctly.

Concerning the assistant for the second: if the main second cannot behead him successfully, then the reserve second should take over. The original second should not fail, but even so, the assistant should observe the legs of the corpse and check if they are thrashing around, and if so, he should cut the victim's throat. This point is of utmost importance for the assistant to the second.

Sometimes a head inspection has to be conducted and the head presented to the inspector(s).[7] To do this, hold the bottom of the neck where it has been cut off and place it on a shaved wooden tray[8] with the head facing the joint and with high quality paper[9] on it; in this way it can be inspected. An informal way of doing this is to hold the topknot with the left hand and place the right hand under the chin so you can present the head for inspection.

Figure 13.7.

It is essential for the inspector to have a close look at the dead body. Keep in mind that he should approach the decapitated corpse and confirm the death. If the head is left connected with the body [by the skin], have it completely disconnected [for verification].

The above things are secret, but with your earnest request, they are here transmitted completely. Do not show this to any other person.

Niki Shinjūrō Masanaga (二木新十郎政長)

Hagiwara Jūzō Shigetatsu (萩原重蔵茂辰)

Tōmi Gen'nai Nobuna (東美源内宣名)

Kitagawa Kin'emon Sadahide (北河金右衛門貞英)

Kishimoto Genshichi Sadanobu (岸本源七貞信)

Sawamura Matsuemon Tadanawa (沢村松右衛門忠縄)

[Transcribed in] Bunka 5 [1808], the Year of Tsuchinoe Dragon

[Transcribed by] Takakuwa Chōzaemon Yoshimasa (高桑長左衛門良昌)

Figure 13.8.

14

DEEP SECRETS AND THE ARTS OF THE SHINOBI

Mubyōshi Ryū contains other elements outside hand-to-hand combat and weapon skill sets. These external elements, like their martial arts, are aimed at self-protection. Samurai skills can be divided into military and civilian arts, meaning some skills are required for military campaigns while other skills are used for self-protection in samurai civilian life. The latter is where the arts of the shinobi and the more esoteric skills join this school's curriculum.

Hagiwara Jūzō himself points out that his school is not primarily a shinobi school, and that the path of the shinobi is not the task the people of the school perform. This means that they are not hired to perform as shinobi for their lord and do not engage in espionage or commando tactics, as that task would have mainly been done by the men in the lord's employ who were from Iga and Kōka, or decedents of those warriors. The result is that this collection of shinobi skills, put together by Hagiwara Jūzō, concentrates on:

- home infiltration
- protection from infiltrators
- safe traveling
- personal vendetta skills
- escape after making a kill
- protection from spirits and other magical elements

The result is that the shinobi skills of Mubyōshi Ryū can be seen as specific to the students' individual needs. This can be observed when compared to other schools that show a strong element of military shinobi skills. Therefore it can be stated with confidence that the Mubyōshi Ryū's shinobi curriculum is almost fully focused on civilian life. To add to this, other deep secrets, including ritual magic, charms, and spells, are mixed in with these shinobi arts, crossing many elements together that help a practitioner defend against men or monsters in the night.

Some of the following scrolls clearly identify shinobi skills from other elements, dividing them from each other, while some scrolls provide an eclectic mix. Overall there is a clear image of a skill set that allows defense against intruders to the home, thieves while traveling, and monsters, which were believed to travel the dark roads of Japan at night. Hence, Mubyōshi Ryū is an exceptional example of the use of the shinobi arts in a time when military action was in rapid decline and a concentration on personal protection was emerging as a prominent feature in samurai life. This section comprises the following scrolls:

- *Mizukagami:* This is one of the better-known named shinobi scrolls in the ninja community, in both Japan and the West. Most likely originally written by Hagiwara Jūzō in the mid-1600s, the earliest known transcription is 1678, in the Cummins Collection. Multiple transcriptions exist in both private and library collections and more continue to appear on the market. Containing the core selection of shinobi skills and other survival tips, this scroll is the foundation of Mubyōshi Ryū's ninja curriculum, for both offense and defense.

- *Mizukagami Kuden no Oboe: Kuden* is Japanese for "oral tradition." This can consist of secret teachings or of those details too difficult to write down in full. It denotes the passing on of information by word of mouth. As time passed and information was not passed on so frequently, oral traditions were sometimes written down. In this case, the oral traditions that expand on the *Mizukagami* scroll were recorded here. Only a single version of this scroll is known to exist.

- *Mizukagami Shinsatsu:* Only a single transcription of this scroll has been found to date. Literally, the title means "a new volume of the *Mizukagami*." the scroll revisits sections of the original *Mizukagami*, giving

*Figure 14.1. The **Mizukagami** on Yahoo Auction. Sadly I did not know this was for sale until after the transaction was finished.*

extra information and detail, but in addition adds multiple new skills. Written at a later date, it is unknown whether the new information contained within it was passed down by the original students of Hagiwara or if these are newer additional skill sets. Much of the information, however, can be seen in the Mubyōshi Ryū kuden list, meaning that those elements must indeed have been inherited from older days, but without a full transmission, it is difficult to assess the dates for each skill. As many do appear in the older kuden list, it can be assumed that these are original teachings. The most distinct difference between this scroll and the original *Mizukagami* is the obvious inclusion of a vastly higher percentage of magical skills, steering away from what we would consider practical and which start to fall outside the shinobi.

The scrolls above account for this school's ninja curriculum, but they also delve deep into magic. In Japan the arts of the shinobi also have a very solid section of magical elements, but here some of the spells and rituals included start to fall outside of the aim of shinobi no jutsu. Therefore there are parts that stand beyond the realm of the shinobi.

THE WATER MIRROR SCROLL (水鏡, MIZUKAGAMI)

Although there are various arts and skills for the bushi, most people are not aware that there are no other elements than flexible (柔), hard (剛), strong (強), and weak (弱), and that only a few people master this principle.

As naturally as water seeks its own level, even someone who has a formidable reputation can be killed if he lowers his guard. Be aware that disasters of all kinds are caused by a lack of vigilance. People tend to be inattentive when they feel too familiar with something and forget basic precautions. Therefore, in order to deal with such inattentiveness, I here record how to overcome an enemy instead of being overcome yourself, and for the prosperity of students to come in the future.

When you walk late at night in places where you feel insecure, you should carry stones in your sleeve that are of an appropriate size to hit someone with. Also, throw one of them into any place where you suspect danger. If anyone is there, they will surely reveal themselves.

When you cross over a river you are not familiar with, try to cross it diagonally upstream. Details are in the oral tradition.

Figure 14.2.

When a storm is raging and you cannot see what is ahead of you, if you find something white or conspicuous anywhere on the ground, do not pick it up. If you do so without care, you will be marked[1] and easily killed in most cases. [To see what it is,] draw your sword and check it with the scabbard, and then leave it there. Details are in the oral tradition.

If you come across mountain bandits, keep your mind calm and pass through as quickly as possible without becoming scared. While traveling for two or three *ri* (5–7 miles) from that point, keep a watchful eye for anyone coming from the front, rear, right, or left. Mountain bandits are usually in a group of six from the servant class.[2] Know that only one will show himself at first while the other five or so will be hiding in a grassy field or somewhere of that nature. In some cases, one may pretend to be ill on the road and ask you if you have medicine. In that case, do not get close to such a person. Also, you should be suspicious if a stranger asks you to travel together in daytime. More details are in the oral tradition.

When you want to flee after killing someone at night and as quickly as possible, you may become disoriented and not know which way is east, west, south, or north. In this case you should try to find a stream and move upstream. It will surely lead you to a mountain.

Once you get onto the mountain, take a position at a high place so as to have a view of the landscape. That will allow you to find where the roads are situated. This is done to observe those chasing you with torches or lights. In this situation, you should think carefully [about your next step].

If they are about to come upon you, and if you are finding it difficult to continue to escape, cut off the tip of your scabbard so that you can breathe through the hole. To do this, submerge yourself in water holding your scabbard with the opening in your mouth. Stab your sword, shortsword, or knife

Figure 14.3.

Figure 14.4.

Figure 14.5.

Figure 14.6.

Figure 14.7.

onto the bed of the water and use it as an anchoring point. There is a certain way of breathing you need to learn. Details are in the oral tradition.

Also if you are injured, it is good to walk in a stream to throw off your pursuers.[3]

If there is snow on the ground, put on your footwear on backward, use a cane on your left side, and walk into a stream. By doing this, your footsteps will be difficult to decipher.[4]

While traveling and staying at lodgings that you think are not secure, observe what the defenses are like at the rear of the house. This should be done in case a fire or robbery takes place. In a building, inspect the following:

- floor
- veranda
- ceiling
- tatami mats: where the mat springs under your inspection, you should check beneath by pulling it up.

In a bedroom, place your things where they are not safe while the light is on, and after the light has been doused, move your gear to where it is safe. Also, use a very uncomfortable pillow. There is a pillow called the Pillow of Crickets,[5] and with it you will wake up even if a cricket comes into your room. If you have a mosquito net in the room, there are things you should be aware of on how to keep your swords at the ready. This is an oral tradition.[6]

You should secure the door by drilling into the ends of the doors. The drill should be made as in the drawing.

This [drill] can also be used when you infiltrate a place where the doors or paper sliding doors are secured tightly, or when you need to climb up onto the roof in the event of a fire or a situation such as this.

Figure 14.8.

Figure 14.9.

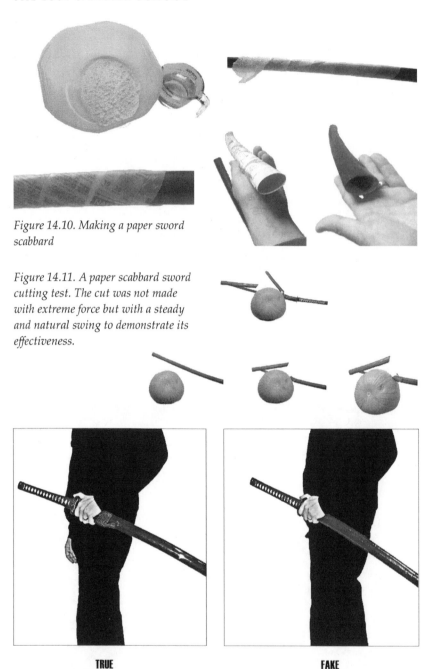

Figure 14.10. Making a paper sword scabbard

Figure 14.11. A paper scabbard sword cutting test. The cut was not made with extreme force but with a steady and natural swing to demonstrate its effectiveness.

TRUE

FAKE

Figure 14.12. The scabbard on the left is made of wood; the one to the right is made of paper.

190

When you have [a servant] carry a lantern for you, it is not good to have him go ahead. Instead, have him on your left side about two or three shaku behind your swords.[7] This is done so that you can get a good view of every direction: front, rear, left, and right.

If someone is approaching you in a relaxed manner with his left hand inside his kimono and his sword in an informal position, do not let your guard down, be it day or night.

If this happens at night, it is possible his sword is in a scabbard that is made of black paper and that he may immediately strike you with the sword without unsheathing it (fig. 14.9).[8] There are more details for what you can do for this. There are five things you should keep in mind in the oral tradition.[9]

If it is daytime, he may hook his scabbard hook[10] into his topknot and draw his sword with only with his right hand and then strike, keeping his left hand in his kimono (fig. 14.13).

Figure 14.13.

If you pass by [an enemy] and put a distance of four or five *chō* (500–600 yards) between you, you may feel relieved and out of danger and consider that there are no more enemies in the area, and you may even talk to someone and let your guard down. Remember, if the man you are talking to strikes at you with a sword that is housed in a black paper scabbard and with correct timing, there will be no chance the strike will fail.

If you find someone has infiltrated your house and want to know [if someone around you] is the infiltrator, call out to him with your own name. This is an oral tradition.

If a large number of *yatō* (night thieves) enter your house, it is seriously inappropriate for you to strike up a light inside the building. If you have to

Figure 14.14.

Figure 14.15.

Figure 14.16.

defend against them in small number, and if you hear them whisper occasionally, if you wish to kill them, stretch rope in the direction where you expect they may come from. Do this at the height of four or five sun [5–6 inches].

Then while waiting for them, you should hold something you think will serve as a shield, and also hold your weapon diagonally, and sweep at them with this weapon.

Remember, if you make a light inside a room, those who are in the darkness outside can see you clearly, and thus it is a dire mistake. It is essential for shinobi to carry lights. More details are in the oral tradition. There are oral traditions when scattering caltrops on a night attack and also teachings on night attack tools.[11]

Even if you do not know when the enemy shinobi will actually come,[12] it is more than likely that you will have a gut feeling concerning the matter. If you feel it appropriate, you should prepare for them. If the shinobi know that

Figure 14.17.

you have noticed [they are there], they may in response copy an animal's call when they approach. Therefore, you should be aware of this and not think it is in fact an animal.

Shinobi have various other techniques, more than just this one [concerning animal noises]. For example, if you hear someone cough at a distance, you should be aware he is close by you. [Shinobi] have a technique to make a cough sound like it is at a distance while actually the cough is very close.

If there is a moat, river, or pond, they sometimes may have prepared a stone of an appropriate size at the side of the water. They do this before they infiltrate. This is done so that if they are detected and chased, they will throw the stone into water [so it will sound like they have escaped that way]. You

Figure 14.18.

Figure 14.19.

should be aware of this and not be deceived by such a trick. More details are in an oral tradition.

If you need to search the house for shinobi[13] who have infiltrated the building, draw your sword with only two or three sun [2–3 inches] of the blade left inside the scabbard. Also, have the scabbard cord stretched out and attached onto your obi belt. Hold something as a shield with your left hand to protect yourself while searching.

Figure 14.20.   *Figure 14.21.*

You can also search with a bow too. To do this, draw the bowstring tight and hold it. Next, hold a second arrow[14] with the left hand, grasping the rear of the shaft with the fingers, search around with the arrowhead. However, it is not easy to search closely because [the arrow] hits here and there [as you move around the room].

If the shinobi [no] mono realizes you are searching for him, he may be crouching in the fire and hearth, keeping himself composed, waiting to take advantage of any chance to escape. Hiding in a hearth is effective because people defending a position are very familiar with the hearth and its position, so it is very likely that they will just pass by it as they usually do. Be warned: if you get close to the hearth to get a light and without care, you may be struck.

Figure 14.22.

Figure 14.23.

Figure 14.24.

When you pursue [someone who has infiltrated], it is essential for you to pay attention to everything. If the infiltrator is careful enough, he might have made arrangements such as [the following two points]:

He may stretch a thin rope across the exit at the height of four or five sun [5–6 inches].

He may cut a door curtain[15] into vertical strips as with a rope curtain,[16] leaving only four or five sun [5–6 inches] [uncut] at the bottom. Also, he may tie up the cords of the two ends of a rope curtain.

Also, he may crouch below steps, if any, and when you step down, he may attack you with the sword. You should be careful about these techniques.

If chased all of sudden, [shinobi] may scatter caltrops as they retreat. If you step on the caltrops, you cannot pursue him, and you will not be able to take even another step.

When they exit out a gate, they will close the doors[17] behind them. This is so it will take you time to open it. Meanwhile they gain about five ken [100 feet] in distance in the time it takes you to open the door. There are things you should learn, whether as a pursuer or if you are being chased. These are oral traditions.

When you are walking and all is normal, if you are called from behind and attacked with a sword, there is a certain way you should draw your own

Figure 14.26.

Figure 14.25.

Figure 14.27.

sword. Also, there is a technique to stop such an attacker without even drawing your sword. This is an oral tradition.

You should make a strong request of a shinobi, asking him to teach you to copy animal or bird calls. The technique is often useful when on a covert activity. In ancient China, at the checkpoint of Hangu Pass, the guards let Lord Mengchang go through the checkpoint since the guards thought that the crow of a cockerel that a retainer of the lord copied was real.[18] Especially when you infiltrate on a night of *kōshin*,[19] copying a cock-crow is a method used. Some people say; "What you do on a kōshin night will be discovered without fail." This proverb seems to be a saying first spoken by thieves. [However, it is also said that] what is done on a kōshin night will not be discovered as easily as on a normal night.

When crossing a wall on a covert infiltration, stand your sword against the wall, and tie the end of the sword cord around your ankle. Next, step on the hilt and hold on to a bracket [above you]. [When you are on top of the wall], retrieve your sword and put it back on your waist, then descend to the ground [on the other side].

If it is difficult to hold a bracket because the wall is too high, use the drill that you are carrying and insert it into the wall so that you can [reach up and] cross over.

Figure 14.28.

Figure 14.29.

Alternatively, use a grappling hook.[20] Generally, when the wall is high and difficult to cross, you should put [the rope of] the grappling hook through your obi at your back with a two-shaku [24-inch] gap from the end of the hook, put the rope across the shoulder, and tie it onto your obi on the front, then cross the wall. Once you get hold of the bracket, you can hook the grappling hook onto it so that you can use your body freely.

It is commonly known that when descending, you should keep calm and put the grappling hook at an appropriate place, and then descend, holding the rope.

Another way to descend is to use a drill as a handhold, descend holding on to it, and then letting go with one hand. Pay attention to your feet, swing out, and jump down lightly, then have the mental feeling of jumping again when you get to three shaku [3 feet] from the ground.

Figure 14.30.

[When you land], you should intentionally move into a forward roll two or three times, one after the other, instead of landing directly on your feet. It is never proper to jump from a point that is too high. If you are going to jump, then you often become *mitsuri* with the heavier part in your top

Figure 14.31.

half and lighter in the lower part of your body. In this case you will hit [the ground] badly; there is no doubt about this. Even if you do not know of these teachings, it is best to concentrate on descending.

Also, consider the quarterstaff useful [when descending[21]].

Those who are knowledgeable in these things tend not to hurt themselves badly. There are various things to be orally transmitted on how to practice these points. There are other teachings on how to jump from a height. To jump from the height of two or three jō [20–30 feet] is an oral tradition.[22]

If the horse you are riding does not want to get on board a ship, dismount from the horse, trace the

Figure 14.32.

Figure 14.33.

character for moon (月) on the horse's bit, and then follow up with the character 賦 in the middle of the horse's forehead.

賦

When you trace this character, hold the horse's mouth with your left hand, trace the last dot in the direction of the ship, and say *"hai"* to the horse.

If there is an unexpected argument and those present in the room are against you,[23] or you have to deal with a large number gathering at night and you are in a room and alone with no one at your side to help, then, because you are vastly outnumbered, you may feel that you cannot defeat all of them, even if your own life is spent in the process. It is difficult for you to do anything outside the path of the bushi.[24] Therefore, you may not able to decide what to do immediately. In this situation, keep calm, determine to die, and try to make your body *in* and your inside [mind] yō.[25] Observe with exactness what the room is like, and fight with tactics.

Approach the light with a calm attitude and without attracting their attention. With correct timing, when you think it is the moment to do so, stand up, grab your sword, and kick out the light with your foot. If the light is a candle,[26] put it out by taking out the wick. Also, you should use the candle stand as a shield to defend yourself with. Take shelter behind something that you have observed beforehand and stay still, keeping yourself as quiet as possible, and attack with full force only when appropriate and in accordance with the situation—attack from behind cover.

In any case, you should hold your *tachi* greatsword diagonally and sweep with it horizontally. Pay attention to all exits. Finally, if you take these above measures, even if there are many formidable people, they may lose all the advantages that they had and may even fight among themselves because of the darkness. Take advantage of these opportunities. Without doubt they will be of aid to you.

If there are three people talking in a room and two of them start arguing and then fighting with swords, you should intervene as follows: draw your wakizashi shortsword and hold it toward the one who seems the most determined, paying attention so that the blade will not turn away,[27] and hold the scabbard in your left hand. Then take a position about two shaku [2 feet] away from the middle of the two of them and keep an eye on both. At the moment they attack each other with swords, try to divide them by flicking up their swords.[28]

If you cannot divide them, after warning them, strike between the wrist and the elbow so that they will drop [their weapons]. It is essential to inform

Figure 14.34.

them that you intend to divide them before you draw out your shortsword. It is also good if you raise a tatami mat from the floor and put it between them, or even to stand a sliding door between them. You should not try to talk about who is right or not concerning the argument. If you try to convince them by talking [about blame] and then draw your shortsword, you will surely be taken as assisting one of them and may possibly be attacked. If you can, it is better to stop them without drawing your sword. These techniques should be left to your judgement and will change according to the situation.

When you serve as a second, assisting someone who is performing seppuku ritual suicide, do as follows:

Position yourself about two shaku to the left of the person who is going to commit seppuku with your swords at the waist. It is essential for you to observe the status of the person. If he looks like he is having regrets about committing seppuku, behead him just as he takes hold of the shortsword. If he looks determined, decapitate him when you see him cut his belly and when his neck straightens.

When he stabs his stomach with the sword and finish cutting, his neck will always tilt to the side. Remember, if you behead him when the head is tilted like this, then you will fail to [decapitate] properly. Make sure to do it when you see his neck positioned straight and upright. However, also remember that, if you concentrate too much on timing, thinking that you have to cut as soon as the neck is in that position, then it will also be inappropriate due to overconcentration. Just do it when you are spirited[29] and when it feels right. Furthermore, you can draw your sword beforehand without being seen by the person who is going to perform seppuku and place it where it is convenient for use.

When the time comes, take a position on the left side of the victim, and at the appropriate time, move your right foot forward so that it is in line with his hip joint. Raise your big toe [from the ground] and point it up and in line with the earlobe of the person committing seppuku. In your mind, imagine cutting from the base of his topknot into the chest. Keep your waist low, and move onto the tip of your right big toe as you cut off the head with one stroke. Do this with double the intensely you can normally muster. You will not fail to cut the head off if you follow this trajectory.

If you do fail to take the head off in one strike, calm yourself, [turn the handle] and grasp your sword with the blade facing upward, and then cut the head off from the front at the throat, and do so without delay.

When someone is forced to kill himself, be very careful and get as close to the person as you can, so that you are almost approaching his right side [even though you are still positioned on the left], then decapitate him with your shortsword [instead of your longsword].

In this situation, you should draw your shortsword before the [ritual] starts and place it on the back of your left hand, and do not take your attention away from the victim performing seppuku. If the victim has hidden intent in his mind and makes a counterattack, do not retreat but instead immediately stab him with your shortsword with the intent to kill. If he commits seppuku without incident, then behead him in the same way as described above.

If you feel apprehensive but do not know the reason why, do not venture out, even if a close friend offers to accompany you. This is because if your life is in serious danger, you will have a sense of gloom—this will happen without exception.

In such a case, feel your pulse. Do this by placing your right hand on your throat pulse and your left hand on the pulse on your right wrist. If they are in the same rhythm, there is no serious danger.

If you are going to kill someone, you should first be determined to die and think nothing of yourself but only of the enemy. The enemy may be determined and vigilant and can readily give himself to any change in accordance to the four ways:[30]

1. flexible (柔)
2. weak (弱)
3. hard (剛)
4. brave (勇)

If this is the case, then know that this is a serious matter. In such a situation you should kill him by employing tactics. The enemy will also plan

Figure 14.35.   Figure 14.36.

against you; therefore it is difficult to determine a single way to proceed. For both sides, there are two ways, known as *sen-go:*

1. *sen* (先), preemptive
2. *go* (後), responsive

There are various and numerous tactics that can be undertaken by those who have mastered themselves well and have settled and stabilized their nerves. These [tactics will change] according to what the enemy residence is like, or what the surroundings are like, and so on; everything cannot be explained here. However, the following is an example:

Figure 14.37.

Figure 14.38.

Realizing you are coming, he may pretend to be ill and defenseless, having no swords, wearing a *tenugui* cloth for an obi sash. He may approach in this defenseless way, preparing his hair and holding a paper string in his mouth.[31] In such a case, he will have hidden a bladed weapon in his hair, and he will attack you by taking advantage of any gap you leave open. He will concentrate on striking straight down with both hands,[32] landing the blow on the forehead. In this he will not fail. This is because he has opted to take the preemptive move.

Therefore, be aware that in this situation, there may or may not be a way to respond. Simply walk toward him without preplanning, make sure it is not too fast but also not too slow, striding up to him steadily and without hesitation. This gives him the opportunity to kill you, so take the advantage of that moment and kill him instead. It is essential to force the enemy to move to an attack that will result in his own death.

This scroll has a small amount of writing concerning shinobi; however, we are not specialized on this matter.[33] If you have a strong enemy that you wish to attack but he is too strong to overcome, and if you are going to conduct a night attack by yourself, you should do so by considering and planning with the above points. If you are determined and ready to die and have prepared with such tactics, then, when you attack, there is no way you will fail to fulfill your aim, no matter how strong the enemy is.

As I have said previously, you should not use these arts in an unrighteous way, and as you have given an oath, I need not make sure of [your intentions] again. However, if you use any of the above for unrighteous purposes, then be warned that you will not able to escape from the punishments brought on you by the gods.

The above scroll is a secret writing; however, as you are enthusiastic and wish to inherit these teachings, I will give it to you now. Take note: you should train yourself earnestly and without negligence.

[The collective names of all those who appear on the multiple transcriptions of this scroll:]

Niki Shinjūrō Masanaga (二木新十郎政長) [This name only appears on one version; in other versions Hagiwara Jūzō is given prime position if he is listed.]

Hagiwara Jūzō Shigetatsu (萩原重蔵茂辰), 1678

Tōmi Gen'nai Nobuna (東美源内宣名)

Kitagawa Kin'emon (北川金右衛門)

Igarashi Kin'emon (五十嵐金右衛門), 1678

Hattori Tokuzaemon Takenori (服部徳左衛門武順), 1797

Horii Shinji (堀井信二), 1797

Ikegami Yōsuke Hisamasu (池上用助久益)

Nagayama Sagozaemon Toyomotsu (永山佐五左衛門豊物)

Okuda Kuzaemon Yoshimichi (奥田九左衛門好道)

Yamada Tsunejirō (山田常次朗), 1819

Izumida Teikyūsai Gento (泉田貞久齊元渡), 1830

Yanase Kihei Yoshitomo (柳瀬喜兵衛義知)

Ishimaru Yatarō (石丸弥太郎), 1848

Morita Kohei (森田小兵衛), 1859

[The following two names are found in the Issō Mutai Ryū version
   of the scroll:]

Ōta Kiyozō (大田清臓)

Kubota Kazue (窪田數衛)

Comments on the Oral Traditions for the Mizukagami Scroll (水鏡口傳之覚, Mizukagami Kuden no Oboe)

[This text is divided in to three subsections.]

When you are going to cross over a river that you are not familiar with, estimate where the shallows are and judge the area to discern the point you should cross from, then cross upstream of this shallow area. To cross, move upstream of the shallows and cross in a diagonal fashion, and then when you are in the middle of the river, change to moving downstream and cross to the other side.

Figure 14.39.

At night when it is raining and you cannot see where you are heading, if there is something white or anything strange on the ground, pull out your sword, loosening the sword slightly from the scabbard, place it under the object, move it by flipping it over, and then pick it up. It is often the case that you may be killed because of such an object.

Hints for dealing with mountain bandits.[34] It is essential to pay attention to everything as taught in writings [on such matters]. Samurai are sometimes found to be without a master and wander from place to place, which is not their wish, but it is required. As that which is martial is that which they do, and if there is no other way that [a samurai] can go, they will become *yama-dachi* (mountain-bandits). If there is anyone available, then work together as a group to achieve this.[35] If alone, have a shortsword of eight sun [9.5 inches] in length that is double edged and with no hand guard.[36] This is to be used as a dagger that is kept inside the kimono. Next, wait at an appropriate place for someone to come by, grab the person by the chest, hold the dagger in the right hand in a reverse grip, and quickly cut his throat. Put *aka* inside the kimono.[37] If someone else happens to pass by, keep the mind calm and say that this man was suddenly ill and that he has been given medicine, and that they should not worry, but just continue on ahead. When no one is around, throw the body from a cliff or somewhere where no one will see it. There are more details that are to be passed on in oral form.

The art of the cricket pillow[38] (邯鄲の枕の事, kantan no makura no koto)

The image is an important aspect to be used in your sleeping quarters and should be transmitted from person to person in front of an altar. When you are in a traveling lodge, perform this method by meditating on the image of a rope that is surrounding the room. To perform this method, trace the characters (in fig. 14.40) with reference to the four directions and the center, then trace the arrow [seen in the image] toward the character for dog (犬). Place this under your pillow. Details on how to perform this are an oral tradition.

Figure 14.40.

207

Figure 14.41.

Figure 14.42.

Figure 14.43.

When sleeping outdoors, again meditate on the image of a rope that is surrounding you. No matter how many *chō* or ri the distance is, the most important element is to have a strong image in mind. There are more oral traditions.[39]

208

When shinobi infiltrate your house, one of the things to keep in mind is the following point: You should call out with your own name, because if you call out to him using one of your retainer's names, a shinobi no mono will be able to deal with this and answer, pretending to be that person. Therefore, you should call out your own name, and if the person answers as you, he must be an intruder.

When a number of shinobi infiltrate, the first thing to do is to make the inside of your house unseen from the outside. Put anything you can find over the lantern(s) so that those outside cannot see the inside. There are many details to consider.

The method of how a shinobi coughs: they sometimes cough with a bamboo cylinder at their mouths. There are other ways to do this, but they are oral traditions.

When you are chasing someone to kill him, and when the distance between you is about

Figure 14.44.

Figure 14.45.

six shaku [6 feet] and you are still out of reach with your katana, dive forward and swipe at his legs. This is called *nedake no kenmon*.[40]

When you are being chased by someone, if you intend to move into a small alleyway, you need to have enough distance between you [and the enemy], and then get in quickly.

How to defend against someone who is attacking from an alleyway with a tachi greatsword: when you cannot draw your own sword [in time], move to the left and make a turn. Next, stop his strike with your left hand by pulling out your katana while still in the sheath.[41]

When a father and son or brothers or close friends are arguing with others, if you have tried to settle the disturbance with reason, but neither of them are

Figure 14.46.

Figure 14.47.

convinced to do so, both may become more violent. If you are in close proximity to your comrade, pretend not to pay any attention but place your hand behind [and hold the scabbard with this hand] and break the seal between the sword and the scabbard.[42]

If you are near the opponent, turn the blade inward.[43] This will aid in advantage and disadvantage.

The above eleven points on how to use the *Mizukagami* scroll have been orally transmitted by Shigenao Sensei[44] and written down here. Even though points concerning the Cricket Pillow have been written down, they should be taught at an altar, and that is why the details have not been given in full.

Comments on Elements of Mubyōshi Ryū's Combat Skills (戦場組打無拍子流中通覚, Senjō Kumiuchi Mubyōshi Ryū Nakadōri Oboe)

Principles of the hidden dagger[45] (懐劔之大事, kaiken no daiji[46])

This is a hint for when you are in the presence of someone of high ranking. If you have an audience with [one of high rank] and desire to carry such a dagger, wear it between your inner and outer kimono. Have the blade pointing downward with the tip of the scabbard toward your thigh and the handle [upward] below your right armpit. When an emergency arises, you should take your kimono off your right shoulder and expose [your arm], draw the [blade], and stab. The hidden dagger is between nine sun, five bu and one shaku, two or three sun [11–15 inches] in length at its longest. It should have

Figure 14.48.

no hand guard.[47] When things are urgent, you can [replace this] with your normal wakizashi shortsword. There is more to be orally transmitted.

The surge of falling rocks and stones (岩石落之事, ganseki otoshi no koto)

When Lord Yoshitsune was successful in the assault on [the steep terrain of] Hiyodori,[48] they collected many vines of the wisteria tree and braided a rope from them, then with branches they made folding ladders, and with these the army advanced. Where the horses could not walk freely, they bound their legs and carried them down where it was too difficult.

Figure 14.49.

Figure 14.50.

Hints for things you should keep in mind for steep areas such as those given above:

In order not to be pushed down from such a high place [during combat], you should drop down with speed [keeping your center of gravity low]—this is an oral tradition.

If you intend to push someone off [a cliff], you should keep a good balance and put both hands on your waist and push him over with your shoulder. This is because if you try to push him off with your hands, the enemy may grab your hands and you will plummet together.

The secret skill of the many-petaled cherry blossom (極意八重桜之事, gokui yaezakura no koto)

[One record of this skill says chrysanthemum.[49]]

This is a secret for man-to-man combat on a battlefield. You should first decide which one of the enemy is your target, keep track of him, and have a good image in your mind. Then approach him gradually, consider the front tassets of his armor as cherry blossom petals and the strings of that section of armor the stamen of the flower. Drop down with your right knee on the ground and your left knee upward, and take hold of his tasset and lift it. During this, draw your sword with your right hand and stab into him. There are more oral traditions about this skill.

If the enemy uses the above skill on you, you should quickly adopt an *in* body. Put your right hand on the enemy's face and push. Also push the enemy's left knee with your left hand. There are more oral secrets here.

The above skill of the many-petaled cherry blossom is a secret of man-to-man combat, and although there are other skills, they are so many and so complex they are not mentioned here. Only what Shigenao Sensei orally transmitted has been recorded.

Figure 14.51.

Figure 14.52.

Secret Ways of Purification *and* Shinobi-Jutsu (極意清浄之品 并忍術, Gokui Seijō no Shina narabini Shinobi-Jutsu)

The formal way of decorating an altar is not easy to perform. Therefore, these days we use an informal way.

To do this:

- Hang an image of your central deity[50] with due respect.
- In front of the image, place a stand and put a votive light on it.
- Offer sake and washed rice [in small bowls; put them] on a thin tray.
- Place a *torii* gate in front of the sake and rice. The gate is one shaku eight sun [21.5 inches] in height.
- In front of that gate, place clear water in a bowl.
- Place a standing screen of six sun [7 inches] in height and eight sun [9.5 inches] in width to the side.

Figure 14.53.

[Method 1]

When you meditate, look at the votive light and imagine it as a great fire. Next, imagine throwing yourself into the fire. After this, put the screen at the rear

Figure 14.54.

214

of the water bowl [blocking out the fire] and think of the water in the bowl as a lake. At this point you should imagine yourself diving into the water. After doing both of these, you have purified yourself with fire and water. You have invited the Buddha—through the image—into your mind.

This is the first method of three.

[Method 2]

Another method is as follows. This is called *tachi haramaki* (太刀腹巻). To perform this, you should draw your sword and say *"On"* and trace the character for fire (火) three times on the front[51] of the sword, and on the reverse side you should write water (水) three times with your finger.

Next, hold an image of the votive light [which is the fire] described above in your mind and stab your tachi greatsword into the imaginary flames. After this, rub the ridge[52] of the sword with your left hand and observe. If you have performed this correctly, [the blade] will be flexible. If it has not been heated by the fire of your mind, however, you should repeat this meditation no matter how many times it

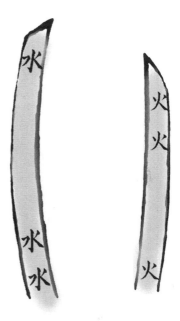

Figure 14.55.

Figure 14.56.

takes. When you want to return the sword to a state before it was infused with fire, trace the character for water (水) close to the tip on the other side. Rub the ridge[53] with your left hand and chant the spell below:

Sugunareya sugunaru tachi wo sugunisite yuge wo harau abiraunken

(すくなれや直なる太刀をすくにしてゆ気をはらふあびらうんけん)

The above is the second method.

[Method 3]

The last way is to meditate with the image described above in mind and try to picture a white fox with him. However, unless the white fox is one thousand years old, it will not work.[54] This way is also applied to *shinobi no hō*[55] to invite Inari (the god of foxes).

Figure 14.57.

Figure 14.58.

These are the three kinds [of purification].

Shinobi (志のひ)

Shinobi are not those who are common. They are given orders by the lord and travel the various provinces carrying secret letters, oaths, and joint signatures.[56]

A Buddha statue used by shinobi for traveling around the provinces is as follows:

One way is to disguise oneself as a pilgrim and have a figurine of Hotoke hanging around the neck that has been hollowed out and made in sections with a secret letter that fits inside the statue. This is called *Hotoke wari no shinobi*.[57]

In our school, we say that you should be extremely careful and prepare for where the enemy is likely to become suspicious and how your secret intentions can be detected. How to carry or hide a secret letter on you is described later, but

Figure 14.59.

if the enemy still considers you suspicious and imprisons you, you should carry a [saw] called a *chinsetsu*[58] this is three sun [3.5 inches] in length. The manner in which you should keep it is also described later. When you are imprisoned, you should take out the chinsetsu and burn it in your mind with mental fire, just as you did with the tachi haramaki [purification spells above]. Then, saw your way out where you think you can best escape. Do this in the middle of the night so that you can move out [in stealth].

There are things that you should keep in mind for when there is a strict policy at checkpoints. Prepare a wooden cylinder of the *kiri* tree of one sun, eight bu [2 inches] in length and one sun, eight bu [2 inches] in width, and then cut it into a triangular form and hollow it out. Next, cut out a heart-shaped hole, wrap [the outside] with expensive brocade, and line the inside with gold leaf,[59] then meditate and put a statue of your guardian deity inside it. You should always carry this guardian deity as protection. When you come to a strictly guarded checkpoint as mentioned above you should put it under your topknot. By doing this you can hide yourself.

How to prepare a secret letter:

Fold paper in to a four-sun [4.8-inch] section, roll it into a cylinder, and secure it with glue. Keep this secret, keep this secret. This is only to be transmitted to one person. The place where you should put the secret letter is into your *shitagi* (under-kimono). Keep this secret, keep it secret.

To carry the chinsetsu [the saw mentioned above], you should sometimes roll it together with the secret letter described above, or alternatively you can place it between your upper gum and the upper lip. This is the deepest of secrets.

The above three secrets and *shinobi-hō* are mysteries from the family of Hagiwara [Jūzō] Shigetatsu, [and these were given to] Sakurai Shigenao. Sakurai Shigenao was extremely enthusiastic and he was able to obtain this. I, also being enthusiastic, was given it by him. The way of the shinobi is myriad and comprehensive. Therefore only the outline is mentioned here.

Figure 14.60.

THE UPDATED WATER MIRROR SCROLL
(水鏡新冊, MIZUKAGAMI SHINSATSU)

There are six points on things about your outward appearance.

1. Know that at night there should no definite method that the allied battle camp follows.
2. At night the spirit of men, be it yours or the enemy's, will be enhanced.
3. Sometimes you will be surprised when a bow or something else that has been put against a wall falls over.[60]
4. [Avoid] sneezing in a battle camp.
5. If people tend to be talkative, it does not show a state of seriousness.
6. Secure the horses in your camp.

To discover the whereabouts of an ambush on a moonless night and when you can clearly see the stars, know that no stars will shine above an ambush if one is present.

One of Yoshitsune's poems[61] says:

Do not go to the direction where no stars can be seen on a pitch-dark night
While on a cloudy night, do not go toward clouds that are shining.

(闇の夜ハ星なき方に行ぬもの　くもる夜ならは雲ひかる方)

Figure 14.61.

Above an ambush, you will not see birds flying and there will always be energy[62] present. In the morning, mist will clear sooner above an ambush. Know that chi will always hang above them.

Shinobi no mono, when trying to gain entrance to a position, will move in various guises, such as beggars. Carefully question and capture [those who are suspicious], take up their hair, or shave their heads in the correct manner,[63] and put them on horseback or put them in an inner room. Also, give them bows, spears, and other weapons. Do this and observe them so that you can detect shinobi no mono.

[Shinobi] conduct their plans by disguising themselves as blind men. To do this, polish the scales of the carp fish with a fine whetstone until they are

Figure 14.62.

Figure 14.63.

very smooth, pierce a hole in the middle of each scale, and then put them over the eyes.

In order to distinguish the two kinds of fire:

- human (人)
- shape-shifter (化)

Trace a cross (+) in the air with your hand in the mudra of Hō (方). Draw your sword and position it toward the fire and observe. If the target is above the hilt,[64] you can say it is a light being carried by a human. If you see it below the hilt, however, it is the fire of a shape-shifter. If it is the fire of a shape-shifter,[65] no matter whether it is in a mountain or a field, you should make a gesture of washing your hands, and chant the following spell three times. With this it will show its true nature:

Hintei Sowaka

(ヒンテイソワカ)

To make this peculiar fire disappear, form the mudra of Nichirin (在, *zai*) and chant the following:

Figure 14.64.

On anichiya marishiei sowaka

(ヲンアニチヤマリシエイソワカ)

After this, the mysterious unknown will disappear.

You should not hit something that illuminates[66] with a wooden stick or cut it, because it will self-replicate [after it has been cut in half].

When you see such a mysterious creature,[67] all that you need to do is to settle your mind. This point holds true not only for mysterious creatures but also for all purposes. Whenever you see people, observe them with a virtuous and clear mind. However, take note that it is difficult to identify a real-world person[68] without the correct teachings. Therefore conduct *goshinpō-kuji* (the rite of *kuji* for protection) when you see these strange creatures.

There is a way to discern what is actually around. Do this by looking over the left sleeve of your kimono. The secret to making this creature show itself is that you should make the seven hand positions (mudra) of the *Kōmyō Shingon* so it will show what it truly is:

[The seven mudras do not appear in the original text and have been added here. The idea is to form these mudras with the hands and chant the sections underneath. Together they form the full chant.]

1. Chiken-in mudra (智拳印)
   Chant: *on abokya beiroshanou* (オン　アボキャ　ベイロ　シャノウ)
2. Gegoko-in mudra (外五鈷印)
   Chant: *maka* (マカ)
3. Goshikikō-in mudra (五色光印)
   Chant: *bodara* (ボダラ)
4. Gebaku nichūhō-in mudra (外縛二中寶印)
   Chant: *mani* (マニ)
5. Gebaku nichū renge-in mudra (外縛二中蓮華印)
   Chant: *handoma* (ハンドマ)
6. Chiken-in mudra (智拳印)
   Chant: *jinbara* (ジンバラ)
7. Hachiyō-in mudra (八葉印)
   Chant: *harabari taya un* (ハラバリ　タヤ　ウン)

[The full chant is: *on abokya beishanou makabodaramani handoma jinbara harabaritaya un.*]

A *shinobi-hi* is a tool that you make in the shape ▲ and of copper. It goes on top of a lantern or light so that it will go dark quickly. If you want it to become light again, take this away. How to make this tool is passed on in oral tradition.

Figure 14.65.

Put tweezers over the opening [of the lantern or light] and put a one *mon* [copper] coin on the light. This has the same effect as the above. Also, you can put toothpicks under the lantern or light.

When you walk along a road at night and you think that it is dangerous, you should put a stone of appropriate size in your sleeve and carry it. Where you think that there is something suspicious, you can throw this stone to discover what is hidden there. Before you throw the stone, you should make a prayer to the gods and put some spit on it (fig. 14.65).

When you come across a vicious creature,[69] know that they hide their toes. You should look at them carefully, as there may be difference with their legs. There are eighteen kinds of differences between human beings [and these creatures]. If you look for those points, you may find that they can move their legs in ways that a human cannot. Therefore pay attention to their legs. When you strike them, you should not cut them on the head, but strike at any lower point. The legs of a shape-shifter[70] are just like a horse.[71]

Figure 14.66.

When it is raining heavily, cloudy, and dark, you cannot see where you are going very well. Never pick up anything white or that stands out. If you pick it up, someone will strike out at you, as this white object will mark you [in the poor visibility]. If you need to pick it up for any reason, you should draw your sword out a small amount and protect yourself. Flip the white object over with your scabbard. This is done because it may poisoned; be aware of this.

Until the fourth hour,[72] if you are walking in the street, walk in the middle of the road. After that time, however, move over to the left or to the right. This is because until this time of the fourth hour, the middle of the road has chi of yō.[73]

Figure 14.67.

Figure 14.68.

Figure 14.69.

During the night, do not take the position with the wind or the rain blowing into your face. If you are in any argument or similar situation, move so that you are not in such a position. Even when you go out the gateway, observe the wind.

If you are in a northern province, footsteps that are not around a castle or a busy street sound out as far as one ri (2.4 miles). If someone is ahead of you, know that it can be dangerous.

After you have killed someone at night and are retreating, if you are unaware of where east, west, north, and south are and do not know what to do, find a watercourse and go upstream so that you can find a mountain. Go onto the mountain and take a position where you can observe whether people are chasing you with torches in hand. This way you can identify any roads or paths, allowing you to construct a way of escape.

If those who are chasing you are close behind and you think it is difficult to get through them successfully, cut off the end of your scabbard so that you can breathe through it, put the open end[74] into your mouth, and then hide in the water. Stab your katana or wakizashi [into the riverbed] and secure yourself with this. There is a method that you must learn concerning the way to breathe for this skill, but it is passed on in oral tradition.

Figure 14.70.

Figure 14.71.

When you are injured on your arm or anywhere else, move into a stream of water. This is done so that people will not be able to follow the trail of blood drops.

Also, when it is snowing, you should put your footwear on backward, hold a branch[75] on the left side, and move into the stream. This is done so that you are not followed.

Figure 14.72.

Figure 14.73.

This is an important point or spell for when you have killed someone and have to move on:[76]

yunde mete ato to saki towa kō no musha naru wo mamoru wa shichiyō no hoshi abiraunken

(弓手免て阿とと先とはかふの
武者なるを守るは七ようのほ
しアヒラウンケン)

Figure 14.74.

When you have someone carry a lantern for you, it is not good to have him ahead of you. Instead have him to your left side, two or three shaku [2–3 feet] behind your swords. This is done so that you have a good view of the front, the rear, the left, and the right. This is especially so when you are on guard duty and during and after the sixth month of the year.[77]

Observe the area around the house [where you are staying] and consider what the defenses are like. You should take into account the prospect of both fire and yatō thieves.

In a house, be very careful around the floor, veranda, ceiling, and where tatami mats are soft on inspection. You should lift tatami mats and check below them thoroughly. Also, take down any decorations and hanging scrolls[78] from the walls.

When you have a retainer of yours in the next room, have him sleep across the door between your rooms. If you are staying upstairs,[79] have him sleep at the bottom of the steps that lead to the entrance to your room.

When you are in your quarters [at a lodging], there are oral traditions for when lamps are still lit and when they have died down. They are as follows: Put both of your swords in a place that is not considered safe [while the lights are up], and after the lights have died down, move them to an appropriate and safer place. Also sleep two shaku, five sun [30 inches] away from the door.

Any pillow you use should be one that will not let you sleep comfortably. Also, there is something called the pillow of crickets. With this you will wake up even if a cricket comes into your house. This is an oral tradition.

Figure 14.75.

How to construct the pillow of crickets:

Cut paper in a square and write down these words as shown (fig. 14.76). The characters to use are listed here:

1. 蘇民 (somin)
2. 無昇 (mushō)
3. 通達 (tsūtatsu)
4. 太刀 (tachi)
5. 犬 (inu)
6. Draw the arrow [and follow the instruction below].

Figure 14.76.

When you write the arrow,[80] create a meditative image. For the vertical line, hold the image of piercing a dog.[81] While drawing this line, [chant] *"on marishiei [sowaka]."*

Figure 14.77.

Write the above on *hōshō* paper, then cut *tatō* paper into a square and seal [the talisman] within the tatō sheet. When you sleep, lay with your head on it. Whenever you are worried in a traveling lodge or similar situation, use this [and you will wake if danger approaches]. If you do not have it with you, write [this spell] in the four corners of the room.[82] More is found in oral tradition.

When the enemy infiltrates and there is a moat, river, or pond in the area, he may have prepared an appropriate size stone beside the water. This is done for the case that if the people of the house wake up and the shinobi is chased, he may throw this stone into water. If you are not aware of this technique, you will be deceived.[83]

Sometimes the person who has infiltrated, if he thinks he has been detected, may keep a level head and step into the hearth and crouch there, trying to take advantage of any gap you show, and will strike and escape. The oral tradition here is that anyone who wakes up will be very familiar with the house, and will automatically avoid this place. Be aware that an infiltrator may wait here and attack those who come close by the fireplace who are trying to get a light.

When you exit to chase an enemy who has infiltrated, there are things you should be aware of, including the following. Oral tradition states that you should be careful about everything. When an enemy has infiltrated, stretch a cord across the entrance, and if there is cloth curtain, you should cut it

Figure 14.78.

Figure 14.79.   Figure 14.80.

vertically and leave four or five sun [5–6 inches] at the bottom [uncut, so that when he exits, he will become trapped inside it]. If it is a screen of rope, you should tie the ends together at the bottom. If there are stairs, he will hide in the next room, and if someone comes down the stairs, he will attack from that position. Be aware of this. If the enemy is chased suddenly, he will scatter caltrops behind him on his way out, and if you step on them, you cannot proceed any farther. When the enemy goes out through a gate, he will shut it, and that will allow him to go five ken [100 feet] farther while you are still trying to open it. There are teachings on chasing or escaping, all of which are skills to be orally transmitted.

When you perform as a shinobi, you should learn to imitate birds and other such things, as it is often useful when you are undertaking shinobi action. In ancient China there was a case where the guards at a checkpoint allowed [Tian Wen] to go through, because one of his men made the sound of a cockerel. You should copy a cockerel particularly on a kōshin night. Some people say whatever you do on a kōshin night will be exposed without fail. This was first said by thieves. Are these things detected with ease or not on this night? As to which is correct is an oral tradition.

To know if there will be an accident on a ship, before you get on board, write the character below on the ground with your big toe, and when you write the final dot, step on it and then look at the captain's face. If there is to be a problem [with the ship], you will see him headless. However, if there is nothing to worry about, then you will see him as normal.

To prevent seasickness [for others], you should pray to [Prince] Yamato Takeru, write the character below toward the deck[84] of the ship, and put the last dot on the head of the person [who is seasick].

Alternatively, you can get on board with a straw hat and carry *Pinellia tuber.* If it is not available, you should scrape and take the clay from a wall [and take that]. Carrying sulfur in your kimono will also suffice. In addition to this, you can prepare twisted paper string and tickle the inside your nose to sneeze before you get on board. Those who shoot muskets do not get seasick.

If you have an engraving of Kurikara Fudō (a dragon wreathed in flame) on your *ko-gatana* knife, then also you will not suffer from seasickness. Ko-gatana and a *kozuka* [small blades attached to a sword scabbard] will protect you from being attacked in vengeance [while traveling], but this does not always hold true with any vehicle.[85]

If you come across mountain bandits, keep your mind calm and pass through as quickly as possible without becoming scared. While traveling for two or three ri (5–7 miles) from that point, keep a watchful eye for anyone coming from the front, rear, right, or left. Mountain bandits are usually in a group of six from the servant class.[86] Know that only one will show himself at first, while the other five or so will be hiding in a grass field or somewhere of that nature.

Figure 14.81. Kurikara Fudō

229

Oral tradition states: mountain bandits will put their left ear to the ground to know [if someone] is strong or weak [by the strength of their footsteps] and also to listen to their voices [to see if they have strong personalities]. Those who are decisive and with a righteous mind, who have a resonant and clear voice, have a strong mind and maintain a tight belly when on a mountain or in a field. When scared, you cannot maintain such a tight belly, and your

Figure 14.82.

voice and footsteps will sound hollow, clench your teeth, maintain a tight belly, and shake the ground with your steps. Also, when scared on a mountain or in a field, chant the spell of *Fudō no Jiku no Ju*; this will give you a strong mind. Those whose footsteps continue to resonate are brave and strong, while those who are weak have light footsteps. It is said that mountain bandits decide if they will fight after they have identified the type of footstep [of their intended target]. Also, they may stretch rope across a road. There is an oral tradition for this case.

If there is a sick person on the road while you travel, who is moaning in pain, asking you for medicine, you should be aware that you should not get close to such a person. Also, if someone you do not know wishes to accompany you in the daytime, then this is also not a safe situation.

Figure 14.83.

Figure 14.84.

When you cross over a river you are not familiar with, you should move diagonally upstream [then move downstream when half way across].

How to know from which direction *tōzoku* thieves will come from:

On the days of the:

- Rat
- Horse
- Cockerel
- Snake
- Boar
- Tiger

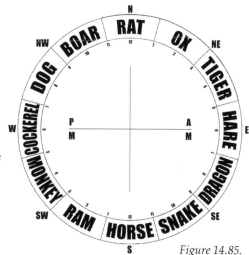

Figure 14.85.

Thieves will come from the eighth direction from the animal for that day.

On the days of the:

- Ox
- Ram
- Dog
- Hare
- Monkey
- Dragon

Thieves will come from the fourth direction for the animal of that day.

You can identify the direction according to the Twelve Earthly Branches.[87]

On a day of Kinoe and Kinoto they will come in the hour of the Dog.

On a day of Hinoe and Kanoe they will come in the hour of the Rat, Tiger, Dog, or Boar.

On a day of Tsuchinoe or Kanoto they will come in the hour of the Rat or the Dog.

On a day of Tsuchinoto and Mizunoe they will come in the hour of the Horse and the Boar.

On the day of Mizunoto and Hinoto they will come in the hour of the Rat.

When you wake up [unexpectedly] while in a traveling lodge or your own house, the things you should pay attention to are:

- if rats are making noise
- if mosquitoes are flying about quickly
- if insects are making noises

If you are in your house, you should check the external areas. There are oral traditions here.

Here is a hint you should be aware of when while you are engaged in duty [around a castle, etc.]: If a retainer or somebody loses his mind, you should bind him inside of his kimono and carry him out as if he is ill. Have his body bound in the kimono and bind his legs [around the height] of one shaku [1 foot], then carry him away.

When someone is bitten by a horse, put water into a wooden trough or a ladle and write the characters 離火消水 with the Two Swords hand mudra,[88] have the person bitten drink three sips, little by little, and pour the rest of the water on to the wound. Also, you can chew raw millet and put the pulp on the wound; this will also work.

When you are stung by a bee, grind the leaf of the taro plant and put it on the sting; this will help. Also, you can write the following on the sting:

南無赤不動明王

Figure 14.86.

(namu aka fudōmyō'ō)

Hayatsukegi (fast fire tool): either put sulfur on both ends [of a taper], or put equal amounts of a decoction of sulfur and camphor on thick paper.

Do not run out of breath smoothing medicine. You should always have, be prepared with, and be aware of the following way: take a blue hand cloth, cut a bundle of straw of the thickness that you can grip, [wrap it with the cloth], and then put it across the mouth.[89]

The art of the shape-shifter at night (夜中妖怪ノ事, yachū yōkai no koto)

This concerns an army at night and is the skill in which shinobi no mono disguise themselves as women. Normally there is nothing particularly dubious about them, but there are oral traditions about this. In this case, if you burn pine resin or cedar resin, this skill will disappear.[90]

Figure 14.87.

If you happen to fight a vicious creature[91] at a malignant place, you should pick up a stone and chant the name of your god, or say "*Yun Hotoke, Yun Kami,*"[92] put your spittle on the stone, and throw it to hit this creature. At this point, a wooden statue and the like may appear by magic. You also should hit this [with the stone]. In Iga, Kai, and Nagato,[93] they perform this tradition.

How to prevent mosquitoes from coming into the room: Write the characters for wind (風) and smoke (煙) on paper and put it under the window. Capture a brown bat[94] and bind it upside down in the east of a room, take its blood, and soak cord in this

Figure 14.88.

blood. Stretch the rope at the height of sleeping level. This tradition is called Yoshitsune's Principle of Sleeping Quarters (Yoshitsune neya no daiji).

How to not shake and shiver from illness: During the three months of spring, grind the flowers of a hemp plant and put it [in] your nose. Also, you can put the juice of the hemp leaves into a bowl, add some water, and mix them. Also, have the morning sunshine reflect on the water and drink it; this will free you from shakes and shivers for one year.

How to stop a baby crying in the night: Stretch a rope that has been soaked with the blood of a gray horse on the roof. Then a talisman should be written as follows:

You should write the talisman (shown in fig. 14.89) on blue paper and make one end to look like a [Chinese] sword. You should put this talisman in [or around] a stove.

A teaching about departure from a poem by Yoshitsune says:

> *If you find a rice husk in your departing meal, it is a sign of luck for your upcoming conflict.*[95]

(門出ニスハリシ食ニモミアラハ　仕合ノヨキスイソウトシレ)

Figure 14.89.

If you hear a crow calling upon your departure, if it is an odd number, it is lucky; if an even number, however, then you should be careful. Also, it is unlucky if an animal crosses your path. When you depart, you should start with the leg of yō (the left leg).

Use an ink stone and rub the ink stone in the ink tray [to create the ink]. When you do this, mix your earwax in the ink. When you go to a battle camp, you should put an ear pick in your ink set.[96] This is the proper way. If you write something for an important matter, mix grated yam in the ink. Alternatively, you can apply [the grated yam] to the writing afterward. This will dispel *yōkai* (monsters), and they will have no power. Also, you can add grated yam, and the writing will not come off.

Figure 14.90.

When you approach a corner of a street, you should observe both the left and the right and pass the corner carefully, as it is not good to turn a corner carelessly.

The principle of birds (鳥類之大事, chōrui no daiji)

In a period of war, how to observe birds that fly away or approach is as follows:

- If the birds are chirping and facing your direction, it is lucky.
- If you are hit with bird droppings, it is bad luck.
- If a bird comes in your room, even if it is a simple hut, it is unlucky.
- If a crane makes a nest [around the house], it is unlucky.
- It is unlucky if [you see] birds flock together.

- It is unlucky if birds make much noise at night.
- If birds chirp in the early hours of the night, they may be made to chirp through shinobi no hō (the ways of the shinobi).[97]

There are more details to be passed orally.

This scroll consists of seventy-five points[98] concerning shinobi, which should be constantly kept in mind. However, [we are] not exclusively on that path. If there is a very strong enemy who cannot be defeated, and you intend to perform a night attack upon him and alone, you should attack with these skills. If you are determined to die when you attack with these skills, no matter how strong the enemy is, there is no chance that you cannot fulfill your aim. These lessons should not be given out, and it is strictly forbidden to use the above teachings for an unrighteous purpose. This is to be acknowledged beforehand with a written oath. Therefore, there is no need to dwell on this anymore. However, if you give it away without permission, you cannot escape the punishment of the gods, as it has been written in an oath.

This scroll is a secret writing that has been transmitted in our family; however, as you are enthusiastic to have this writing, I will give all of this to you. Do not expose this to others.

Let it be so.

The first month of Kōka 2 [1845], a Year of the Snake

Figure 14.91.

15

RITUAL MAGIC

Esoteric teachings and ritual magic have been present throughout much of Mubyōshi Ryū's teachings, displaying the time frame in which the skills were born. Previously, any magical skills were teachings within another section, such as the magical teachings attributed to or complementary with shinobi skills. The following is an overview of the magic to be found in Mubyōshi Ryū, predominantly inserted into the school from the traditions of Bishamon-den and the sword school Shinjin Ryū.

THE ART OF KUJI

Kuji is a famous ritual and a misunderstood art. The reason for this is that it is extremely old, predating the samurai, and is found in various forms and is performed for various reasons. Many sources have differing teachings, causing confusion as to what kuji actually is and why it was performed.

Kuji should be considered a nine-word ritual prayer for self-protection, divided into two basic forms. First, in fixed two-handed postures called mudra, where each word is represented by a single hand position. In this version, the samurai would make each hand posture as he spoke the correct spell. Second, a grid network is constructed of nine lines, each representing a single word of the prayer, with a tenth word written over the grid of nine lines.

A samurai would use these protection rituals when he felt in danger. He might simply perform all nine hand postures with their accompanying mantras as a form of spell, or he might make a grid in the air or on paper, where he would write down a tenth word in the center of the grid, depending on which situation he faced, as explained below.

The following two kuji scrolls were written in the nineteenth century by a student of Mubyōshi Ryū, but it is not certain which version the founder of the school used.

The Principle of Kuji (九字之大事, Kuji no Daiji)

1. For Rin (臨), use the Daiitokubō-in mudra (大威徳棒印).

Figure 15.1.
Daiitokubō mudra

2. For Pyō (兵), use the Daikongōrin-in mudra (大金剛輪印).

Figure 15.2.
Daikongōrin-in mudra

3. For Tō (闘), use the Gejishi-in mudra (外獅子印).

Figure 15.3.
Gejishi-in mudra

4. For Sha (者), use the Naijishi-in mudra (内獅子印).

Figure 15.4.
Naijishi-in mudra

5. For Kai (皆), use the Gebaku-in mudra (外縛印).

Figure 15.5.
Gebaku-in mudra

6. For Jin (陣), use the Naibaku-in mudra (内縛印).

Figure 15.6.
Naibaku-in mudra

7. For Retsu (烈), use the Chiken-in mudra (智拳印).

Figure 15.7.
Chiken-in mudra

8. For Zai (在), use the Nichirin-in mudra (日輪印).

Figure 15.8.
Nichirin-in mudra

9. For Zen (前), use the
   Hōbyō-in mudra
   (宝瓶印).

*Figure 15.9.
Hōbyō-in mudra*

Figure 15.10.

[The Ishida Tarō collection states the
   following:]

Go through this ritual three times.
Then clap three times [the first two
   claps are silent, and the third clap
   is with sound].
[The Morita Kohei collection gives the
   following date.] The fourth month
   of Ansei 6 [1859] (安政六年四月)
From Yoshitomo (義知)
To Mr. Morita Kohei (森田小兵衛殿)

The Soldier's Way of Jūji (兵法十字法, Heihō Jūji Hō)

[In this system, you create the nine-line grid and then, depending on your
situation, write the correct character in the center.]

*Figure 15.11. The kuji nine-line grid.
The dot represents the place where one
of the characters listed below should
be written.*

1. Use *ten* (heaven) before you meet high ranking people (高位對面之時).

2. Use *ryū* (dragon) when you cross the sea or river by boat or bridge (海河舟橋渡時).

3. Use *ko* (tiger) when you go through a large field or deep mountains (廣野深山行時).

4. Use *ō* (king) when you go to battle or meet a thief (合戰盜賊向時).

5. Use *mei* (life) when you eat without protection (無心計飯食時).

6. Use *shō* (victory) when you quarrel or have a confrontation (問答對決靜時).

7. Use *ki* (demon) when you fight illness or go to an evil place (病人向又魔所行時).

8. Use *sui* (water) when many people gather (大衆交時).

9. Use *dai* (large) when you are happy or something positive has happened (萬喜善事之時).

10. Use *gyō* (to go) when you move to war or depart a place (出陣出行之時).

Write the correct character where the dot is on the kuji grid, and you will avoid and escape various difficulties or danger. Now I give you this. Live deeply and believe in your true mind. Do not show or give this to anyone.

[The Ishida Tarō collection adds the following instruction]:

Symbolically wash your hands without water (karachōzu, から手水)

Wash your hands without water
Perform the sacred cuts and hand postures
And your body will be purified as a sky without clouds is clear

から手水　渇してかけて　きりむすひ　身尓ハけがれぬ浮雲もなし

Repeat this three times.
The fourth month Ansei 6 [1859] (安政六年四月)
From Yoshitomo (義知)
To Mr. Morita Kohei (森田小兵衛殿)

THE SCROLL OF THE STAR HAGUN (破軍星之巻, HAGUN SHŌ NO MAKI)

Antony Cummins says: This scroll is a collection of astrological secrets that are based on an understanding of the heavenly bodies, and in particular, the dipper asterism in the constellation Ursa Major. They are at the start difficult to digest, but with perseverance, their meaning becomes clear. They are also an invaluable look at the spiritual and religious side of the samurai, helping us understand their beliefs and magic systems.

The Secrets of Military Astrology (軍敗秘傳, Gunbai Hiden)

CONTENTS

PART 1. THE PRINCIPLE OF HAGUN (破軍之大事, HAGUN NO DAIJI)

Antony Cummins says: In the constellation Ursa Major, this is the dipper asterism in the form of a dragon. The planet Venus is represented here by the word *kanawa hoshi.* The dipper asterism is an important factor in samurai warfare.

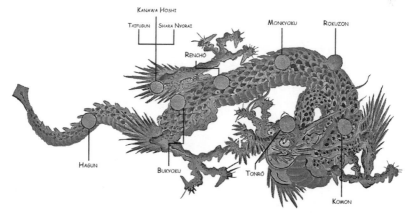

Figure 15.12. The image of the Ursa Major dipper asterism in the form of a dragon. The star Hagun is known as Alkaid in the West.[1]

PART 2. UNDERSTANDING THE POSITION OF HAGUN (破軍在處之事, HAGUN ARU TOKORO NO KOTO)

Antony Cummins says: A samurai army had to know where the star Hagun was. It represents defeat and can be an ill omen if it is in the wrong position in relation to the army. Therefore, knowing its position was important. The following list describes where the star will be. The Hour of the Dog is 7 p.m. to 9 p.m.

In the first month, [Hagun] will be in the direction of the Tiger
at the Hour of the Dog (正月　戌之時　在寅之方ニ).
In the second month, [Hagun] will be in the direction of the Hare
at the Hour of the Dog (二月　戌之時　在卯之方ニ).
In the third month, [Hagun] will be in the direction of the Dragon
at the Hour of the Dog (三月　戌之時　在辰之方ニ).
In the fourth month, [Hagun] will be in the direction of the Snake
at the Hour of the Dog (四月　戌之時　在巳之方ニ).
In the fifth month, [Hagun] will be in the direction of the Horse
at the Hour of the Dog (五月　戌之時　在午之方ニ).
In the sixth month, [Hagun] will be in the direction of the Ram
at the Hour of the Dog (六月　戌之時　在未之方ニ).
In the seventh month, [Hagun] will be in the direction of the Monkey
at the Hour of the Dog (七月　戌之時　在申之方ニ).
In the eighth month, [Hagun] will be in the direction of the Cockerel
at the Hour of the Dog (八月　戌之時　在酉之方ニ).
In the ninth month, [Hagun] will be in the direction of the Dog
at the Hour of the Dog (九月　戌之時　在戌之方ニ).
In the tenth month, [Hagun] will be in the direction of the Boar
at the Hour of the Dog (十月　戌之時　在亥之方ニ).
In the eleventh month, [Hagun] will be in the direction of the Rat
at the Hour of the Dog (十一月　戌之時　在子之方ニ).
In the twelfth month, [Hagun] will be in the direction of the Ox
at the Hour of the Dog (十二月　戌之時　在丑之方ニ).
The above revolve and come around again as listed above
(以上如是次第ニ廻).

PART 3. THE ART OF KNOWING THE AUSPICIOUS AND INAUSPICIOUS WHEN GOING TO BATTLE — ORAL TRADITION (軍ニ出ルニ知生死ヲ事　傳, IKUSA NI DERU NI SEI SHI WO SHIRU KOTO)

Antony Cummins says: The following information is connected to the zodiac and to establishing luck. A person inquiring into his or her horoscope needs to understand how to find the elements known as *honmyō* (luck) and *ganshin* (bad luck). This is done by using the person's birth sign and counting around the zodiac a listed number of spaces. See the chart in figure 14.85. This section also has a selection of magical spells to be chanted.

七星之中ニ本命元辰雲暗ハ軍サニ不可出

本命ト云ハ生レ年ニ當ル星ヲ云也

元辰ト云ハ亥丑卯巳酉未此年ヲ陰ト云

生レタル星ヨリ六ツ目ニ當ル星ヲ元辰ト言也

子寅辰午申戌此年ノ人ヲ陽ト云

此生レ年ノ星ヨリ八ツ目ヲ元辰ト云

此外泰山府軍一字金輪ハ如上謂

亦夕星之本地モ如面テ謂フカ此外有重之秘事

Honmyō (本命) is your birth element [and is very lucky]. It can be found in the constellation Ursa Major. When Ganshin (元辰) [an inauspicious element] is threatening, you should not go to battle. Your honmyō is associated to the zodiac sign you belong to.

If your honmyō is negative [Boar, Ox, Hare, Snake, Cockerel, Ram], then count around the zodiac signs six places [from your birth starting point; this will give you your element of ganshin so that you can work your horoscope].

If your honmyō is positive [Rat, Tiger, Dragon, Horse, Monkey, Dog], then count around the zodiac signs eight places [from your birth starting point; this will give you your element of ganshin so that you can work your horoscope[2]].

Kuden Senkin Bakuden (口傳　千金莫傳)

An oral tradition that should not be transmitted even for a thousand gold coins

[A magic spell to be chanted:]

heichō, riken, tanin, tahō, gashu, honrai, hokuto ōkami, shichi nan, sokumetsu, fukuju, zōchō, honmyō, ganshin, tōnen, sokusei, taizan fugun, ichiji kinrin, kyū kyū nyoritsu ryō

(兵調利劔他人他寶我聚本来北斗大神七難即滅福壽増長

本命元辰當年即生泰山府軍一字金輪急急如律令)

[A free translation:]

Military harmony, sharp swords that include Buddhist wisdom that renounces evil passions, others' treasure, of my people, and of myself, know that the god Hokuto Ōkami immediately removes the seven misfortunes and gives long life and happiness. Of honmyō and ganshin, know that which brings luck for this year.

Praise the gods Taizan Fugun, Ichiji Kinrin—so mote it be.

Yakushi Nyorai's magic spell for removing illness and pain (薬師消咒, yakushi shōshu)

on korokoro sendari matougi sowaka

(唵呼盧呼盧戰駄利摩橙祇莎波訶)

Ichiji Kinrin's magic spell (一字金輪咒, ichiji kinrin shu)

noumaku sanmanda bodanan boron

(曩莫三曼多没駄南 *(in Sanskrit, boron)*

Repeat [the above] 100 times.
毎日二百返奉唱者万騎之中雖戦
軍不負手モ不負北計七日生泰山
府軍不可謹軍之時千返間無者
百返急者二十一返門口 (Sanskrit)
如是毎日朝夕ニ手ヲ洗口ヲ漱可奉
唱者也七難即滅ツ七福即生来ト云云

When you chant *noumaku sanmanda bodanan boron*:
Two hundred times every day, your army will not lose a battle, and
    there will be no injury in battle, even if there are ten thousand enemy
    mounted riders.
One thousand chants in a battle cannot be done, so do it one hundred
    times if you have no time.
Twenty-one times if you are in a hurry when you start something.
Chant it every morning and every evening after washing your hands
    and rinsing your mouth.

If this is done, the seven misfortunes will disappear immediately, turning to the seven fortunes, and long life and happiness will be secured.

PART 4. THE SEVEN MANTRAS OF URSA MAJOR (七曜之真言, SHICHIYŌ NO SHINGON)

Antony Cummins says: The seven stars of the dipper asterism in Ursa Major each have their own story and god. This section shows a person which god is associated with their star. I was born in the Year of the Horse, which shows me which star I fall under and which spell I should use.

Mantra 1. The star Phecda (貪狼星, tonrō shō)

This star protects a person who was born in the Year of the Rat.

(子ノ年ノ人ヲ守, ne no toshi no hito wo mamoru)

This star's guardian god is Senju Kan'non. (本師　千手観音真言ニ曰)

The god's mantra is:

on darani sowaka

(唵多羅尼婆嚩訶)

Mantra 2. The star Merak (巨門星, komon shō)

This star protects a person who was born in the year of the Ox and the Boar. (丑亥之年ノ人ヲ守, ushi i no toshi no hito wo mamoru)

This star's guardian god is Seishi. (本師　勢至　真言ニ曰)

The god's mantra is:

on kukirudara un sowaka

(唵狗盧多羅吽婆嚩訶)

Mantra 3. The star Dubhe (禄存星, rokuzon shō)

This star protects a person who was born in the Year of the Tiger and the Dog. (寅戌之年ノ人ヲ守, tora inu no toshi no hito wo mamoru)

This star's guardian god is Amida. (本師　阿弥陀　真言ニ曰)

This god's mantra is:

on harasarakukin sowaka

(唵波羅旧羅吒禁婆嚩訶)

Mantra 4. The star Megrez (文曲星, monkyoku shō)

This star protects a person who was born in the Year of the Hare and the Cockerel. (卯酉之年之人ヲ守, u tori no toshi no hito wo mamoru)

The star's guardian god Monju. (本師　文殊　真言ニ日)

This god's mantra is:

on iritarataran sowaka

(唵伊哩叱羅多乱婆嚩訶)

Mantra 5. The star Alioth (廉貞星, renchō shō)

This star protects a person who was born in the Year of the Dragon and the Monkey. (辰申之年ノ人ヲ守, tatsu saru no toshi no hito wo mamoru)

This star's guardian god is Fugen. (本師　普賢　真言ニ日)

This gods mantra is:

on kotoni un sowaka

(唵戸陀尼吽婆嚩訶)

Mantra 6. The stars Alcor and Mizar (武曲星, bukyoku shō)

This star protects a person who was born in the Year of the Snake and the Ram. (巳未之年ノ人ヲ守, mi hitsuji no toshi no hito wo mamoru)

This star's guardian god is Miroku. (本師　弥勒　真言ニ日)

This god's mantra is:

on kimatouro sowaka

(唵機摩登爐婆嚩訶)

Mantra 7. The star Alkaid (破軍星, hagun shō)

This god protects a person who was born in the Year of the Horse. (午之年ノ人ヲ守, uma no toshi no hito wo mamoru)

This star's guardian god is Kokūzō. (本師　虚空藏　真言ニ日)

This god's mantra is:

on hasatakanta un sowaka

(唵波旧叱漢陀吽婆嚩訶)

Part 5. Extracts from *Sangoku Sōden*, a Book of Divination, the Twenty-Eight Mansions (三國相傳之抜書　二十八宿, *Sangoku Sōden no Nukigaki Nijū-Hasshuku*)

Antony Cummins says: This section has not been included. It consists of a list of the twenty-eight lunar mansions and their positive and negative connotations for a samurai. The original image is shown (fig. 15.13).

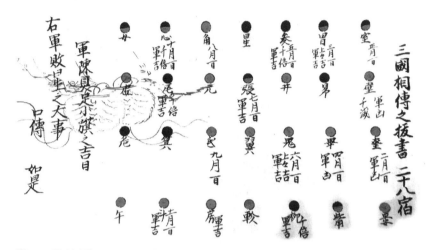

Figure 15.13. The twenty-eight lunar mansions from the Ishida family's Mubyōshi Ryū scrolls, stored in the Amagasaki Municipal Archives (尼崎市立地域研究史料館蔵石田太郎氏文書)

右此一巻雖秘貴殿多年御所望
感信心深軍敗之内抜出其外秘蜜
之真言并先師傳来之口決兵法之
結要令附属写自今以後雖志輩
有就風流若輩之強郷不可有授
受信心見届以神文盟誓可有
傳受者仍如件

The above is a secret scroll.

As you have been hoping to obtain this for a long time and you are
faithful, I have gathered and written extracts from military astrology,
secret magic spells, and oral traditions that are military tactics from
former masters.

> In the future, this should not be transmitted to any immature students, even if they are strong and have studied with ambition [the ways of] our school.
>
> After seeing through his devoutness, this should be transmitted.
>
> Swear this with a written pledge.
>
> Niki Shinjūrō Masanaga
>
> Hagiwara Jūzō Shigetatsu
>
> Tōmi Gen'nai Nobuna
>
> Kitagawa Kin'emon Sadahide
>
> Gotō Shinsuke Suketomo
>
> Mizuno Jūzō
>
> Written in Tenmei 7 [1787] (天明七年)
>
> On the second day in the twelfth month (十二月二日) (花押)
>
> Given to Kitagawa Gorobei (北川五郎兵衛　殿)

THE ART OF SELF-PROTECTION

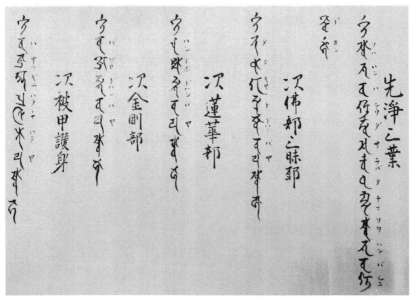

Figure 15.14. The goshinpō ritual from the Ishida family's Mubyōshi Ryū scrolls, stored in the Amagasaki Municipal Archives (尼崎市立地域研究史料館蔵石田太郎氏文書)

Goshinpō is a short ritual of five components with the objective of surrounding the samurai with spiritual armor. Each of the five stages builds on the purity and spiritual defense of the warrior, until in the end he is given divine protection against his enemies. Each stage consists of a mudra hand position and a mantra spell. For a deeper description of the ritual of goshinpō, see *Invisible Armour* by Serge Mol.[3] Mol's translations of the mantra are used below, and the images were provided by Gabriel Rossa. Goshinpō may also be known as *goshinhō* or *goshinbō*.

Self-Protection (護身法, Goshinpō)

1. 浄三業
Om sowa hanba shiuda saraba tarama sowa hanba shudo kan
Om, all beings are pure by nature, I myself am pure by nature.
Use the Jōsangō mudra (fig. 15.15).

Figure 15.15. Jōsangō mudra

2. 佛部三昧耶
Om tatagyato dohanbaya sowaka
Om, I pay tribute to the victorious that is born, so be it.
Use the Butsubu Sanmaya mudra (fig. 15.16).

Figure 15.16. Butsubu Sanmaya mudra

3. 蓮華部
Om handobo dohanbaya sowaka
Om, I pay tribute to the lotus that is born, so be it.
Use the Rengebu mudra (fig. 15.17).

Figure 15.17. Rengebu mudra

4. 金剛部

Om bazoro dohanbaya sowaka

Om, I pay tribute to the family of all *vajras*, so be it.

Use the Kongōbu mudra (fig. 15.18).

Figure 15.18. Kongōbu mudra

5. 被甲護身

Om bazara gini hara chihataya sowaka

Om, I pay tribute to Agni, goddess of lightning, who lashes out flames, so be it.

Use the Hikō Goshin mudra (fig. 15.19).

Figure 15.19. Hikō Goshin mudra

16

KUDEN—ORAL TRADITIONS

Again, this is simply a list, and therefore only the names remain, which can lead to confusion. Luckily, however, some manuals were written later in the school's history, such as the *Mizukagami, Mizukagami Kuden no Oboe,* and *Mizukagami Shinsatsu.* These writings recorded some of these oral traditions in full. This list has been inserted here, and whether the skill is missing or has been recorded is written below each. In Total there are 158 skills, and approximately 50 of them have been recorded throughout this book in the different scrolls, meaning that almost seventy percent of the oral traditions are missing.

The list is still of great interest as it provides an understanding of the skills involved within the school and allows us to peer into the way of the samurai. Remember that without context, some of the skills can seem abstract or may even be misleading.

Mubyōshi Ryū Oral Traditions (無拍子流口傳之部, Mubyōshi Ryū Kuden no Bu)

1. Quick Kuji (早九字, hayakuji)
   [Quick ritual of kuji, a defensive spell]
2. To Imbue the Greatsword (太刀腹巻, tachi haramaki)
   [Found in the *Mizukagami Kuden no Oboe* scroll, this skill is to write characters on the blade of the sword for purification purposes.]
3. Dismounting a Man from a Horse (下馬落, geba otoshi)
   [Found in the *Bishamonden Kenjutsu* scroll, not translated in this book; a spell to make a mounted enemy fall]
4. The Cricket Pillow (邯鄲の枕, kantan no makura)
   [A spell creating an imaginary rope that surrounds the sleeping warrior and wakes him if an intruder enters]
5. Mystery of Staunching Blood (血留の奇, chidome no ki)
   [Missing]

6. The Way of Kuji (九字法, kuji hō)
   [The full ritual of kuji]

7. The Way of Jūji (十字法, jūji hō)
   [The full ritual of jūji, a protection spell consisting of kuji plus one character]

8. The Way of Self-Defense (護身法, goshinpō)
   [Defensive spell]

9. The Principle of the Helmet (甲の大事, kabuto no daiji)
   [Missing]

10. The Principle of the Horse (馬の大事, uma no daiji)
    [Missing]

11. The Principle of Armor (よろ以の大事, yoroi no daiji)
    [Missing]

12. The Principle of the Sword (太刀の大事, tachi no daiji)
    [Missing]

13. The Principle of Water (水の大事, mizu no daiji)
    [Missing]

14. The Principle of Filth (汚穢の大事, owai no daiji)
    [Missing]

15. Stopping a Sword (白刃どり, shiraha dori)
    [Missing]

16. Securing a Horse at the Legs (志者つなぎ, shiba tsunagi)
    [Missing]

17. The Art of Boarding a Ship (舟尓乗事, fune ni noru koto)
    [A magic spell to see if the ship will sink on its journey]

18. The Principle of No Fire (無火の大事, muka no daiji)
    [Missing]

19. The Way of the Narrow Path (細道の法, hosomichi no hō)
    [To hide in alleyways when being chased]

20. The Principle of Distance (間門の大事, kenmon no daiji)
    [Found in the *Mizukagami Kuden no Oboe* and *Shinkan no Maki* scrolls. To dive forward and strike people at the lower leg with the sword when running.]

21. The Principle of Courtesy (禮の大事, rei no daiji)
    [Missing]

22. The Teaching of the Moon on the Water (水月の位, suigetsu no kurai)
    [Found in the *Bishamonden* and *Bishamonden Kenjutsu* scrolls. A concept often found in samurai literature concerning the reflection of

the true mind. A mirror is placed on an altar to clean both the mirror and the mind simultaneously.]

23. The Principle of Honing Oneself (執行の大事, shugyō no daiji)
    [Missing]

24. The Way of Three Gods (三神能法, san jin no hō)
    [Found in the *Bishamonden* scroll; no explanation is given.]

25. The Principle of Sleeping Quarters (寝屋の大事, neya no daiji)
    [Found in the *Mizukagami Shinsatsu* scroll. This skill is to use blood to attract mosquitoes away from a sleeping person at night.]

26. The Way of Killing Thieves (盗人死する法, nusubito shisuru hō)
    [No specific teaching found, but multiple articles fit this title in the *Mizukagami* scroll.]

27. Not Moving the Inside to the Outside (内外江出ぬ法, naigai e denu hō)
    [Missing]

28. The Way of the Dog that Lies Down (犬臥之法, inu fuse no hō)
    [Missing]

29. The Way of Arresting Criminals (犯人越留る法, han'nin wo tomeru hō)
    [Missing]

30. The Way of Stopping People (足留之法, ashidome no hō)
    [Missing]

31. The Way of Crossing Over an Unknown River (不知川越法, shiranu kawa wo kosu hō)
    [Found in *Kuden no Oboe* and *Mizukagami Shinsatsu*. It is to cross diagonally upstream at first and then move downstream.]

32. The Way of the Light Body (身加路き法, mi karoki hō)
    [Found in the *Mizukagami;* to have a lightness in form when jumping from a high place]

33. The Way of the Immortal Fire (万年火法, man'nen-bi no hō)
    [Missing; possibly low light and long-lasting torch]

34. The Way of the Ten-Thousand-Year Torch (万年松明, man'nen taimatsu)
    [Missing; most likely an alternate version of the previous item]

35. The Way to Know if a Sick Person Will Live or Die (病人生死知法, byōnin seishi wo shiru hō)
    [Missing]

36. Breathing in Water (水中息する, suichū iki suru)
    [Found in the *Mizukagami;* to cut down the scabbard of the sword and breathe through it]

37. The Way Purifying the Hands (から手水法, kara chōzu hō)
[Found in the *Mizukagami Shinsatsu* scroll; see the poem at the end of "The Soldier's Way of Jūji" section in chapter 15. To imagine and symbolically wash the hands to rid the area of evil.]

38. The Way of Hiding in Grass (草隠連の法, kusagakure no hō)
[Found in the *Bishamonden* scroll; no explanation is given.]

39. The Way of Illuminating a Dark Night (闇夜明キ法, yamiyo akaruki hō)
[Missing]

40. To Stop a Running Horse (者世馬留る, hase uma tomeru)
[Missing]

41. To Send a Person to Sleep (人越祢むらす, hito wo nemurasu)
[Missing]

42. To Remain Awake (我祢むらぬ, ware nemuranu)
[Missing]

43. Dangerous Epidemics (やく病深, yakubyō fukashi)
[Found in the *Bishamonden Kenjutsu* scroll. It involves a magic talisman against epidemics.]

44. Understanding Night Attacks (夜討を知法, youchi wo shiru hō)
[Missing]

45. The Way of the Blindfold (目隠之法, mekakushi no hō)
[Missing]

46. The Way of the Three Gods of War (三闘神之法, santōshin no hō)
[Possibly found in the *Bishamonden* scroll]

47. The Way of Goddess of Gyokujo (玉女神之法, gyokujoshin no hō)
[Missing; Gyokujo is a goddess in Taoism.]

48. The Way of Walking at Night (夜行之法, yakō no hō)
[Missing]

49. The Way of Walking in Daytime (昼行之法, chūkō no hō)
[Missing]

50. The Way of the Drawstring Pouch (袋巾着法, fukuro kinchaku no hō)
[Small bag used to hold daily things or sometimes fuses]

51. The Way of the Floating Candle (蝋燭飛法, rōsoku tobasu hō)
[Missing]

52. The Way of Avoiding Lightning Strikes (雷不落法, kaminari ochinu hō)
[Found in the *Bishamonden Kenjutsu* scroll; not recorded here]

53. Understanding Death (絶命知法, zetsumei wo shiru hō)
[Missing]

54. The Way of Identifying Decapitated Head Types (首実検法, kubi jikken no hō)
[Missing]

55. The Way of Taking a Pulse (見脈法, kenmyaku hō)
[Found in the *Mizukagami* scroll; used to identify if a warrior's pulse rate is erratic and thus foretelling of an upcoming danger]

56. Attending to the White Part of a Sick Horse's Eye (馬白眼直法, uma no shirome naosu hō)
[Missing]

57. The Way of Making a Horse Lower Itself (馬伏之法, uma fuse no hō)
[Missing]

58. To Confuse [the Enemy] (無明の酒, mumyō no sake)
[Found in the *Shinkan no Maki* scroll; a weapon, normally a powder, to confuse the enemy]

59. The Way without Opening (無の阿け法, mu no ake hō)
[Missing; the translation of this title can drastically change depending on the context. This translation may not reflect the teachings.]

60. Gandō Lantern がんとう火, gandō hi)
[A hooded lantern]

61. The Principle of Knowing if an Emergency Is Taking Place (大事来知, daiji kuru wo shiru)
[Missing]

62. The Precept against Unnecessary Killing (殺生させぬ, sesshō sasenu)
[Found in the *Bishamonden* scroll]

63. How to Avoid Coming across People (人尓不逢法, hito ni awazaru hō)
[Missing]

64. Victory on All Fronts (前後勝法, zengo katsu hō)
[Missing]

65. The Space in the Middle of Combat (大小の当り, daishō no atari)
[Possibly the concept found in the *Shinkan no Maki* scroll about rhythm and timing]

66. Knowing When People Have Fallen Asleep (寝入りたる越知, neiritaru wo shiru)
[Missing]

67. How to Send People to Sleep (人越寝入ス, hito wo neirasu)
[Missing]

68. The Way of Shooting (射ぬきの法, inuki no hō)
[Missing]

69. The Way of Arson (火事出る法, kaji deru hō)
[Missing]

70. The Way of Drawing Someone Out (人呼出ス法, hito yobidasu hō)
[Missing]

71. The Way of Stone inside a Pocket (懐中石の法, kaichū ishi no hō)
[To carry a stone in the sleeve of the kimono]

72. The Way of Fire inside a Pocket (懐中火の法, kaichū hi no hō)
[Missing]

73. The Way of Rope during Travel (道中縄ノ法, dōchū nawa no hō)
[Missing]

74. The Way of Taking a Bath (風呂ヘ入時法, furo e iru toki no hō)
[Missing]

75. The Way of Passing in the Midst of the Enemy (敵中通る法, takechū tōru hō)
[Missing]

76. To Stop Fighting (喧嘩留様, kenka tome yō)
[Found in the *Kuden no Oboe* and *Mizukagami* scrolls; to prepare for and discourage personal eruptions that may turn to violence]

77. Straight Throwing Blades (竿手利釼, sao shuriken)
[Missing]

78. The Way of Passing along a River Edge (川縁通法, kawa fuchi tōru hō)
[Missing]

79. The Way of Discussing and Persuading (論逢とくる法, ronjiai tokuru hō)
[Missing]

80. The Way of Signaling with Fire (火越志めす法, hi wo shimesu hō)
[Missing; literally, "showing fire"]

81. The Way of Creating Fire (火越なす法, hi wo nasu hō)
[Missing]

82. The Way of Crossing over a Castle and Moat (堀城越す法, hori shiro kosu hō)
[Missing]

83. The Way of Shrinking without Overextending (不延ちゞます法, nobezu chijimasu hō)
[Missing]

84. Concerning Those You Meet while Traveling (道中逢者, dōchū au mono)
[Missing]

85. Not Using Large Steps (足ニ大足出来ぬ, ashi ni ōashi dekinu)
[Missing]

86. The Art of Knowing People's Inner Thoughts (人心内知事, hito no kokoro no uchi wo shiru koto)
[Missing]

87. The Emanating Light of a Statue of Buddha (佛像光出ス, butsuzō hikari dasu)
[Missing]

88. The Way of Curing Bed-Wetting (夜者゛り留法, yobari tomeru hō)
[Missing]

89. To Change between Evil and Good (悪ニ善ニする, aku ni zen ni suru)
[Missing]

90. Kicking and Pushing with a Long Stride (けをし大足, keoshi ōashi)
[Missing]

91. The Way of Planting an Idea in Someone's Mind (論人ニ付法, ron hito ni tsukeru hō)
[Missing]

92. The Way of Extracting Toad Oil (飛きの油取様, hiki no abura toriyō)
[Missing]

93. The Way of Knowing if Someone Approaches (人来知法, hito kitaru wo shiru hō)
[Missing]

94. The Way of Saving Those Who Have Been Strangled (首〆人生す法, kubi shime hito ikasu hō)
[Missing]

95. The Way of Saving a Suicide Victim (自害人生す法, jigai hito ikasu hō)
[Missing]

96. The Way of Saving Those Who Drown (水溺人生法, mizu oboreru hito ikasu hō)
[Missing]

97. To Revive a Dead Person in a Winter Camp (冬陣死人生ス, fuyujin shinin ikasu)
[Missing]

98. To Be without Shortness of Breath When Running (走時息不切, hashiru toki iki kirezu)
[Probably, using a small bundle of straw wrapped in cloth]

99. The Way of Swatting the Mosquito (蚊を討法, ka wo utsu hō)
[Missing]

100. The Way of Swatting Flies (者いを討する, hai[1] wo utasuru)
    [Missing]

101. Reversal of the Scabbard End (こじ里返, kojiri gaeshi)
    [Missing]

102. Grabbing the Hilts of Swords (柄取逢法, tsuka toriau hō)
    [Missing]

103. Thy Way of the Stopping Body Movement (身動不成法, miugoki narazaru hō)
    [Missing]

104. The Way of Changing People at Night (夜人変ル法, yoru hito kawaru hō)
    [Missing]

105. The Way without Water (水無法, mizunaki hō)
    [Missing]

106. Sword Thievery (刀とら連たる, katana toraretaru)
    [Most likely, the act of securing swords when asleep]

107. To Carry Oil and Fire at Night (夜油火持出ス, yoru abura hi mochidasu)
    [Missing]

108. To Hold a Lantern with the Hand (手提灯持, te chōchin wo motsu)
    [Multiple light-based skills appear in the text.]

109. The Way When You Encounter a Wild Boar and a Bear (猪熊逢法, ino kuma au hō)
    [Found in the *Bishamonden Kenjutsu* scroll; not translated in this book]

110. The Way When You Encounter a Bandit (山達ニ逢法, yamadachi ni au hō)
    [Points on mountain bandits are found in the *Mizukagami, Mizukagami Kuden no Oboe,* and *Mizukagami Shinsatsu* scrolls.]

111. Traveling Alone (飛とり旅, hitori tabi)
    [Small hints are found within some teachings.]

112. The Way of the Inside of a Mosquito Net (かやの内法, kaya no uchi no hō)
    [To use a sword to look from below the net]

113. Encountering a Monster (化生者ニ逢, keshōmono ni au)
    [Found in the *Mizukagami Shinsatsu;* magical spell to discover if there is a monster present]

114. The Knowledge of the Chaser (追掛者心得, oikakeru mono no kokoroe)
    [Multiple skills found in the *Mizukagami Shinsatsu* scroll, such as caltrops, trip wires, and positioning]

115. Projectile Weapons for Capturing (飛道具捕, tobi dōgu tori)
[Some elements remain, but many are missing.]

116. The Way of Capturing a Person You Meet (逢人捕法, au hito toru hō)
[Missing]

117. The Way of Not Feeling Pain (無痛可成法, mutsū narubeki hō)
[Missing]

118. The Way of Making the Jittoku (The Tool of Ten Uses) (十徳拵様, jittoku koshirae yō)
[Tool found in the *Dōgu no Maki* scroll, but details unknown]

119. The Coup de Grâce (と〻め指法, todome sasu hō)
[Missing]

120. One Thousand Uses of the Spear (鑓千徳, yari sen toku)
[Missing]

121. The Way of Stopping a Stabbing Sword (突刀取法, tsuku katana toru hō)
[Missing]

122. The Place Where You Should Grab Armor (よ路以手掛所, yoroi te wo kakeru tokoro)
[Missing]

123. How to Hold the Reins of a Horse (馬手綱摂, uma tazuna wo toru)
[Missing]

124. The Way of Observing the Formation of Clouds (雲立見法, kumo dachi miru hō)
[Missing]

125. The Throwing Fire Arrow (なけ火矢, yakitsuke hiya)
[Missing]

126. Horse Striking (馬能当リ, uma no atari)
[Missing]

127. Close Distance Arrow Strike (矢際当リ, chikai atari)
[Missing]

128. Tools to Have on Hand When Traveling (旅手道具, tabi te dōgu)
[Multiple tools and skills are taught for traveling.]

129. The Direction of Those Who Chase (追掛者方角, oikakeru mono no hōgaku)
[Missing]

130. The Way of Approaching a Horse (馬逢者法, uma au mono no hō)
[Missing]

131. The Tradition of the Manji (万字習, manji no narai)

     [The tool named *manji* is found in the *Dōgu no Maki* scroll. It appears to be a combat tool with a swastika-formed head. Skills are unknown, but it is an art form that was taught in the main Keibukan school.]

132. War Helmet Wings (吹返し具, fukikaeshi gu)

     [Missing]

133. The Way of the Invisible Hat (隠帽子法, kakure bōshi no hō)

     [Missing]

134. The Secret of Words When Fighting (喧嘩口上秘傳, kenka kōjō hiden)

     [Missing]

135. The Way to Discover if There Is Water or Not (水有無法, mizu ari nashi no hō)

     [Missing]

136. The Way of Kuji (九字法, kuji hō)

     [Repeat of article 6]

137. To Be Surrounded by Fire (火包ま連る, hi tsutsumareru)

     [Missing]

138. How to Extinguish Cholera (ころ里取, korori tori)

     [Missing]

139. The Way of Using the Fox (狐遣ひ法, kitsune tsukai hō)

     [Found in the *Mizukagami Kuden no Oboe* scroll; a ritual involving a fox with nine tails found in Japanese folklore]

140. The Way of the Sage (仙術之法, senjutsu no hō)

     [Missing]

141. Dispelling Nightmares (悪夢退ル, akumu shirizokeru)

     [Missing]

142. The Way of Writing on a Stone (石ニもの書法, ishi ni mono kaku hō)

     [Missing]

143. The Way of Inserting a Wish into Wood (木ニ志之込法, ki ni kokorozashi no komeru hō)

     [Missing]

144. The Posture of the Shinto Gateway (鳥井構, torii no kamae)

     [Found in the *Bishamonden* and *Bishamonden Kenjutsu* scrolls, and in Shinjin Ryū, but not translated here]

145. The Way of War (軍佐法, ikusa no hō)

     [Missing]

146. Horseback Riding (馬乗様, uma nori yō)

     [Missing]

147. The Knowledge of Loyalty and Filial Piety (忠孝心得, chūkō kokoroe)
[Some parts are discussed in the *Shinkan no Maki* scroll.]

148. Knowledge of Ritual Suicide (切腹心得, seppuku kokoroe)
[Found in the *Kaishaku narabini Seppuku Dōtsuki no Shidai* scroll]

149. The Knowledge of Beheading (介錯心得, kaishaku kokoroe)
[Found in the *Kaishaku narabini Seppuku Dōtsuki no Shidai* scroll]

150. When a Horses Missteps (馬足踏違, uma ashi fumi tagaeru)
[Missing]

151. The Way of Wind (風之法, kaze no hō)
[In combat, to stand with the wind to the rear]

152. To Get a Sleeping Person to Talk (寝多る人物云ス, netaru hito mono iwasu)
[Missing]

153. To Predict If the Following Day Will Be of Ill Luck or Not (明日吉悪知, asu yoshi ashi wo shiru)
[Missing]

154. The Way of Hiding in Clouds (雲隠法, kumogakure no hō)
[Missing]

155. Changing a Timid Person into One of Strength (物恐人強する法, mono-oji suru hito tsuyokusuru hō)
[Missing]

156. Swimming for Those Who Are Poor Swimmers (水心無川ヲおよく, mizugokoro naku kawa wo oyogu)
[Missing]

157. The Principle of Not Striking (無伐大事, utanu daiji)
[Missing]

158. The Principle of Invincibility (無敵之大事, muteki no daiji)
[Missing]

17

MUBYŌSHI RYŪ SAVED

Well, not quite, but a stepping stone toward such a goal has been achieved. In truth all samurai schools are of importance, and if possible, all should be recorded and saved. At this point, the "mirror" of Mubyōshi Ryū is not fully clear, but it has without doubt been cleaned enough that we can see a reflection of the school. It is, of course, a shame that so much of the school has been lost, but equally it is a joy that much was recorded.

The tale of Hagiwara Jūzō and his struggle for revenge and survival can be seen in the devious tricks that he acquired and his focus on reprisal. It must be reiterated that Niki Shinjurō has an equal part to play, or is at least considered as a tutor to the founder. Together they formed a great school that lasted for generations and still clings to life today, albeit in a reduced fashion. The current grandmaster, Uematsu Sensei, has the difficult task of keeping it alive and also now trying to identify where the skills have been changed over time and whether or not to try to bring them back to their original form. Herein lies a great lesson for all those who study from old schools—a lesson that teaches that ancient lineage does not mean that the teachings remain the same, and that over generations, differences creep into the skills. Each ancient samurai school differs in the variations they have acquired, and each master will be responsible for trying to maintain the original teachings.

Without doubt, however, change has crept in. Mubyōshi Ryū can be classed as one of those schools where a larger portion of change has occurred, but it also benefits from multiple transcriptions and recordings of the skills involved. Above all, we should live with the satisfaction that a samurai under the threat of blood feud perfected these skills and fought off many enemies, and that we, alongside the current grandmaster, have the ability and—if it may be said—the duty to bring these skills back to life as they were once taught.

It is with great joy that these teachings have been left for another generation and that this book will create a foundation for future study. Such study must be directed toward reconnecting with how the skills were originally laid down and understanding the environment that they were created in. It is with absolute sincerity that I ask those who have been touched by this tale to take up the torch and help carry Mubyōshi Ryū into a new generation. The key is to spread the story of this school through social media as well as traditional avenues, bringing the teachings to a whole new audience. For those who have the strength of mind, I request that you study the school. Everything you need for a proper foundation is in this book, and all that is required is that you make contact with the main dōjō, first build a relationship, and then find a way to visit Japan to study with the current grandmaster. Good luck, and maintain the correct strength of mind.

Figure 17.1.

18

BONUS MATERIAL: CHŪ-KODACHI AND SHURIKEN SKILLS FROM THE UEMATSU FAMILY

無覚流, MUKAKU RYŪ

In 1679, Uematsu Tanomonosuke, under the guidance of Suga Gensai Masaie, developed Mukaku Ryū, a samurai school of chū-kodachi (shortsword) and shuriken-jutsu (the art of the throwing blade). The tradition has been passed down in the Uematsu family from that time until now and is taught by Uematsu Yoshiyuki Sensei. While other branches did form, he is considered the primary lineage. The skills of his school are being revealed for the first time to anyone in any language outside the school, and it is a privilege to share these ancient skills with the world. I personally hope that these teachings reach dedicated students, and that those wishing to fully engage with these skills—who may also hopefully become licensed teachers—will visit japan to study under the grandmaster.

The scrolls of Mukaku Ryū in Uematsu Yoshiyuki's care are all handwritten by him from his family teachings, which, of course, does not cement his school in history. However, upon researching the school, a collection of three Mukaku Ryū scrolls were found on the rare book market in Tokyo and were sold as Edo Period scrolls of Mukaku Ryū. This scroll set was found by Mieko Koizumi and me, ensuring that no tampering occurred. Even after the branch schools had spent possibly hundreds of years apart, the teachings in the school remained, in title and name, the same, as seen in figure 18.1.

THE MUKAKU RYŪ LINEAGE

The grandmaster lineage as given by Uematsu Sensei:

1. Uematsu Tanomonosuke Yoshiharu (上松頼母介義治)
2. Uematsu Gondayū Yoshinaga (上松権太夫義長)

3. Uematsu Shin'emon Yoshisada (上松新右衛門義祇)

4. Uematsu Kuranoshin Yoshichika (上松藏之進義局)

5. Uematsu Uneme (Kazuma) Yoshishige (上松采女(主馬)義蕃)

6. Uematsu Shinzaemon (Shin'emon) Yoshitoyo (上松新左(右)衛門義豊)

7. Uematsu Kuranoshin Yoshitsugu (上松藏之進義次)

8. Mori Gohō (森悟峰)

9. Uematsu Torao (上松寅雄)

10. Uematsu Ichiji (上松一二)

11. Uematsu Yoshiyuki (上松義幸)

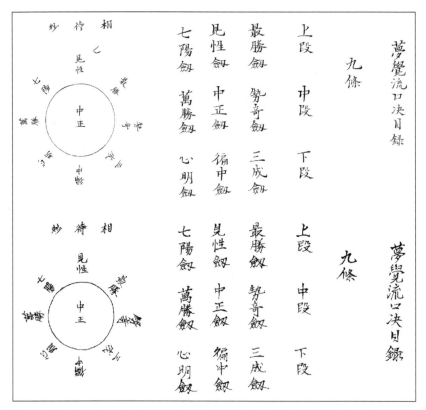

Figure 18.1. Grandmaster Uematsu's scroll (below) and the Edo Period scroll (above) found by Antony Cummins and Mieko Koizumi. The skill sets remain the same in both.

The Kodachi Sword Skills of Mukaku Ryū (無覚流中・小太刀, Mukaku Ryū Chū Kodachi)

Antony Cummins says: *Kodachi* literally means "smaller greatsword," a small tachi. In this case the "t" sound in tachi becomes "d." The kodachi is the main sword used in the Mukaku Ryū system.

Figure 18.2. A section of Grandmaster Uematsu's scroll and his drawing of one of the skills.

Basic Chū-Kodachi Sword Skills in Mukaku Ryū (無覚流中・小太刀, Mukaku Ryū Chū Kodachi)

Grandmaster Uematsu says: This skill is done both to the left and the right.

Figure 18.3. Sanpōgiri (三方切)

Figure 18.4. Kotezume
(小手詰)

Figure 18.5. Ōzume
(大詰)

Figure 18.6. Kakegiri (掛斬)

Figure 18.7. Migikiri Hidarikiri (右切左切)

Figure 18.8. Ainuki (相抜)

Grandmaster Uematsu says: This is a fast cross-walk where you move to the side of the opponent before he fully draws his weapon. The walk is shown in figure 18.9.

Figure 18.9.

Figure 18.10. Surinuki (摺抜)

Grandmaster Uematsu says: This step has small jumps to the side. In our school the swordsman will move with speed and a small leap to cut the enemy.

Figure 18.11. Kaerimi (返身)

Figure 18.12. Unryū (雲瀧)

Figure 18.13. Kumotsuke (雲附)

Figure 18.14. Hiryū (飛瀧)

Grandmaster Uematsu says:
When you have defended against an overhead cut, crouch and slice the inside of the opponent's leg.

Figure 18.15. Hien (飛燕)

Figure 18.16. Raikō (雷光)

Figure 18.17. Kasumigiri (霞切)

Figure 18.18. Tappi (達飛)

Figure 18.19. Enkai (猿廻)

Figure 18.20. Enpi (猿飛)

THE NINE POSTURES (九條, KUJŌ)

Grandmaster Uematsu says: The following nine positions are the guards and stances of our school. They are divided into three sections: upper, middle, and lower. You strike in the direction the blade naturally wishes to move in.

Upper Position (上段, Jōdan)

Grandmaster Uematsu says: The first three are in the upper position.

Figure 18.21. Saishōken (最勝剣)

Figure 18.22. Kenshōken (見性剣)

Figure 18.23. Shichiyōken (七陽剣)

Middle Position (中段, Chūdan)

Grandmaster Uematsu says: The second three are in the middle position.

Figure 18.24. Seikiken
(勢旁剣)

Figure 18.25. Chūseiken
(中正剣)

Grandmaster Uematsu says: This guard is also to stab from.

Figure 18.26. Manshōken
(萬勝剣)

Lower Position (下段, Gedan)

Grandmaster Uematsu says: The third three are in the lower position.

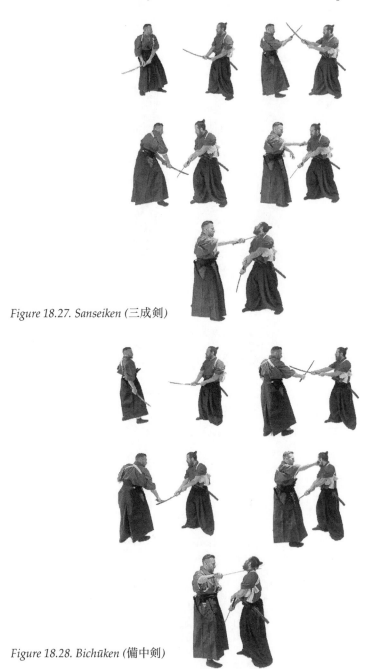

Figure 18.27. Sanseiken (三成剣)

Figure 18.28. Bichūken (備中剣)

Figure 18.29. Shinmyōken (心明剣)

Grandmaster Uematsu says: This is the end of the nine sword positions and their applications.

THE ART OF KUJI NO IN OF MUKAKU RYŪ (九字之印, KUJI NO IN)

Figure 18.30. The Kuji section in Grandmaster Uematsu's scrolls, with the associated gods and Sanskrit equivalent

The nine positions of the Kuji ritual:

- Rin (臨) is associated with the deity Bishamonten (毘沙門天).
- Pyō (兵) is associated with the deity Jūichi-men Kan'non (十一面観音).
- Tō (闘) is associated with the deity Kongō Nyoirin (金剛如意倫).
- Sha (者) is associated with the deity Fudō Myō'ō (不動明王).
- Kai (皆)is associated with the deity Aizen Myō'ō (愛染明王).
- Jin (陳) is associated with the deity Shō Kan'non (聖観音).
- Retsu (裂) is associated with the deity Senju Kan'non (千手観音).
- Zai (在) is associated with the deity Miroku Bosatsu (弥勒菩薩).
- Zen (前) is associated with the deity Daikokuten (大黒天).

Antony Cummins says: Kuji is found in many schools and is a recurring theme in samurai teachings. On the whole the outline is the same, but each school may have their own secrets and usages. The kuji nine-step ritual is also a preparation for jūji—the tenth symbol when using esoteric magic.

How to perform the ritual of *kuji no in:*

Step 1: The Sword Hand Position

Grandmaster Uematsu says: Place your fingers into your hand as shown in figure 18.31. This symbolizes the sword. You then withdraw this "blade" from its "scabbard." The hand now becomes the sword, ready to perform the ritual of kuji.

Figure 18.31.

	2. Pyo	4. Sha	6. Jin	8. Zai
1. Rin				
3. Tō				
5. Kai				
7. Retsu				
9. Zen				

Figure 18.32.

Step 2: Draw the Grid in the Air

Grandmaster Uematsu says: Draw all nine lines to form the grid in front of you. We have a secret tradition in our school about the third line.

Secret tradition: The secret tradition is to flick the fingers out to the right on the third line, as shown in figure 18.33.

Figure 18.33.

Step 3:

Grandmaster Uematsu says: When the ninth line is finished, make a low guttural shout, saying the sounds "a-un."

Antony Cummins says: "A-un" represents the beginning and the end of all things. This is said with power but not said too loudly.

Step 4:

Grandmaster Uematsu says: Hold up the sword fingers and blow the energy away.

Figure 18.34.

Figure 18.35.

Figure 18.36.

Step 5:

Grandmaster Uematsu says: Place the sword fingers back in their scabbard. Now that the ritual is done, you have hidden your power of intent. You are now ready to kill your enemy.

The deepest secret of kuji in Mukaku Ryū: In Mukaku Ryū, kuji is used to help the samurai kill an enemy. When a samurai of this school wishes to kill a foe, he has to hide his killing intent. Therefore, before he approaches the target to make his kill, he performs the ritual out of sight. Doing this dispels the killing intent, making the samurai's intentions invisible to the adversary.

Antony Cummins says: The enemy may feel the samurai's intent to kill, therefore this ritual dispels and hides the intent. The samurai then approaches the enemy with less energy emanating from him.

Once performed, a samurai may restore his lost power by chanting the following spell three times:

On kirikyara harahara futaran Pasotsu Sowaka

Kuji can also be performed with a real sword:

Figure 18.37. Grandmaster Uematsu performing the ritual of kuji with a sword

Mukaku Ryū Shuriken-Jutsu (無覚流手裏剣術)

Grandmaster Uematsu says: This is the hidden element of martial arts that lies below the surface. It can also be known as *onken-jutsu* (hidden blades) or *an-kenjutsu* (dark blade art). It is used to defeat an enemy, both distant and close. This is achieved by holding [the blade] and hiding it without it being noticed by the opponent. Even small blades of five sun [6 inches] can overcome a larger blade of three shaku [3 feet].

Concerning Shape (形状之事, Keijō no Koto)

There are many shapes of shuriken, each according to its school, including these, among others:

- *bōjō* (spike)
- *jūji* (cross)
- *hiragata* (plate)

Train and consider how to throw and stab with them.
[Types of Shuriken recorded by the current Grandmaster:]

Figure 18.38. Katori Shintō Ryū: square cross section (角型, kaku-gata)

Figure 18.39. Enmei Ryū: knife-bladed (短刀型, tantō-gata)

Figure 18.40. Shirai Ryū: round cross section (丸棒型, marubō-gata)

*Figure 18.41. Mukaku
Ryū: square cross section,
with angled edge (四角型,
shikaku-gata)*

*Figure 18.42. Tōden Mōen
Ryū [no title]*

*Figure 18.43. Yagyū Ryū:
cross style (十字型, jūji-gata)*

*Figure 18.44. Tsugawa Ryū:
plate (平型, hira-gata)*

*Figure 18.45. Negishi
Ryū: eight-sided (八角型,
hakkaku-gata)*

The Art of Posture and Form (構形之事, Kamae Kata no Koto)

When throwing and striking with a shuriken against the enemy, adopt the appropriate method for each shuriken.

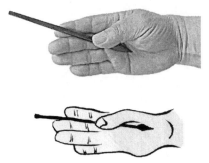

Figure 18.46. Reversed

Grandmaster Uematsu says: The shuriken spins over only half a turn before the spike hits the target.

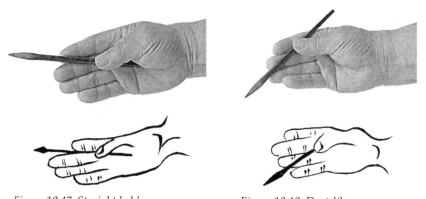

Figure 18.47. Straight hold   *Figure 18.48. Dart-like*

Grandmaster Uematsu says: The shuriken is thrown in a similar [yet not the same] way as in the Western sport of darts.

Gauging Distance (目測之事, Mokusoku no Koto)

Correctly estimate the distance between you and the enemy, judge the advantages and disadvantages, and throw in an appropriate fashion so as to defeat the enemy.

Throwing the Blade (打剣之事, Uchi-ken no Koto)

Anytime that you strike with the blade, throw and gain victory with the intention to kill the enemy.

Skills with the Hidden Palm Blade (掌剣型之事, Shōken-gata no Koto)

[Skills with the hidden palm blade are the following skill sets:]
Palm blade: basic form (掌剣型, shōken-gata)

Figure 18.49. Basic palm blade from the scroll and its modern replica

Palm blade: cross form (十字掌剣, jūji shōken)

Figure 18.50. Cross palm blade from the scroll and its modern replica

Grandmaster Uematsu says: Hide these in the palm of your hand, and with a flicking motion, allow the spike to come into position, as shown in figure 18.51.

Figure 18.51.

Figure 18.52. An example of the secret weapon in use

Mukaku Ryū Skill List

Antony Cummins says: The following is a list of the skills found in Mukaku Ryū's tradition. Note that the target changes from side to side; make sure to check your starting posture in relation to the target.

Figure 18.53. Forward posture (正面打, choku-uchi)

Figure 18.54. Sideward posture (横打, yoko-uchi)

Figure 18.55. Rear-turning posture (後転打, kōten-uchi)

*Figure 18.56. Stationary throwing
(不動打, fudō-uchi)*

*Figure 18.57. Quick throwing
(速転打, sokuten-uchi)*

Grandmaster Uematsu says: This is to hold a bunch of shuriken in your left hand and to throw them in quick succession with your right hand.

Antony Cummins says: If you are left handed, hold them in your right hand and throw with your left. This is about holding the shuriken in the nondominant hand and throwing with the dominant hand.

*Figure 18.58. Throwing from kneeling
(膝打, hiza-uchi)*

Figure 18.59. Moving in and throwing (遠近打, enkin-uchi)

Grandmaster Uematsu says: In this skill you can hide one blade while allowing the enemy to see a blade in your other hand. This takes the enemy's focus away from your hidden weapon. Next bring the hidden shuriken into position—which may require you to flip it—and then throw it at the enemy. Another method is to hide both blades in your hands.

Pretend to throw the shuriken, but in fact do not [instead use the action as a feint]. When the enemy [reacts] and lets his guard down, throw it at him.

Antony Cummins says: This is to pretend to throw a shuriken at the enemy. When he reacts to defend himself, quickly make the throw for real and hit him as he comes out of his first defense. This has a two-heartbeat feel, in that you pretend to throw, and almost on the second beat, you really throw.

Throw a shuriken and pretend to have finished throwing [all your blades]. However, hide a single blade [in the left hand] and use it to pierce the enemy's eye. This skill is used as a final measure.

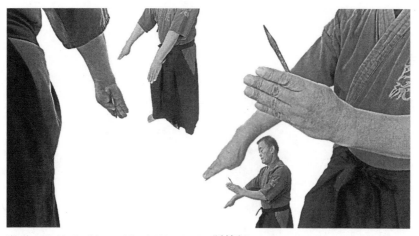

Figure 18.60. Striking with a hidden blade (隠持打, inji-uchi)

Figure 18.61. The deceptive fox throw
(狐疑心打, *kogishin-uchi*)

Figure 18.62. The crab-eye throw
(蟹目打, *kanime-uchi*)

Antony Cummins says: This skill is to have either a hidden blade or Mukaku Ryū's secret weapon in your left hand. When you throw a shuriken, flip the hidden blade into the correct position and stab the enemy in the eye.

*Figure 18.63. The fire
blade of confusion
(火乱剣, kaenken)*

*Figure 18.64. The fire
blade of confusion*

Throw the knife that you are holding in your right hand at the enemy.

Antony Cummins says: This skill is to throw a knife at the enemy so that he cuts the thrown blade out of the air with his sword. As he defends himself against the thrown blade, you should strike him down.

The above is our scroll and list of shuriken-jutsu (skills with the hidden blade).

[Praise] Hachiman Daibosatsu
[Praise] Bishamonten
1679[1]
The founder of the school was Uematsu Tanomonosuke Yoshiharu.
The current grandmaster of Mukaku Ryū is Uematsu Yoshiyuki.
Complied in 2005 [from our ancient ways].

This is the end of Mukaku Ryū's teachings.

APPENDIXES

The following appendixes are for Mubyōshi Ryū alone and deal with statistical information alongside the Japanese transcriptions. Mukaku Ryū does not feature here. All were compiled by Antony Cummins and Mieko Koizumi and have been recorded here to help with future research, both Japanese and Western, in the hope that others will also take up the torch and help to save this dying art.

以下、巻末に無拍子流に関する資料と概略・伝書の翻刻等を掲載する。(無覚流については、ここでは触れていない)これらの資料は、アントニー・クミンズ、小泉美江子が収集し、将来、日本と西洋の両方で無拍子流の研究に役立つことを、また、伝統を受け継ぎ消えゆく技を守っていく一助となることを願って、ここにまとめたものである。

APPENDIX A.
MEASUREMENTS AND NUMBERS

Throughout the original text, various names, tools, recipes, and skills involve a myriad of Japanese measurements, which have been translated in the text in their original form. Words such as *shaku*, *ryō*, and *bu* will become familiar as you progress through the text. To aid understanding, the following table allows conversions to several formats.

Measurement	Character	Metric	U.S./Imperial
LENGTHS			
rin	厘	0.3 millimeters	0.01 inches
bu	分	3.03 millimeters	0.11 inches
sun	寸	3.03 centimeters	1.19 inches
shaku	尺	30.3 centimeters	11.93 inches
ken	間	1.81 meters	5.96 feet
chō	町	109.1 meters	357.9 feet
ri	里	3.92 kilometers	2.435 miles
MASS OR WEIGHT			
bu/fun	分	0.37 grams	0.013 ounces
momme	匁	3.75 grams	0.132 ounces
ryō	両	37.5 grams	1.32 ounces
kin	斤	600 grams	21.16 ounces

Appendix B.
Subjects and Schools Taught at the Keibukan Military School of Kanazawa

The following table shows the subjects and schools taught in the years 1828 and 1854.

Section	Subject	School (1828)	School (1854)
射術 Shajutsu Projectiles	杢馬騎射 Mokubakisha Shooting on horseback		小笠原流 Ogasawara Ryū
	弓術 Kyūjutsu Archery	吉田流 Yoshida Ryū	吉田流 Yoshida Ryū
馬術 Bajutsu Horsemanship	馬術 Bajutsu Horsemanship	大坪流 Ōtsubo Ryū	大坪流 Ōtsubo Ryū
		大坪流荒木掛 Ōtsubo Ryū Arakigakari	大坪流荒木掛 Ōtsubo Ryū Arakigakari
		斎藤流 Saitō Ryū	斎藤流 Saitō Ryū
		八条流 Hachijō Ryū	八条流 Hachijō Ryū
刀術 Tō jutsu Sword arts	剣術 Kenjutsu Swordsmanship	中条流 Chūjō Ryū	中条流 Chūjō Ryū
		冨田流 Toda Ryū	
		新陰流 Shinkage Ryū	新陰流 Shinkage Ryū
		柳生流 Yagyū Ryū	柳生流 Yagyū Ryū
		神伝流 Shinden Ryū	

Table continues on next page.

Section	Subject	School (1828)	School (1854)
		深甚流 Shinjin Ryū	深甚流 Shinjin Ryū
		真甚流 Shinjin Ryū	真甚流 Shinjin Ryū
		義経神明流 Yoshitsune Shinmei Ryū	義経神明流 Yoshitsune Shinmei Ryū
			運籌流 Unchū Ryū
			水野一伝流 Mizuno Ichiden Ryū
			神信影流 Shinshinkage Ry
		真心陰流 Shin no Shi'nin Ryū	
			神相流 Shinsō Ryū
		伊賀流 Iga Ryū	伊賀流 Iga Ryū
	長巻柄太刀 Nagamaki tsuka tachi Pole-arms with sword blades		神武流 Shinbu Ryū
	中巻 Nakamaki Large war sword with long handle		山口流 Yamaguchi Ryū
	長刀 Naginata Halberd	神相流 Shinsō Ryū	神相流 Shinsō Ryū
			心鏡流 Shinkyō Ryū
			神道流 Shintō Ryū
	居合 Iai Quick drawing	多宮流 Tamiya Ryū	多宮流 Tamiya Ryū

Section	Subject	School (1828)	School (1854)
		民弥流 Tamiya Ryū	民弥流 Tamiya Ryū
		浅加流(浅賀流) Asaga Ryū	浅加流(浅賀流) Asaga Ryū
		山岸流 Yamagishi Ryū	山岸流 Yamagishi Ryū
		相心流 Sōshin Ryū	
鎗術 Sōjutsu Spearmanship	鎗術 Sōjutsu Spearmanship	宝蔵陰流 Hōzōin Ryū	宝蔵陰流 Hōzōin Ryū
		大島流 ŌShima Ryū	大島流 ŌShima Ryū
		大島当流 Ōshima Tō Ryū	大島当流 Ōshima Tō Ryū
		原田流 Harada Ryū	原田流 Harada Ryū
		機流早槍 Kiryū Kudayari	機流早槍 Kiryū Kudayari
		観通流 Kantsū Ryū	観通流 Kantsū Ryū
		堀流 Hori Ryū	堀流 Hori Ryū
鎖鎌 Kusarigama Sickle and chain	鎖玉術 Kusaridama jutsu Sickle and chain	瀧流 Taki Ryū	瀧流 Taki Ryū
			心鏡流 Shinkyō Ryū
小具足 Kogusoku Jūjutsu 捕物 Torimono Capture	柔術 Jūjutsu Grappling	無拍子流 Mubyōshi Ryū	無拍子流 Mubyōshi Ryū
		一相無拍子流 Issō Mubyōshi Ryū	一相無拍子 Issō Mubyōshi Ryū
			一惣無躰流 Issō Mutai Ryū

Section	Subject	School (1828)	School (1854)
	躰術 Taijutsu Grappling	長尾流 Nagao Ryū	長尾流 Nagao Ryū
			伯州流 Hakushū Ryū
	組打 Kumiuchi Grappling	無拍子流 Mubyōshi Ryū	無拍子流 Mubyōshi Ryū
		一惣流（一相流） Issō Ryū	一惣流（一相流） Issō Ryū
		清剛玉心流 Seigō Gyokushin Ryū	清剛玉心流 Seigō Gyokushin Ryū
	棒術 Bōjutsu Quarterstaff	神岡流 Kamioka Ryū	神岡流 Kamioka Ryū
		戸田金剛流 Toda Kongō Ryū	戸田金剛流 Toda Kongō Ryū
			戸田流 Toda Ryū
	卍術 Manji jutsu Close combat with a swastika-shaped weapon		卍術 Manjijutsu (unknown, considered a restraining art or an aid to capturing criminals)
	陰術 In jutsu (unknown)		神道流 Shintō Ryū
炮術 Hōjutsu Gunnery	炮術 Hōjutsu Gunnery	not taught	荻野流 Ogino Ryū
		not taught	豊島流 Hōshima Ryū
		not taught	自得流 Jitoku Ryū
		not taught	酒井流 Sakai Ryū
兵術 Heijutsu Art of war	軍螺 Gunra Military signals	武田流（甲州流） Takeda Ryū (Kōshū Ryū)	武田流（甲州流） Takeda Ryū (Kōshū Ryū)

Appendix C.
Keibukan Military School Lesson Timetable

The following table shows the times when lessons were given in the main military school, the Keibukan. Of course, lessons were also given in each school's respective dōjō. The list appears to date to the late Edo Period.

Day	Time	Subject	Instructor
朔日 1st day	朝 morning	弓術 Kyūjutsu Archery	吉田彦兵衛 Yoshida Hikobei
二日 2nd day	同 as above	鎗術 Sōjutsu Spears	筒井常右衛門 Tsutsui Tsuneemon 筒井善左衛門 Tsutsui Zenzaemon 筒井勘助 Tsutsui Kansuke
三日 3rd day	同 as above	弓術 Kyūjutsu Archery	吉田権平 Yoshida Gonbei
四日 4th day	同 as above	弓術 Kyūjutsu Archery	吉田才一郎 Yoshida Saiichirō
五日 5th day	同 as above	剣術 Kenjutsu Swordsmanship	山森武太夫 Yamamori Takedayū 木村喜右衛門 Kimura Kiemon
同 as above	夕 evening	剣術 Kenjutsu Swordsmanship	木村藤兵衛 Kimura Tōbei

Table continues on next page.

Day	Time	Subject	Instructor
六日 6th day	朝 morning	鎗術 Sōjutsu Spearmanship	原田又右衛門 Harada Mataemon
同 as above	夕 evening	馬術 Bajutsu Horsemanship	片山久右衛門 Katayama Hisaemon
七日 7th day	朝 morning	剣術 Kenjutsu Swordsmanship	山崎次郎兵衛 Yamasaki Jirobei
同 as above	夕 evening	馬術 Bajutsu Horsemanship	星野高九郎 Hoshino Takakurō 小池伴太夫 Koike Bandayū
八日 8th day	朝 morning	居合 Iai Quick drawing	中村八兵衛 Nakamura Hachibei
同 as above	夕 evening	馬術 Bajutsu Horsemanship	高桑津左衛門 Takakuwa Tsuzaemon 明石数右衛門 Akashi Kazuemon
九日 9th day	朝夕 morning and evening	剣術 Kenjutsu Swordsmanship	八島金蔵 Yashima Kinzō
十日 10th day	朝 morning	剣術 Kenjutsu Swordsmanship	神保三八 Jinbo Sanpachi
同 as above	夕 evening	鎗術 Sōjutsu Spearmanship	土田武右衛門 Tsuchida Takeemon
十一日 11th day	朝 morning	剣術 Kenjutsu Swordsmanship	矢野久左衛門 Yano Hisazaemon
同 as above	夕 evening	馬術 Bajutsu Horsemanship	斎藤久之助 Saitō Hisanosuke

Day	Time	Subject	Instructor
十二日 12th day	朝 morning	剣術 Kenjutsu Swordsmanship	山森武太夫 Yamamori Takedayū
同 as above	夕 evening	居合 Iai Quick drawing	白江金十郎 Shirae Kinjūrō
十三日 13th day	朝 morning	居合 Iai Sword drawing	富永半助 Tominaga Hansuke 岡山森江 Okayama Morie
同 as above	夕 evening	馬術 Bajutsu Horsemanship	佐野久喜次 Sano Kukitsugu
十四日 14th day	朝 morning	剣術 Kenjutsu Swordsmanship	木村惣太夫 Kimura Sōdayū
同 as above	夕 evening	剣術 Kenjutsu Swordsmanship	笠間九兵衛 Kasama Kyūbei
十五日 15th day	朝 morning	同 as above	平井茂右衛門 Hirai Shigeemon
同 as above	夕 evening	同 as above	馬淵順左衛門 Mabuchi Junzaemon
十六日 16th day	朝夕 morning and evening	鎗術 Sōjutsu Spearmanship	関和太夫 Seki Kazudayū
十七日 17th day	朝 morning	鎗術 Sōjutsu Spearmanship	加藤三内 Katō Sandai
同 as above	夕 evening	馬術 Bajutsu Horsemanship	田中源五衛門 Tanaka Gengoemon
十八日 18th day	朝 morning	居合 Iai Quick drawing	筒井常右衛門 Tsutsui Tsuneemon
同 as above	夕 evening	組打 Kumiuchi Grappling	萩原又六 Hagiwara Mataroku

Day	Time	Subject	Instructor
十九日 19th day	朝夕 morning and evening	居合 Iai Quick drawing	武藤市郎兵衛 Mutō Ichirōbei
二十日 20th day	朝 morning	軍螺 Gunra Military signals	小嶋七右衛門 Kojima Shichiemon
同 as above	夕 evening	馬術 Bajutsu Horsemanship	安田安左衛門 Yasuda Yasuzaemon
二十一日 21st day	朝 morning	長刀 Naginata Halberd	岸清八郎 Kishi Seihachirō
同 as above	夕 evening	居合 Iai Quick drawing	高畠安右衛門 Takahata Yasuemon
二十二日 22nd day	朝 morning	剣術 Kenjutsu Swordsmanship	南保太右衛門 Nanpo Taemon
同 as above	夕 evening	柔術 Jūjutsu Grappling	池上用助 Ikegami Yōsuke

APPENDIX D.
SCROLL LIST AND COLLECTION RECORD

This table is a list of the main scrolls used for this book. They constitute the bulk of knowledge on Mubyōshi Ryū that survives to this day, the main scrolls have been listed with their current location for future researchers to investigate.

Title	Romanized Form	English Translation	Transcription Dates	Current Location
[水鏡]	[Mizukagami], title not on scoll	[The Water Mirror]	1678	The Cummins Collection
水かゞ美序	Mizukagami Jo	The Water Mirror: The Beginning	undated	The Cummins Collection
水鏡之巻序	Mizukagami no Maki Jo	The Water Mirror Scroll: The Beginning	undated	The Cummins Collection
無拍子流和序	Mubyōshi Ryū Yawara Jo	Mubyōshi Ryū Jūjutsu: The Beginning	undated	The Cummins Collection
介錯并切腹胴附之次第	Kaishaku narabini Seppuku Dōtsuki no Shidai	The Manners for Assisting with Seppuku	undated	The Cummins Collection
無拍子流和序	Mubyōshi Ryū Yawara Jo	Mubyōshi Ryū Jūjutsu: The Beginning	1777 and 1863	The Cummins Collection

Table continues on next page.

Title	Romanized Form	English Translation	Transcription Dates	Current Location
[無拍子流和序] 居捕之巻 立合之巻 外之物勝負之巻 心鑑之巻 縄之巻 道具之巻 組討之巻	[Mubyōshi Ryū Yawara Jo] Idori no Maki Tachiai no Maki Tonomono Shōbu no Maki Shinkan no Maki Nawa no Maki Dōgu no Maki Kumiuchi no Maki	[Mubyōshi Ryū Jūjutsu: The Beginning] The Scroll of Sitting Combat, The Scroll of Standing Combat, The Scroll of Other Skills for Victory, The Scroll of Reflecting on the Mind, The Scroll of Rope Skills, The Scroll of Tools, The Scroll of Grappling and Striking	undated	The Cummins Collection
水鏡序巻	Mizukagami Jo no Maki	The Water Mirror Scroll: The Beginning	1859	The Nakashima Collection
毘沙門傳抜書用方	Bishamonden Nukigaki Mochiikata	The Selected Use of the Tradition of Bishamon	1698	Kinsei Shiryōkan-Tamagawa Library
水鏡之巻 <無拍子流水鏡 之巻伝授書>	Mizukagami no Maki (Mubyōshi Ryū Mizukagami no Maki Denjusho)	The Water Mirror Scroll (Teaching of Mubyōshi Ryū Water Mirror Scroll)	1859	Kinsei Shiryōkan-Tamagawa Library
水鏡口傳之覚	Mizukagami Kuden no Oboe	The Oral Traditions and Memorandum for the Water Mirror Scroll	undated	Kinsei Shiryōkan-Tamagawa Library
水鏡新冊	Mizukagami Shinsatsu	The Water Mirror New Book	1845	Kinsei Shiryōkan-Tamagawa Library
無拍子流和序	Mubyōshi Ryū Yawara Jo	Mubyōshi Ryū Jūjutsu: The Beginning	1805	Kinsei Shiryōkan-Tamagawa Library
無拍子流免許目録	Mubyōshi Ryū Menkyo Mokuroku	The Listings and Certificates of Mubyōshi Ryū	1792	Kinsei Shiryōkan-Tamagawa Library
極秘伝忍書 <中将(家)流平 法手術之次第>	Gokuhiden Shinobi no Sho: Chūjō (ke) Ryū Heihō Tejutsu no Shidai	The Secret Tradition of Shinobi Writings: Chūjō Ryū Military Tactics	1776	Kinsei Shiryōkan-Tamagawa Library
無拍子流立合之 巻免許状	Mubyōshi Ryū Tachiai no Maki Menkyo-Jō	A Certificate for: The Scroll of Mubyōshi Ryū Standing Combat	undated	Kinsei Shiryōkan-Tamagawa Library

Title	Romanized Form	English Translation	Transcription Dates	Current Location
無拍子流和序 免許状	Mubyōshi Ryū Yawara Jo Menkyo-Jō	A Certificate for: Mubyōshi Ryū Jūjutsu: The Beginning	undated	Kinsei Shiryōkan-Tamagawa Library
外之物勝負之巻 免許状	Tonomono Shōbu no Maki Menkyo-Jō	A Certificate for: The Scroll of the Other Skills for Victory	undated	Kinsei Shiryōkan-Tamagawa Library
道具之巻免許状	Dōgu no Maki Menkyo-Jō	A Certificate for: The Scroll of Tools	undated	Kinsei Shiryōkan-Tamagawa Library
縄之巻免許状	Nawa no Maki Menkyo-Jō	A Certificate for: The Scroll of Rope Skills	undated	Kinsei Shiryōkan-Tamagawa Library
無拍子流居捕之 巻免許状	Mubyōshi Ryū Idori no Maki Menkyo-Jō	A Certificate for: The Scroll of Mubyōshi-Ryū Sitting Combat	undated	Kinsei Shiryōkan-Tamagawa Library
無拍子流戸田流 など相守に付誓 紙血判書	Mubyōshi Ryū Toda Ryū nado Aimamorini tsuki Seishi Keppansho	The Blood Oaths for Mubyōshi Ryū, Toda Ryū, etc.	1855–1907	Kinsei Shiryōkan-Tamagawa Library
無拍子流和序	Mubyōshi Ryū Yawara Jo	Mubyōshi Ryū Jūjutsu: The Beginning	1789	Kinsei Shiryōkan-Tamagawa Library
無拍子流居捕之巻	Mubyōshi Ryū Idori no Maki	The Scroll of Mubyōshi Ryū Sitting Combat	1789	Kinsei Shiryōkan-Tamagawa Library
無拍子流乳切 木之巻	Mubyōshi Ryū Chigiriki no Maki	The Scroll of Mubyōshi Ryū Weigh and Chain	1789	Kinsei Shiryōkan-Tamagawa Library
縄之巻	Nawa no Maki	The Scroll of Rope Skills	1789	Kinsei Shiryōkan-Tamagawa Library
心鑑之巻	Shinkan no Maki	The Scroll of Reflecting on the Mind	1789	Kinsei Shiryōkan-Tamagawa Library
組討太刀打之巻	Kumiuchi Tachi-uchi no Maki	The Scroll of Fighting with a Sword	1789	Kinsei Shiryōkan-Tamagawa Library
外之物勝負之巻	Tonomono Shōbu no Maki	The Scroll of Other Skills for Victory	1789	Kinsei Shiryōkan-Tamagawa Library
棒袖岡流目録	Bō Sodeoka Ryū Mokuroku	The Listings for Sodeoka Ryū Quarterstaff	1789	Kinsei Shiryōkan-Tamagawa Library

Title	Romanized Form	English Translation	Transcription Dates	Current Location
無拍子流初位四王之大事伝授目録	Mubyōshi Ryū Shoi Shiō no Daiji Denju Mokuroku	Mubyōshi Ryū: The Lower Grade: The Principle of the Four Devas	1858	Kinsei Shiryōkan-Tamagawa Library
無拍子流組討之大事等伝授目録	Mubyōshi Ryū Kumiuchi no Daiji nado Denju Mokuroku	The Principles of Mubyōshi Ryū: Fighting	1858	Kinsei Shiryōkan-Tamagawa Library
無拍子流護身法大事伝授目録	Mubyōshi Ryū Goshinpō no Daiji Denju Mokuroku	The Listing of Tradition: The Principle of Mubyōshi Ryū Magical Self-Protection	1859	Kinsei Shiryōkan-Tamagawa Library
無拍子流兵法十字法	Mubyōshi Ryū Heihō Jūji Hō	The Way of Mubyōshi Ryū Military Magical Protection	1859	Kinsei Shiryōkan-Tamagawa Library
無拍子流九字之大事伝授目録	Mubyōshi Ryū Kuji no Daiji Denju Mokuroku	The Principles for Mubyōshi Ryū Kuji Magical Protection	1859	Kinsei Shiryōkan-Tamagawa Library
毘沙門伝剣術	Bishamonden Kenjutsu	The Tradition of Bishamon Swordsmanship	1770	Kinsei Shiryōkan-Tamagawa Library
水鏡之巻	Mizukagami no Maki	The Water Mirror Scroll	undated	Kinsei Shiryōkan-Tamagawa Library
水かがみ	Mizukagami	The Water Mirror	undated	Kinsei Shiryōkan-Tamagawa Library
池上用助伝水鏡巻	Ikegami Yōsuke Den, Mizukagami no maki	The Water Mirror Scroll Transmitted by Ikegami Yōsuke	1847	Kinsei Shiryōkan-Tamagawa Library
一惣無体流水鏡序	Issō Mutai Ryū Mizukagami Jo	Issō Mutai Ryū: The Water Mirror: The Beginning	1858	Kinsei Shiryōkan-Tamagawa Library
居捕之巻・心鑑之巻	Idori no Maki; Shinkan no Maki	The Scroll of Sitting Combat; The Scroll of Reflecting on the Mind	undated	Kinsei Shiryōkan-Tamagawa Library
組討之巻免許状	Kumiuchi no Maki Menkyo-jō	A Certificate for: The Scroll of Fighting	undated	Kinsei Shiryōkan-Tamagawa Library
免許状	Menkyo-jō	A Certificate	undated	Kinsei Shiryōkan-Tamagawa Library

Title	Romanized Form	English Translation	Transcription Dates	Current Location
無拍子流伝授許状	Mubyōshi Ryū Denju Kyojō	A Certificate for: Mubyōshi Ryū Initiation	1820	Kinsei Shiryōkan-Tamagawa Library
袖岡流棒術免状	Sodeoka Ryū Bō Jutsu Menjō	A Certificate for: Sodeoka Ryū Quarterstaff	1813	Kinsei Shiryōkan-Tamagawa Library
兵法「阿日耶摩利天勝負之巻」	Heihō: Anichiya Mariten Shōbu no Maki	Military Tactics: The Scroll of Victory by Anichiya Mariten	1785	Amagasaki Municipal Archives
兵法「無拍子流和序巻」	Heihō: Mubyōshi Ryū Yawara Jo no Maki	Military Tactics: Mubyōshi Ryū Jūjutsu Scroll	1785	Amagasaki Municipal Archives
兵法「組討太刀討之巻」	Heihō: Kumiuchi Tachiuchi no Maki	Military Tactics: The Scroll of Fighting with a Sword	1785	Amagasaki Municipal Archives
兵法「乳切木之巻」	Heihō: Chigiriki no Maki	Military Tactics: The Scroll of Weights and Chains	1785	Amagasaki Municipal Archives
兵法「心鑑之巻」	Heihō: Shinkan no Maki	Military Tactics: The Scroll of Reflecting on the Mind	1785	Amagasaki Municipal Archives
兵法「縄之巻」	Heihō: Nawa no Maki	Military Tactics: The Scroll of Rope Skills	1785	Amagasaki Municipal Archives
皆目書序（兵法無拍子流秘伝書）	Kaimokusho (Heihō: Mubyōshi Ryū Hidensho)	Complete Skill List (The Military Tactics and Secret Scroll of Mubyōshi Ryū)	1786	Amagasaki Municipal Archives
兵法「破軍星之巻」軍配秘伝	Heihō: Hagun Shō no Maki Gunbai Hiden	Military Tactics: The Scroll of the Hagun Star and the Secret of Disposition for Battle	1787	Amagasaki Municipal Archives
兵法「居取立合之巻」	Heihō: Idori Tachiai no Maki	Military Tactics: The Scroll of Sitting and Standing Combat	around 1781–1788	Amagasaki Municipal Archives
水鏡序	Mizukagami Jo	The Water Mirror: The Beginning	1848	Libraries of Kanazawa City
護身法之大事	Goshinpō no Daiji	The Principle of Magical Self-Protection	1713	Hata Shunroku Family Documents

Title	Romanized Form	English Translation	Transcription Dates	Current Location
中通居捕之巻 立合之巻六	Naka Dōri Idori no Maki Tachiai no Maki (6)	The Middle Grade: The Scroll of Sitting Combat; The Scroll of Standing Combat (6)	1936, from an 1808 scroll	Hata Shunroku Family Documents
中通乳キリキ之巻	Naka Dōri Chigiriki no Maki	The Middle Grade: The Scroll of Weights and Chains	1936 (1808)	Hata Shunroku Family Documents
中通居合之巻	Naka Dōri Iai no Maki	The Middle Grade: The Scroll of Quick Drawing	1936 (1808)	Hata Shunroku Family Documents
許之巻外物勝負之巻序七	Kyo no Maki Tonomono Shōbu no Maki Jo (7)	A Scroll Certificate for: The Scroll of Other Skills for Victory: The Beginning (7)	1936 (1808)	Hata Shunroku Family Documents
許之巻毘沙門伝拾二	Kyo no Maki Bishamon Den (12)	The Certificate for: The Scroll and Tradition of Bishamon (12)	1936 (1808)	Hata Shunroku Family Documents
棒袖岡流巻一	Sodeoka Ryū no Maki (1)	The Scroll of Sodeoka Ryū Quarterstaff (1)	1936 (1808)	Hata Shunroku Family Documents
介錯并切腹胴附之次第	Kaishaku narabini Seppuku Dōtsuki no Shidai	Manners for Assisting with Seppuku	1936 (1808)	Hata Shunroku Family Documents
無拍子流和序	Mubyōshi Ryū Yawara Jo	Mubyōshi Ryū Jūjutsu: The Beginning	undated	Kawakita Municipal Library
心鑑之巻	Shinkan no Maki	The Scroll of Reflecting on the Mind	undated	Kaburaki Yukio Family Documents
深甚流秘伝書（内容は『水鏡』に同じ。(前欠)の為、おそらく標題不明のところ、他の深甚流伝書と共に保管され、この標題が付けられたと思われる。）	Shinjin Ryū Hidensho	The Secret Scroll of Shinjin Ryū [incorrectly titled by a Japanese researcher; actually Mizukagami]	1745	Komatsu City Library
無拍子流和序	Mubyōshi Ryū Yawara Jo	Mubyōshi Ryū Jūjutsu: The Beginning	1804	Uematsu Yoshiyuki Sensei

APPENDIX E.
JAPANESE TRANSCRIPTIONS

For the benefit of prosperity and to ensure the hard work of the Warabi Sōsho Club remains documented, the following sections are the scrolls transcribed from their original form. They have been simplified and in parts modernized—a common feature of Japanese transcriptions. This also includes a history of the school in Japanese by Mieko Koizumi.

文書で辿る無拍子流

無拍子流は、加賀藩で生まれた武術である。主に柔術 (和) が伝承されているが、『加賀藩経武館武藝小伝』 [示野喜三郎, 1975]によると、「無拍子流は、いわゆる総合武術であって、術の包含するを列挙すると、柔・棒・剣・鎖玉・筒矢・乳切木・縄・呪術の多数にのぼると云う。」そして、流祖を金子吉兵衛 (吉平) 正武、遠祖を二木新十郎政長としている。

金子吉兵衛の時代に全盛期を迎えた無拍子流は、時を経てその技を伝える者も次第に減少していった。現在、この無拍子流を伝承しているのは、金沢近郊にある無心館総本部道場の上松義幸館長のみである。そのため、無拍子流の歴史については、各地に残されている伝書および金沢近辺の地域で編纂された数点の研究書を手がかりに推し量るしかない。本書の執筆、翻訳にあたり、できる限りの史料を調べ、江戸時代の創始当時から現在までの無拍子流の姿を解き明かそうと試みた。

　まず、その伝系であるが、金沢の近世史料館に無拍子流の伝書がいくつか残されており、それらの奥書によれば、遠祖・二木新十郎政長から始まり、萩原重蔵茂辰、東美源内宣名へと伝授され、諸弟子へと続いていく。遠祖とされる二木新十郎政長という人物については、不詳であるが、『剣聖草深甚四郎』 [川北町教育委員会, 1990]に以下の記述がある。

『深甚流剣法師伝』(文化9年,1812年) によれば、「当国与力組に二木次郎左衛門という者あり。慶尊院は二木に本免を伝えて、泉州に帰る」とある。この二木次郎左衛門はたぶん、二木新十郎政長と同一人物だと思われる。

二木新十郎政長は、加賀藩能美郡草深村の草深甚四郎[1]が創始した深甚流剣術を甚四郎の弟子である泉州の山伏・慶尊院から伝授されている。しかし、二木新十郎政長の弟子・水野忠左衛門道長の『免許之巻』の序文には、「のち、わが師[2]、かの

術我意にまかせ、元祖の教えに背き、他流に淫溺す」とある。また、深甚流『かな目録』には、「二木権之丞 (二木新十郎と思われる)」という名が線で囲まれ、印が付けられていることから、二木新十郎が深甚流の伝系から外されたと考えられる。(『剣聖草深甚四郎』 [川北町教育委員会, 1990])

現時点では、推測の域を出ないのだが、無拍子流には、深甚流の本義である「水鏡[3]」や、「浮舟」「浪枕」「筏」など、深甚流の技と同名の技もあり、間積りを表す「見門 (間門)」という深甚流独特の言葉が無拍子流の伝書にも見られることから、遠祖といわれる二木新十郎が深甚流に我流の技を加え、無拍子流を生み出したとも考えられる。

萩原重蔵茂辰は、二木新十郎政長から無拍子流及び深甚流を伝授されている。その人物については、文化5年(1808)高桑長左衛門の写本『許之巻　毘沙門伝拾二』(畑俊六家文書) の奥書に見ることができる。(『剣聖草深甚四郎』 [川北町教育委員会, 1990])

要約すると、「茂辰は武神の加護を受け、三十二回の危機を逃れたが、そのうち七回は命の危険に曝された。若い頃、不意に人を討ち、その仇討ちのために九年間、昼夜を問わず敵に命を狙われた。茂辰は武芸に励み、諸流を探し、師を頼むこと数多に及んだ。先祖の恨みを買い、何度か危険な目に合うこともあったが、命の難は逃れた。敵の為にこれらの業を学び受け、自ずと家芸となった」ということが記されている。また、彼自身、『水鏡 (水かがみ)』という伝書をいくつか書き残している。この伝書には、屋敷に忍び込む時、塀を乗り越える時、旅の宿で眠る時などに敵を警戒し危険に対処する忍術的要素を含んだ業が記されている。無拍子流の伝書の奥書は二木新十郎から始まるものが多いのだが、『水鏡 (水かがみ)』に関しては、萩原重蔵の名前だけが書かれているものが数点あり、その中の一点が、先に述べた最も古いと思われる無拍子流の巻物 (延宝6年、1678年) であった。以上のことから、最初に伝書を残した人物は萩原重蔵で、二木新十郎から伝授された教えをもとに無拍子流を確立し、自ら『水鏡 (水かがみ)』を書き残したとも考えられる。

東美源内宣名 (?～1715) は、金沢の浪人であった。深甚流の剣術及び無拍子流の和義 (柔術) を萩原十蔵 (重蔵) に学び、それを門人に教えて生涯を送った。(『加能郷土辞彙』 [日置謙, 1942])

　無拍子流の伝書では、まず、二木、萩原、東美・・・と続き、その後、諸弟子へと伝授されている。私達が収集した伝書の奥書からすべての名前を並べてみると、東美源内宣名から三人の弟子 (北川金右衛門貞英、東美治内照久、嶋野善左衛門直賢) へ相伝され、伝授の枝が広がっていく。

この三人の弟子の一人、嶋野善左衛門直賢に伝授された無拍子流を受け継いだのが、石川県野々市市にある無心館総本部道場の館長、上松義幸先生である。次に、上松先生の伝書に従って、無拍子流の伝系を見ていきたい。今回、嶋野善左

衛門直賢から南部庄助篤圀までの人物に関する文献は見つからなかったため、金子吉兵衛正武以後の人物について記述する。

二木新十郎政長

萩原重蔵茂辰

東美源内宣名

嶋野善左衛門直賢

永井各務方叔

土川覚右衛門貴好

南部庄藏篤慶

南部庄助篤圀

金子吉平正武

山崎惣助

道清屋甚七

曽野幸助

岸井[4]清藏

西村興三兵衛

西村清太郎

上松義幸（哲舟）

　最も古い無拍子流伝書は萩原重蔵が延宝6年（1678年）に書いた『水鏡』であったが、この年代から判断すると、二木、萩原、東美の生きた時代は、加賀藩五代目藩主[5]、前田綱紀（1643～1724）の時代であろう。綱紀はわずか3歳で家督を継ぎ、藩政は80年にわたる。学問・文芸を奨励し、「加賀は天下の書府」と言われる程、自家を含む古文書の保管にも熱心であった。武術に関しては、江戸初期から各地で様々な武術流派が発展し、道場の数も増えていく。そして、江戸中期以降になると、武士だけでなく町民・農民も余暇の楽しみとして武術を学ぶようになった。

金子吉兵衛[6]**正武**（1795～1858）は、少年時代より武芸を好み、やがて武芸百般に通じたが、特に柔術・小太刀の術・呪術に長けていた。父は能美郡牧島に在住し、百石扶持の穀倉役人であった。正武は小松城付足軽となり、現在の小松市園町に住む。彼の武名は加賀藩中にも評判が高く、時の十三代藩主[7]、前田斉奉から足軽扶持の他に米二俵を与えられ、国家老、村井氏からも米五俵を賞与されていた。柔術を学んで熟達し、文政（1818年以降）から天保の頃（1830年頃）にかけて、園町の邸宅横に三間半×七間の瓦葺きの道場を開いた。

　正武については、「筵の敷き流し渡り（水面に筵を浮かべ、その上を速足で渡る）」や「夕方出発し、稽古をつけた後、十数里の道のりをその日のうちに戻ってきた」など、不思議な逸話が残っており、彼の道場の近くにあった来生寺では、本堂で正武が畳返しの術を公開した際、弟子達に何時でも何処からでも打ち込むように

命じ、弟子が打ちかかると、さっと畳をまくってその下に身を隠し、隠れたと思うと
向こう側に出てくる。時には五メートルもある天井に彼の身体がへばりついている
という早業に、弟子達は無刀の彼に翻弄されたという。また、呪術が得意で、まじ
ないによって病気を治したという。特に瘧（マラリヤ熱の一種）を落とし、歯痛を止
めることに優れていたため、歯痛おこり落としの神として、彼の碑の石粉を薬として
用いる者もいたそうだ。

　金子吉兵衛正武には、忍者を連想させるような超人的な逸話が多い。それは、彼
がいかに優れた武芸の達人であったかを物語っている。この達人に教えを請う多く
の弟子達に技を伝授し、無拍子流の最盛期を迎え、やがて無拍子流の祖と言われる
ようになったのであろう。彼の弟子達によって建てられた墓碑の一つは小松市営墓
地内に、もう一つは来生寺の近くにある。示野喜三郎氏は、「更に本当の墓は別の
所にあると云う伝えがあるが、その墓の所在は今以て不明である。」と述べている。
　（『加賀藩経武館武藝小伝　, 1975』[示野喜三郎, 1975]）

山崎惣助[8]は、師である金子吉兵衛正武の道場を手本として、自らの道場を建てたと
思われる。彼の道場跡について、以下の記述がある。「山崎健次氏（山崎惣助の曾
孫にあたる）の前庭に三間×五間半十六坪余三十三畳見当の道場が建てられ、後に
一部増改造もあった跡があるが今も残り、昭和二十年（1945）まで稽古があった。
但しその頃は土間に筵敷きで正当な無拍子流の稽古であったかは不明であるが、建
てた当時は金子吉兵衛道場の見取りを踏襲していると思われる。今は、道場面影を
残しつつ全体を納屋に使用している。」この道場がいつ頃建てられたものか不明で
あるが、山崎健次氏の祖母が昭和の初め頃に嫁いで来られた時には既に道場があ
ったという。（『加賀武術の遺蹤』[示野喜三郎, 1992]）

　示野喜三郎氏が確認した平成3年（1991）に存在していた道場跡の建物が、現
在、どのような状態であるか問い合わせてみたが、道場であった建物は既に建て
替えてしまったため、当時の姿は残っていないようだ。

道清屋甚七、曽野幸助、岸井清藏

　金子吉兵衛正武の弟子であり、園町にある金子吉兵衛正武の墓碑の台石側面に
門弟世話人として名前が刻まれている。

西村興三兵衛[9]は、安政頃（1854年頃）、加賀藩の武術学校である経武館で無拍子
流を教授していた。また、経武館において、どのような術かは不明だが「陰術」の神
道流師範でもあった。また、戸田金剛流も修得していたようである。（『加賀藩経武
館武藝小伝　, 1975』[示野喜三郎, 1975]）

経武館

寛政四年（1792）、加賀藩十一代藩主[10]、前田治脩（1745～1810）は、尊敬する祖
父・綱紀の遺志を継いで、現在の兼六園内の梅林辺りに藩校（明倫堂と経武館）を

創設した (後に仙石町に移転)。約5500坪の敷地内に、文学校としての明倫堂と武学校としての経武館が隣接して建てられた。経武館の師範は加賀藩の陪審、与力、足軽の中から家柄に関係なく、諸流の上手を任命して開校された。修業課目は当初、馬術・鎗術・剣術・柔術・居合・組討・軍螺の七課目であったが、次第に課目も加えられ、通算すると十九課目五十八流派に達し、武芸十八般を網羅していた。

柔術の流派を見ると、無拍子流・一相無拍子流・一惣無躰流[11]の三流派が経武館で教授された。この三つの流派に共通する伝書がある。一相無拍子流の石丸弥太郎[12]の写本『水鏡序』(嘉永元年、1848年、金沢市立図書館所蔵)、一惣無躰流の大田清蔵[13]の写本『水鏡序』(安政5年、1858年、近世史料館春風文庫所蔵)、経武館で無拍子流を指導していた池上用助の写本『池上用助傳水鏡巻』(弘化4年、1847年、近世史料館村松文庫所蔵)である。これらの内容はすべて萩原重蔵の『水鏡』(または『水鏡 (水かゞみ) 序』『水鏡之巻序』)と全く同じである。

一相無拍子流は一相流と無拍子流を合わせて折衷した流派であり、一惣 (相) 無躰流も同様に、無拍子流から分派していった。『剣聖草深甚四郎』 [川北町教育委員会, 1990]の中に「無拍子流柔術」の説明があるが、そこで一惣無躰流についても触れている。

柔術無拍子流
業目多く総合武術。一相無躰流の大田鍋次郎[14]在印の無拍子流目録伝書は七項目のみで、組討に必要な業に絞り込んで表示している、しかるに、藩末の伝書に至ると刀術目録を付加し、業が増えて肥大化し大田系の専門化と別の道を歩んでいる。

この時代、多くの学徒が経武館で武術を学び、同時に各自が師の道場へ通って武芸に励んでいた。また、優秀な者を選ぶために藩侯自らその武術を検閲するなど、藩も武術を奨励していた。経武館の時代は、加賀藩武術の最盛期であったといえるだろう。

加賀藩十三代藩主[15]、前田斉奉 (1811〜1884) の藩政時代、嘉永6年 (1853) にペリーが浦賀に来航する。次第に鎖国から国外に目を向けざるを得なくなり、海防が説かれるようになると、藩の軍備も西洋式へと変化していく。異国船の侵略に備えるため、軍事研究機関として、安政元年 (1854)、洋式兵学校・壮猶館が設立された。経武館は、明治元年 (1868) に壮猶館と合併されて閉校となり、開校76年の歴史を閉じた。

西村清太郎 (1869〜1919) は、明治2年、石川郡富奥村中林区に生まれる。家は農家で、十七歳頃から農業の暇をみて金沢に赴き、町田半兵衛より撃剣、体術、棒、薙刀、鎌、鉄尺の諸技を学んだ。明治36年 (1901)、中林に演武場を建て、久我公爵より「武道館」の書三字を賜る。明治から大正年間に多くの門下生を生み出した。弟子の数は二百人を下らず、武徳会石川県支部を創設し、大正7年 (1918) に

は富奥村剣道会を創設するなど、剣道の普及に力を注いだ。また、武道のみならず、農産業、地域振興にも貢献した。大正8年 (1919)、門下生によって道場横に記念碑が建てられた。

中林春日神社の秋祭りに行われる獅子舞は、中林地区に道場を構えていた西村清太郎が始めたもので、祭り当日はこの記念碑の前でも獅子舞の演武が行われる。

- 上松先生が通った道場は中林にある西村清太郎 (1869〜1919) の道場であったが、伝書に名前が記されている上松先生の師・西村清太郎氏は、年代から見ると明治2年 (1869) 生まれの西村清太郎ではなく、同名の子孫であるとも考えられる。また、西村興三兵衛と西村清太郎の血縁関係についても現在、確認中である。

加賀の殺し獅子

　石川県各所で行われている獅子舞には、大きく分けて能登の舞い獅子、加賀の殺し獅子がある。加賀の獅子舞は、江戸時代以前、一向一揆の民が国を治めていた頃から存在したとされ、天正11年 (1583) に前田利家が金沢へ入城した際に、祝いの獅子舞が行われたそうだ。江戸時代末期の天明の頃には祭りや行事のたびに獅子舞が行われ、地域の民俗芸能として発展してきた。昭和40年に金沢市の無形民俗文化財に指定されている。

　この加賀獅子は、加賀の武術と大変深い繋がりがある。巨大な獅子頭と笛、太鼓、三味線、尺八、胴竹持ちや尾持ちがすべて中に入れる大きさのカヤ (胴体) が特徴で、獅子が舞うというよりも、馬の尾で作られたシャンガンを頭につけた棒振りが棒や剣、薙刀、鎖鎌などを使って獅子に立ち向かう。それは、まるで武術の演武を見ているかのようだ。棒振りは、棒術、剣術、薙刀、柔術、居捕りなどの武術が応用され、武術同様、流派が生まれた。最盛期には約40もの流派があったとされ、中でも二大流派といわれるものが「土方流」と「半兵衛流」である。

　土方流は、1801〜1804年の頃、金沢市の山の上町に道場を構えていた浪人・土方常輔と土方惣右衛門、近代では名人・土方丈五郎らにより剣術、体術、棒術、薙刀などの武芸を応用した棒振りを指導したことに始まり、主に浅野川以北から河北郡で広まった。

　半兵衛流は、金沢の地黄煎町に道場 (無拍子流、水野一伝流など教授) を構えていた町田半兵衛久定 (1832〜1909頃) が生み出した流派で、柔術や薙刀、居合、鎖鎌などに工夫を加えて編み出され、主として犀川以南から石川郡にかけて広まった。半兵衛は百姓であったが、昭和28年、武家の渡辺家を再興して継いだことから、「渡辺半兵衛」と名乗り、半兵衛流の棒振りは、紺地に「渡りトンボ」(「渡」と「トンボ」の絵) を染め抜いた袴を着用するようになった。当時は、渡りトンボの袴を履くことを許可された弟子のみが着用できた。

　無心館総本部道場のある野々市市では、現在、荒町 (本町一丁目)、中町 (本町三丁目)、西町 (本町四丁目)、粟田、中林の地区で半兵衛流の獅子舞が受け継が

れている。半兵衛の弟子・西村清太郎も中林にあった自分の道場で獅子舞を始めている。加賀全土で、各地域にある道場からそれぞれ独自の棒振りが生まれていったと思われる。町田半兵衛は、西村清太郎の師であった。無拍子流を修得した彼らが作り上げた獅子舞の棒振りには、無拍子流の形も含まれているのかもしれない。

上松義幸

1948年1月1日、九州の長崎県に生まれる。9歳の時、佐賀県鍋島の禅宗の勝福寺で得度。10歳の時、伯父・森悟峰住職より武道を伝授された。1971年、石川県門前の総持寺で修行。後に24歳で道場を開いた。

無拍子流を西村清太郎氏より継承。無心館総本部道場では、無拍子流古柔術の他に袖岡流棒術杖道、新陰流居合抜刀術、琉球那覇手昭霊流空手、無覚流中・小太刀、無覚流手裏剣術を指導している。無覚流においては、須賀玄斉の門人であった流の創始者・上松頼母介義治より先祖代々継承された正統な十一代宗家である。

以上、上松先生に伝授された伝書をもとに、現在に至る無拍子流の伝系を辿ってみた。

『剣聖草深甚四郎』[川北町教育委員会, 1990]の中に、今も存続する経武館の武芸流派について次のような記述がある。

平成のいま、命脈を辛うじて保つ経武館の武芸は、深甚流剣術、心鏡流鎌術、それに長尾流躰術の三流のみで、経武館閉校から百二十年を経過し、経武館当時の正確さは望めないが、長尾流躰術は巷間伝承から復元に努力し、正伝として示野喜三郎が中興している。心鏡流鎌術は、武田清房氏が後継者の育成に精を出されており、深甚流は、川北町の深甚会の方々が、巷間伝承から最近整理された埋没小伝書と比べ合わせて復元されている。

ここには「三流」と書かれてあるが、加賀藩で生まれ、経武館で伝授された無拍子流は二木新十郎、萩原重蔵の時代から現在に至るまで、脈々と受け継がれていたのである。よって、現在も継承されている経武館武術は、この三流に無拍子流を加え、四流とすることができるだろう。

二木新十郎から西村清太郎まで伝授された無拍子流が消滅の危機を迎えていた頃、上松先生は知人から西村清太郎氏の道場を紹介され、通うようになった。上松先生は、不思議な縁の積み重ねで無拍子流を継承することになったという。ある時、偶然訪れた黒壁山薬王寺の住職から、無拍子流の金子吉兵衛正武も以前、その寺を訪れたという話を聞いた。またある時は、先生の道場に柔術と空手の稽古に通っていたお弟子さんが、町田半兵衛の子孫であることを知り、彼の家まで巻物を見せてもらいに行ったこともあるそうだ。

　私が無拍子流について調べ始めた理由も、奇跡的な偶然と縁によるものである。古文書を読むために、地域の古文書勉強会に問い合わせ、活動を休止していた会を再開してもらい、私は初めて古文書勉強会に参加した。数人のメンバーで、アントニーが近世史料館から取り寄せた『極秘伝忍書』を読み合わせていった。そして、そのわずか10日後、信じられないような出来事が起きた。神保町の古書展でガラスケースに展示されていた巻物に目がとまり、広げてみると標題は破れて失われていたもののなんとなく見た事のあるような文字がいくつか並んでいた。それを告げるとアントニーは3000円でその巻物を購入した。購入後、すぐに巻物を開いて再確認してみると、そこには第1回目の古文書勉強会で読み合わせをした『極秘伝忍書』と一字一句同じ文章が書かれていたのだ。全身に鳥肌が立った。その巻物が、萩原重蔵の『水鏡』（延宝6年）であった。この『水鏡』は、延宝六年　萩原十藏安信と記されており、調査した数十点の無拍子流伝書の中で最古のものである。その後、それが無拍子流の巻物で、現在も無拍子流が石川県の無心館総本部道場で指導されていることを知り、上松先生と連絡を取り合うようになった。先生の武術に対する熱い思いと、熱心に稽古に励むお弟子さん達に出会い、これまで集めた情報をできる限り伝えなければ・・・という天命のようなものを感じ、ひたすら調査を続けた末、ようやく本書の出版にこぎつけることができた。無拍子流について、伝書、目録以外の史料は少なく、限られた情報源からの寄せ集めではあるが、今後の無拍子流の継承と研究に役立つことを願い、ここに書き留めた次第である。

　平成27年6月、新たに無拍子流の巻物を発見した。不思議なことに、これらの巻物は金沢ではなく尼崎にあった。巻物を所蔵している尼崎市立地域研究史料館の石田太郎氏文書の目録を見ても、ほとんどが鉄道関係の史料であり、その中に無拍子流の巻物があることに違和感を覚えた。

　調べてみると、石田太郎氏は、明治34年（1901）に鉄道会社に就職し、鉄道技師として勤務していた。大正7年（1918）にウラジオストックに渡航しシベリア・東支鉄道の調査を行い、後に神戸鉄道局長、神戸市電気局長等を務めた方で、このことから鉄道関係の史料が多いことがわかった。そして、目録の備考欄に書かれた「石田家先祖北市屋弥三右衛門」の名前を頼りに検索してみると、石田氏のご先祖が加賀藩出身であることがわかった。おそらく石田氏は加賀藩で無拍子流を修得したご先祖の巻物を家伝書として保管し、神戸へ移住されたと思われる。（その後、石田氏は、神戸から尼崎へ転居されたそうだ。）無拍子流と思われる巻物10点のうち8点の巻物は、1785年〜1788年頃、水野重蔵光豊から伝授されたものであり、金沢で収集した史料にはない内容も含まれていた。

　石田太郎氏文書は、平成7年（1995）の阪神淡路大震災直後、尼崎市立地域研究史料館が被災資料救済活動の呼びかけを行った際に、尼崎市で被災された石田太郎氏のご子息から寄贈された史料であった。同史料館によると、震災後の被災史料救出保全活動では、従来知られていなかった史料が発見されることも多か

ったそうだ。今回、尼崎で無拍子流の巻物に出会えたこともまた、運命的な偶然と
いえるのかもしれない。

　最後に、無心館総本部道場・館長の上松義幸先生をはじめ、無心館東京支部の
ジョー・スウィフト氏、写真撮影にご協力いただいた道場のお弟子さん方、根気よく
写真の確認作業にお付き合いいただいた無心館本部道場師範代・川崎悠貴氏、無
心館総本部道場での座談会にお集りいただいた野々市市中林獅子舞保存会の代
表・向田誠市氏、深甚流剣術の形を継承する川北町草深甚四郎顕彰会・深甚会
の上田宏一氏と上登正人氏、獅子舞の写真とビデオをご提供いただいた野々市市
本町一丁目青年会・橋場祐介氏、向田氏と共に中林春日神社で獅子舞の実演と説
明をしてくださった西崎幹夫氏に心から感謝を申し上げます。皆様のおかげで、こ
の本を通して多くの方々に無拍子流についてご紹介できることを嬉しく思います。

　　　　　平成二十八年一月吉日

　　　　　　　　　　　　　　　　　　　　小泉　美江子

水鏡序

夫武士の技藝多端なりといへ共
柔剛強弱の四つの外に出す
是をしらさる者はおほく
此理をまなひ得る者はすくなし
されは水のひくきにつくかことく
大剛の名有人といふとも
ゆるみをうつにうたすといふ事なし
よろすのわさはひは気のゆるみより出くる事を知るへし
其ゆるみというはなつみてかたよる所に有
是みな意のために其の本をうしなうかゆえ也
しかはあれ共手たてという事あれは
敵にはかられさらん事をしらしめんとして
人をはかる品々をしるしあつめて
後のならえるもののたすけとするものなるべし

一　夜中心許なく思ふ道を行時は
　　　人にあたりて能ほとの石を袖に入てもつへし
　　　是は気つかいに思ふ所へ右の石を打て見るに
　　　必其體あらわすもの也

一　案内を知らさる川を越申時は
　　　川上へすちかえにこすもの也　　口傳

一　雨天かきくもり行先も見えさる時は
　　足もとに白きもの其外何によらす
　　眼にかかるもの有といふ共ひろふべからず
　　心得なく是をひろえは目しるしになりてきらるる事多し
　　是は刀を抜鞘にてはね返し取へし　　口傳

一　やまたち¹⁶に逢申時は
　　先我心を能おさめて臆する事なく足はやにとおり
　　さて其二三里に間は前後左右より来る人に
　　かならすこころゆるすべからす
　　まつ定りたる山たちといふは中間六人のもの也
　　一人は出て残る五人は能所に草に臥也
　　又無心許道はたに病人有りてくるしけなる声にて
　　薬なと所望するもののあらは心得近つくへからす
　　又はくちにもしらさるものの道つれ無心許候　　口傳

一　夜中人などあやめてのかんと思ふ時は
　　東西南北をも不見明いかゝせんと思ふ時は
　　流を尋出しそのみなかみへのほれはかならす山有者也
　　さて山中へ入ては高みよりひきみの見ゆる所に居て
　　たいまつなともちて尋来る人のていにて道路を知へし
　　菟角深く思案有へき所也
　　さて追手透間なく来りのかれがかたく思ふ時は
　　刀の小尻を少切いきの出るほと穴をあけ
　　こい口を口にくわえ水底に沈身をかくし
　　刀脇差にても小刀にても水底にさし込
　　是を力に取付いる也
　　いきのつきやうに習有　　口傳
　　手なと負たる時も流の中を行たるが能也
　　是はのり¹⁷をとめられぬ用心也
　　又雪降たる時はきものを跡先にはき
　　杖を左につき流の内に入て行へし
　　足跡をとめられんため也

一　旅にて気つかい成宿と思ふ所にては
　　其家のうらへ出て要害を能見置へし
　　是は火事夜盗などの入たる時のため也
　　扨家の内にては床縁天井畳の落入て
　　やはらかなる所に心をつけ

畳をあけて是を見置へし
寝所に入ては燈の有内
我大小荷物を勝手の悪敷所に置
火消て後勝手の能方へ取りなをし
枕はいかにもしにくき枕をすへし
又邯鄲の枕[18]とて其の座敷の内へ
虫の入ても目のさむる事も有
又蚊帳をつりたる時は
大小の置様に習有　口傳
さて戸尻にきりもみをしたるかよし
きりの拵えやう如斯

(Figure 14.8)
戸障子を能かためたる所へしのひ入にもよし
火事の時やねなどへ上るにもよし

一　ちょうちんを持する事我より先へ持たせたるは悪し
我左の方大小より弐尺はかり跡に為持たるよし
此時は前後左右ともに能見ゆる也

一　左の手を懐に入て打物をかたねなるほと
ぬかりたる躰にもてなし来るものあらは
夜昼共に心をゆるすべからず
夜は黒き反古を鞘のやうに袋にこしらへ
しら刃を包かたよりすくにうつ事有もの也
昼はおりかねを我かみわけに懸て
右の手計にて抜打に
左の手を懐中しなから討事あり
扨其所はや四五町も行過候得は必心ゆるみ
前後左右より来る人を我がかたうど[19]のように思ひ
互に物語なとしかけ心をゆるすもの也
そのとき彼者時分を窺反古にて包みたる刀にて打つに
はつるる事なし

一　我家の内へ忍ひ入たるものを知て
とがめ申には我名を呼へし　口傳

一　我屋敷の内へ大勢夜盗来る時は
先内に火をともす事大きに悪し
人すくなくしてふせかんと思ふ時は

ときどきさゝやき声などしてきかせきらんと思はゝ
夜盗爰より忍ひ入べきと思ふ口に
ほそひきを高さ四五寸計に張
手ころなるものを楯にもち
打物をしやに取て拂切にすへし
又内に火をともしたる時は
外の闇き所より内を見るに能見えて悪し
故に忍ひといふは火を持つ事第一也　　口傳

一　忍び来る時は不知しても必我心に覚有物也
　　其時心得て気つかいすへし
　　其時忍人心得てちくるいの来るやうにする事有
　　時にちくるいと思ふへからず
　　忍ひといふは色々手立有といへり
　　又遠所にかすかにせきなとする事あらは
　　必近所に人有と知へし
　　近所にてするせきを遠所にてするやうにきこゆる習あり
　　彼者しのひ入時は近所に堀川池のあれは
　　其ふちに能ほとの石を置て内に入物也
　　是は出き合追出る時
　　右の石を彼水の中に打込にくへきたくみなり
　　是等の事心得て気をとらるる事なかれ　　口傳

一　しのひ人内に入たるをやさがしするには
　　刀を抜懸切先を二三寸程鞘の内に残し
　　下緒をのへて其先を我帯に付
　　左の手に能物を楯にもち身をかこいさかすへし
　　又弓にて尋る事も有
　　早矢[20]を存るまゝに引込能かつてに納
　　乙矢[21]を押手の人さしゆひにけらくひをはさみ
　　その矢尻にてさかすへし
　　されとも弓にては爰かしこにつかへ
　　思ふ様に尋る事難成
　　其時悪者家をたつぬと思へは
　　能心を納め囲炉裏の中に入り臥て
　　敵のゆるみを窺い見てはつす事有へし
　　扨いろりの中に身をかくす事起合候者共
　　常々見置たるゆへに彼いろりを皆人除て通者也
　　是を心得なく火なとともしに近寄きらるる事有へし

一　追出候時は諸事に心をつくる事肝要也
　　　彼者大事に思ひて忍ひ入時は
　　　入口に高さ四五寸計にほそひきを
　　　張申かのうれんのあれは
　　　上より下へすだれのことく切さき
　　　下四五寸はかり残し置申か
　　　又縄すたれなれは左右のはつれを取て
　　　むすひ置事も有
　　　扨次々の間に段などあれば伏て身をそはめ
　　　彼段よりおり申所を斬事有
　　　此手立を心得へし
　　　急に追懸らるゝ時
　　　其道の通にひしといふものをまく事も有
　　　此ひし足に踏立ては一足も行事なるへからす
　　　又門を出申時後手に尻戸を引立行者也
　　　追出るもの是をあけんとするに五間宛行き過るもの也
　　　扨追懸らるゝにも追出るにも習有
　　　是は何もわさなり

一　常のことく行時我後より声を懸斬時
　　　刀の抜様に習有
　　　ぬかすしてもまたとめるわさ有　口傳

一　しのひしのひに鳥類ちくるいのまねをもし習へし
　　　忍の時入事多し
　　　昔もろこしかんこくの関[22]をも
　　　鳥のそらねにはかられて通したるためしあり
　　　殊更庚申の夜忍入に鶏の真似する大事有
　　　或人の云は庚申の夜したる事は
　　　必あらわるゝものと云傳へたり
　　　是は盗人の申出したる事かと覚候
　　　庚申の夜したる事は常の夜よりはあらわれんなり

一　忍びてへいを越時は刀をへいに立懸
　　　下緒の先を取てむすひ足くひにかけ
　　　鍔を踏てうて木に取付
　　　刀を取て腰に指越へし
　　　若其へい高くして棟木に取付事難成は
　　　彼きりを取出し打立て越へし

又とりかきを懸てこしたるもよし
とかくへい高くして越がたき時は
越へき以前にとりかぎより弐尺はかり縄をのこし
我後の帯に引通し
其まま後より肩を縄を越て
前の帯に縄の先を留て越へし
うて木に取付け候わば
かのかきをうて木に懸て我身を心易くつかふへし
又おり候時は常々如申心を能納て下に重みをつけ
かぎを能所に懸て右の縄をくりてさがりたりもよし
又右のきりをもみ立是を力に取付
ふらりとさがり片手をはなし足計に心をつけ
地きは三尺計上よと思ふ所にて飛へし
拟地に足付よと覚申時態ところひ
二つ三つかえるへし
必高き所より飛事悪敷候
飛んと思へは取上かみつりに成て下軽く成故也
此時は身を強打事無疑也
此習を知すしても
下る事計覚はや六尺の徳あり
いわんや心得たる人は身を打事すくなし
かやうの事おも稽古の仕様に色々口傳有

一　乗たる馬舟にのらさる時馬より
　　おりて轡のはみに月と云字を書
　　馬のひたい辻の上に賦と云字を書て
　　左の手にて口を取
　　賦と云字の点を舟の中へ打込
　　はいと声を懸申す也

一　夜中大勢出座有て口論に及所に
　　其座敷の人数皆一本に成
　　我一人の時誰を相手にもとるへきやうなけれは
　　命を捨ても多勢に無勢なれは
　　可叶共不覚され共
　　武士の道にはつるる事も成がたし
　　如何せんと思ふ時は我心を能納
　　死をやすくして體を陰にして
　　内に陽を含其座の勝手の様子能見置て

行を以て討へし
其手立と云は
心静に人々の気のつかさるように
燈の方により時分を能伺立上り
打物に手をかけんと思ふ時
足にて燈をけかへし申すか
又蝋燭の時はしんを取やうにもてなし
火を消其燭台を楯にして身をかこい
其座勝手兼て見置たる所に身をそはめ
節に當り分別して身をしつみくわし申すか
又伏て切たるもよし
何れも太刀をしやに取なくりたる太刀にてすくに拂へし
四方の口々に心を付けるべし
この手立てに逢うては大剛の者大勢有りと云うとも
誠を失いことごとく配軍²³して闇きゆへ
同士打有物也
此時却て敵の真をうはひ取
我加勢と成事無疑

一　三人居て咄其内両人口論して斬合候時
我一人してさへ可申様は我脇刺を抜
両人の内思切たると見ゆる方に脇刺を持
刃のまわらさる様に克見定
扨左の手に鞘を持両人切合候
中墨より弐尺計脇にくわして
両人切出すうこきの頭を能左右に眼をくはり
はねて分けへし
それにて不分は能断
手首よりひしの間を打落へし
先我脇刺を抜さる以前にて
さへんと能しらする事肝要也
畳を起して間へはね懸候か
又戸障子を隔ての云い分に候はば
間の戸を立切分けたるも吉
前の言分の理非の批判必無用にて候
善悪の批判によりさゑんと思ふて
脇指を抜候へは助太刀と心得て
必きらるる事有

可成事に候はば無刀にて行を以さへ申か能候
是等の心得節に當何によらす取いさへし

一　かひしやく仕様は切腹人より弐尺ばかり左に
　　大小を指ながらひかえて
　　先切腹人の躰を能見る事肝要也
　　彼者未練なる躰に見へ候はば不移時刻
　　脇差を取所をはや討へし
　　又慥成躰に見へ候はば一脇刺引廻
　　首の録にすわるをあいつに討へし
　　つき立申初と引き廻し申す納とに
　　必ず首其方へかたかる²⁴もの也
　　此所を討は討損るもの也
　　只首の録にすわるを見て討へし
　　されとも首の録にすわり申を
　　討んとはかり心得候へば
　　亦是になつみ²⁵討損る事有へし
　　我気に乗たる拍子を討へし
　　前に切腹人の見ぬやうに刀を抜て取合
　　勝手の能方に置たるもよし
　　首討申かねは切腹人の左の方に廻
　　時分を伺我右の足を切腹人のももの付根へ踏出し
　　爪先をそらし大指の頭を切腹人の耳のたぶの通りに見へし
　　たふさ²⁶をかけてむねの内へ打込と思て
　　我右の足の大指の頭をかねに成程腰をすえて
　　我心の一倍に強討落へし
　　此かねにあいては討損る事有まし
　　万々に一討損る事あらは
　　我心を能納其刀を
　　すくに刃を上へ取直し
　　前よりふゑを手はやにかき落すへし
　　又押腹切らする時は能心得て
　　是は切腹人の右に廻り成程身をちかく直り
　　脇刺を以討へし
　　是は初より抜我左の手のかうの上に納
　　切腹人に心の目を放し申間敷候
　　若彼者隔心有て働候はば其座を不去
　　脇指にてすくに指殺へし

如常切腹仕候はば
前のかねに合て首を討へし

一　我に覚なくして心に気つかい成事有時
　　したしき者なと友なわんと云共
　　必ず禁足あるへし
　　我命に大事の有時心うかさるもの也
　　此時は心得てけんみやく²⁷を取へし
　　其取りやうは右の手にて我喉の脈を取
　　左の手にて右の脈を取合見るに
　　一拍子に打はくるしからす

一　仕者の時は先我死を能定
　　身をなくして敵計にして可行
　　敵も又儀に當死をやすくして
　　常に柔剛に身を任せゆるみのなき者は
　　是は大事の討者也
　　此時は行を以て討へし
　　敵にも又手立有
　　一筋に定かたし
　　此二つの内に先後の二つ有
　　心を能定気のすわりて動のなき人に有へし
　　理行の事敵のすまひや家の様子により
　　色々数多候得は是又定かたし
　　去共當座にひとつの行あり
　　敵我を見懸丸腰になり病気の躰にもてなし
　　手拭帯なとして成程ゆうにぬかりたるていに見せ
　　髪をさはきひきさき紙を口にくわへ
　　髪をゆいゆい出る事有
　　是は必後さはきかみの下に白刃の打物を隠置
　　こなたのゆるみを伺只一太刀と思
　　おかみ討に討へし
　　はつるる事なし是は敵に先有故也
　　此時に先の請返し様有り有もなく
　　無もなく無と思ふ心もなく
　　早くもなく遅くもなく
　　つるつるとあゆみ行くに
　　其の時敵我を討んと思う心出来するもの也
　　其気の頭を討へし

331

敵我と行當り
自害するように仕懸申事肝要也
此一巻之内少々忍ひの事書記といへとも
よの常に是を専らとするにはあらず
若討て不叶強敵有て
我一人として夜討にせんと思ふ時
此忍の行を以て可討儀に當
死をやすくして此行を以てうたんに
いかなる強敵と云共
心に不叶と云事不可有
道なき事に右乃習を御取出しやうなきに
前に誓紙を以堅いましめ候はば
今更改申に不及候へ共
すしなき事に此習を御取出し候はば
誓紙の神罰のかれかたかるへき者也

右一巻雖爲秘書貴殿
深依御執心令相傳訖猶
以和義之稽古無怠慢可
被勵勉者也
萩原十蔵

水鏡口傳之覚 　（金沢市立玉川図書館近世史料館所蔵）

一　案内をしらざる川を越る時は
　　瀬とおもふ所の川上を見立
　　其川上より筋違に上の方へ渡り
　　半途過て水に順ひ川下の方へ越る事也

一　雨天にて行き先も見えぬ夜なと
　　足本に白くみえまたは何にてもあやしきものあらは
　　刀をぬきこい口を違て指込
　　それにてはねかへしてとるへし
　　是を目印にして討へきはかりある事也

一　やまたちの事逢たる時の心得は
　　書にあることく万事心を付る事かん要也
　　又士といふものは義によつて心外流窄する事ある也
　　其時は常に武を業とする故
　　外に一命をつなくへき便なき時は

山立を業とする也
仕様は其ともに成へきものあらは心を合すへし
又我身一人の時は八寸斗の短刀を両刃に拵
鍔無しにして懐刃としよき場所をこしらへ
往来の人を勝手能所にまちうけ
左の手にて胸をとり右の手にて短刀を逆手に持
すぐにのんとをおしきり懐中へあかをいるる事也
自然其所へ往来きたらは我心を能おさめ
急病にて薬をもちゆるなどといい
構無とをりたまへと声をかけ
往来静てムクロをがけまたは人しれぬ所へ捨る事なり
猶口傳多き事也

一　邯鄲の枕の事
(Figure 14.40)
　太刀　四　　　蘇民　一
　犬　五　　←六
　通達　三　　　無昇　二
　右は寝屋の大事也壇にて相傳の事也
旅宿にて一と間に此法にて縄をはる観念にて行へし
行ひ様は右之字四方中と心にて書き
犬のけんとうにあて、↑[28]此字を枕の下に書く事也
書き様に口傳あり
また野宿なとにては何町何里にても縄を張る也
観念第一也口傳

一　我やへ志のひ入たる時の心得に我名をよふといふは
　　家来なとの名をよふ時は自然忍の者のはからひにて
　　對る事もあらむと我名をよふなり
　　夫を對るはいよいよ曲者なり

一　志のひ大勢入たるときは
　　まづ家内を外よりみへぬ様にすへし
　　あんとうには何にてもかけて
　　外のみへぬ様にすへし習い多あり

一　志のひのせき仕様竹の筒を口に当てする事あり
　　又外にも仕様さまざま有口傳

一　人をおひ懸討ときは

其間六尺斗にも成いまだ刀のとゝかぬ所にて
身を捨足をなぐへし
是を名付けて寝長ヶのけむもむといふ也

一　人に追懸らるゝときは
　　小路なとへいらむと思はゝ
　　道の矩をとり急に入る事也

一　こう路より打かける太刀を不抜して留様は
　　左へよりかへりさまに刀のさやなから
　　左の手にて我身をかこふ也

一　親子兄弟またはしたしき朋友なと
　　外人と口論におよひ段々詞を尽し
　　さへるといへとも双方無承引
　　もはや事に及むとする時は
　　したしき方にちかくおらは気のつかぬふりにて
　　後の方へ手をまわし鞘を抜口に直すへし
　　又一人の相手のかたに居らは刃を内の方へ直すべし
　　是にて先後はなはだある事也

右十一ヶ条は用方水鏡之書
重直先生口傳之趣書記畢
邯鄲之枕之事雖書記
壇上之事也依而不記委曲者也

戦場組討無拍子流中通覚
一　懐劔之大事
　　尊長高位のまへ出るときの心得也
　　左様の帯刀にて出るときは下着と上着との間にさす事也
　　指様は刃を下へしこじりをももの方へ指込
　　柄を右の脇の下におく也
　　扨事あらば右のはだをぬきそのまま抜突事也
　　懐劔寸は九寸五分より壱尺弐三寸を不越也
　　尤無鍔を用ゆしかりといへとも
　　急成ときは常の脇刺おも用る也
　　猶口傳あり

一　岩石落之事
　　義経公ひよとり越をおとしたまふ時の事也

藤つるを多くあつめ縄にして木の枝をたたみ
階子のごとくにして人数を段々押たまひしと也
馬は輪乗にて乗たおし四足をからげおろししと也
中々馬上にておとすべき所にあらす

一　常の心得は右に准したるがけなどにては心得ある事也
突おとされぬこころ得は早く臥する事也口傳
人をつきおとさんとおもはゞ
我身のろくをきはめ両手を腰にすへ
かたにて突きおとす事也
手にておとす時は其手をとれはともに落る故也

一　極意八重桜之事　　　　　　一本は八重菊とあり
戦場組討の極意なり
まず戦場にいたくおもひ入たる敵一人に目を懸
み込て観念する事第一也
扨段々詰寄て敵の前くさずりを桜の花と見
おどし糸を蕊と見たて左のひざをたて右を臥し
左の手にて草摺を揚右の手に刀をぬき突込也
業にて口傳あり

一　敵より右の仕かけをするときは
はやく陰の身に直り右の手にて面へあたり
敵の立てたる足を左の手にてなけかえへす事也口傳

右八重桜は組討極意なり
此外中通雖有手数業繁多故除
之則重直先生口傳之趣記之畢

極意清浄之品并忍術
一　壇の本かざりは容易におこなひかたし
よつて當時やつして かさる也
そのときは本尊を奉懸そのまへに机をかさり
其上に燈明をおき
へぎ に御酒あらひ米をそなへ
そのまへに長さ壱尺八寸の鳥居をおき
其前に鉢に清水を入備へ
そのわきに高さ六寸幅八寸両足の板のついたてをおく也
扨観念は右の燈明を心の中にて大火に観念し
其火の中へ我身を投込事なり

　　　扨右のついたてを鉢の後へ遣し
　　　右の鉢の水を湖水に観念し
　　　此中へ身を投込なり
　　　もはや火水を以て身を清めたるによつて
　　　我心中へ本尊を勧請したる事也
　　　是三品の一品也

一　　今一品は太刀腹巻なり行様は刀をぬき
　　　おんと唱え指表に火を三ツ＜火火　火如此指にて書き
　　　裏に＜水　水水如此書最前の燈明の段を観念して
　　　心火の中へ太刀を突込左の手にてしのきをこき見る也
　　　成就すれは能自由にまかる也
　　　焼けさる内何篇にても右の観念する事也
　　　左身は水と云う字を切先へよせて書くなり
　　　扨右の刀をもとのことくする時は
　　　すくなれや直なる太刀をすくにして
　　　ゆ気をはらうあびらうんけん
　　　と唱へしのきを左の手にてこくなり
　　　是にて二品也

一　　今一品は初の本尊を観念することくにして
　　　白狐を心中へ納る事也
　　　千年以上の白狐ならては用に不立也
　　　是忍の法にも入事にて則稲荷勧請なり
　　　以上三品

　　　志のひ
一　　志のびといふは常の事にあらず
　　　主君より命をうけ諸国へ音蜜の連判状を持てありく事也
　　　諸国流布の志のひ用る仏
　　　先は六部行脚の躰にもてなし胸に佛の一躰懸
　　　其仏の中をくり張つがひにして中へ蜜状を納る事あり
　　　是佛割の志のひといふ也

一　　当流にては密意露顕せんとほつして
　　　敵に見とかめらるる所を能工夫する事なり
　　　一身の中に密状納所したため様奥に記
　　　猶も敵うたかひて牢者する時は三寸ばかりの
　　　沈切を兼て持事也納所奥に記

拠牢の内にて右の沈切を出し
心火にて太刀腹巻のことく焼
我出んと思ふ一方を切やぶり
夜半に及んて自由に出る也

一　関所なときびしき時は兼て心得有事なり
　　其心得とは如此[小さな筒]の桐の木の
　　長さ一寸八分切口も一寸八分の木を三角に作り
　　中をすき亥の目をあけ表を錦にてつつみ
　　この中を金紙にて張初の三品の観念をし
　　此中へ本尊を入なり
　　常に守りとして懐中し
　　右のことくなる所にてわげの下へはさむ事也
　　是にて我身をかくす事也

一　密状したため様は本紙写し四寸斗打巻
　　上をよくつつみ勝魚木の形にしてふのりにてかためる也
　　可秘〃〃
　　一子相傳の習事也

一　密状納所は下着へ入る、事なり
　　可秘〃〃

一　沈切納所は右の密状の間へ巻込事も有
　　または上はぐき上口びるの間へ入る事もあり
　　是等秘中の秘なり

右極意三品并忍法者
萩原茂辰家秘也
櫻井重直依執心深免許之
予又以執心櫻井重直附与之
忍法者依事繁大綱記已

水鏡新冊　（金沢市立玉川図書館近世史料館所蔵）

水鏡序
夫武士技藝多雖爲端
柔剛弱強之四ツ之外ニ不出
是ヲ不知者多
此理ヲ為得学者少シ
去ハ水之下知ニ付

337

大剛之有名人 ゟ 云共

緩討不討云事ナシ

萬之災気ノ緩山寄出事ト可知

其緩ト云ハ泥て片寄處有

是皆爲意其本失故也

然者方便ト云事有ハ

敵之謀コトハ不相事令知

敵討品々記シ集メ（カ）て

後之習ヱル者之爲助而已

外ニ見様六ツ有ル事次ニ記

一　夜中陣中味方之サ法不定事

一　夜中味方敵方ヨリ氣力進ム事

一　立掛ヲク弓抔タヲレシ（カ）物ヲトロキスル事

一　又陣中ニ鼻ヲヒル事

一　トカク物ヲ言事ウハヒビキ斗スル事

一　味方陣屋ノ馬イホフ事

一　伏勢ヲ見ル事是ハ闇ノ夜ニ星之サヤカト有リテモ
　　伏勢之空ニハ星無キ事義経之御哥ニ
　　闇の夜は星なき方に行ぬものくもる夜ならは雲ひかる方

一　又伏勢之上ニ飛鳥行ヲ見タス其外心勢アリ
　　先伏勢有ル上ハ朝キリ霞早ク上ル也
　　ヲノレト心気タナ引也

一　陣屋ヱ忍之者入ルニハ品々形ヲ替
　　或ハ乞食抔之様出立来ル者ノ也
　　夫ヲ能ク穿鑿仕て捕ヱ髪月代抔ヲサセテ
　　馬ニノセ亦座席ヱ出シ色々仕リ
　　弓鑓抔ヲ爲持様々ニ仕て見也夫ニて忍者ヲ知事也

一　盲人ニ成テ謀事ヲスルニハ鯉之イロコ[29]ヲアハセドニテ能クスリ
　　何程モウスクシテマン中ニ釘ニテ穴ヲ明
　　夫ヲ眼中ヱ入レ右之コトクナシ面ニ[30]ヌル事也

一　人化ニツ之火ノ見様ハ方之印ニテ十文字書キ
　　刀ヲ抜テ向イニアテ見ルニ
　　鍔ヨリ上ニ見ユルハ人ノ持タル火也
　　下之方ニ見ユルハ化者ヲ火也

一　山野ニヨラス変成火ノ時カラ手水[31]ヲツカイ
　　ヒンテイソワカト三度唱シハ生ヲアラハス
　　亦日輪ン之印ヲ結ヒ

ヲンアニチヤマリシヱイソワカト唱レハクハイキヱル事

ヒカリ物抔枝ニテウタヌ事切ハ数多ク成事

一　是ハ化生之者ヲ見ルニハ先我心ヲ定ル事サキノ者タモレハ[32]

一　我心サヘ定レハヨシ此ヶ条ケシヤウ之者ニカキラス萬便ニ通ル

　　事スヘテ者ヲ見ルハ心明徳ヨリ見ル事然共ホン人ハ習ナク

　　テハ見ルル事カタシ故ニ変物見ルニハ護身法九字ヲナスヘシ

一　亦我左ノタモトヨリ見様アレ共極意ハ光明眞言之七印

　　ヲムスヘハ何ト云本性ヲアラハス事

一　忍火ト云ハ道具也▲此形ニ銅子ニて拵ヱ行燈之火口ニカブセ申

　　セハ則クラク成ル亦明ニ仕度時ハ右之道具ヲ取也

　　但シ道具拵様ハ　　　　口傳

一　又火口ニケヌキヲ置夫上ヱ銭一文ノセレハ右之通ニ成事同シ

　　行燈ノ下ニ楊枝ヲク事

一　下カハラケ[33]ニ水入レヲケハ化生ノ物火ヲケサス[34]事

一　夜中無心元ト思道ヲ行時ハ敵ニ當リテ能キ程ノ石ヲ袖ニ入テ

　　持ヘシ是ハ氣遣ニ思フ所ヱ右之石ヲ打テ見ルニ必其躰アハル[35]者也

一　右之石ヲ打時神ヲ祈リ石ニツハキ[36]ヲ付打事

一　夜中悪物出合之時足之ツマ先ヲカクス者也

　　能気付見ルニ足ニタカイ[37]有人ニ替ル事十八所有リ

　　此所ヲ見ルニ人ニコト成[38]所人之不及足遣多クアリ

　　トカク足ニ気付見ル之事切時ハ頭ヲ切ラス下ヲ切ル事

　　化物ノ足ハ前トル馬ノ如シ[39]

一　雨天カキ曇行先モ見ヱサル時足元ニ白キ物其外何ニ不寄

　　眼ニ掛ル物有ト侭ヨ捨[40]ヘカラス

　　心得ナク是ヲ取ル時ハ目印ニ成テ切ル事有

　　是ハ若捨ハ子ハ[41]カナハヌ時刀ヲ抜カケ身ヲカコイ鞘テ

　　刎返シテ取ヘシ右何ニヨラス毒ヲ付ヲク事有リ

　　心得アルヘク事

一　夜中四ツ時迄ハ道ノ中ヲ通ル事四ツヨリハ左右ヲ行事陽気

　　四ツ迄ハ中ニ有ル事

一　夜中ニ風雨ノトモヒカヱル事口論等ニハナリカハル事

　　門外ヱ出ルトモ風見分ヲク事

一　北國ニ有拗夜之足音城辺或ハ往来多キ所ニアル

　　除レハ足壱里先ヱ行ナリ先江人行トモ刀[42]大事也

一　夜中人抔討テ退ント思時東西南北モ見分ス如何ンセント

　　思フ時ハ水之流ヲ尋出シ其水上登レハ山有ル者也拗山中ヱ入ツテ

　　高キヨリ下キ所ヲ見ヱル所ニ居テ明松ナソヲ持尋来ル人之躰テ

　　道路ヲ可知トカク思案工夫分別可然所也

　　　扨追手透間ナク来リ退シ方ナク難逃ト思時ハ
　　　刀之小尻ヲ少シ切息ノ出ル程穴ヲアケテコイ口ヲロチニクハヱテ
　　　水之中ニ沈ミ身ヲカクシ刀脇指ニテモ水底ニ指込ミ
　　　是ヲチカラニ取付居ル也息ノシ様ニ習有口傳
一　手抔負タル時モ流ノ中ヲ行キタルカ能也
　　　是ハノリヲトメラレヌ用心也
　　　亦雪フリタル時ハはき物[43]ヲ跡先[44]ニハキ枝ヲ左ニツキ
　　　流ノ中ニ入ツテ行ヘシ跡ヲトメラレヌタメ也
一　人ヲ討テ退ク時ノ大事ハ
　　　弓手[45]免テ[46]あと先とむかふの武者なるを守るは七やうのほし[47]
　　　アヒラウンケン
一　提灯ヲ持スル事我ヨリ先江為持タルハ悪シ我左ノ方
　　　大小ヨリ二三尺斗跡ニ為持タルカ吉
　　　此時ハ前後左右共ニ能見ユル也ニ
　　　張リ之時ハ格別六月下旬ヨリハ欠猶更事
一　其家ノ内ヱ廻リ要害ヲ能見置ヘシ
　　　是ハ火事夜盗抔入タル時之為也
一　家ノ内ニテハ床縁天井畳落入和カ成所[48]ニ心ヲ付
　　　畳ヲアケテ能見ヲクヘシコト大福掛物ハスヽヘシ
　　　家来ハ居ル脇ノ間我ヲル入口ニ子サスヘシ[49]
　　　若ニカイ抔ハ[50]入口ハシコ下ニ寝スヘシ
一　寝所ニ入テハ焼火ノ有ル内亦焼火消テ後口傳ト云儀ハ
　　　我大小落物ヲ勝手ノアシキ所ニ置キ
　　　火消テ後勝手悪敷方直シ戸障ら貳尺五寸余ヨケテ子ル事
一　枕ニハイカニモ任ニクキ枕ヲ可致
　　　亦カンタン之枕とて其屋敷ノ内ヱ虫ノ入テモ目ノ覚ル事アリ口傳

[(Figure 14.76)参照]
　　　邯鄲ノ枕調様
　　　必此紙ヲ四角ニ切
　　　此文字ヲ如此四方ニ書可申事
一　蘇民　二　無昇　三　通達　四　太刀　五　犬　六↑
　　　ヲンマリシエイソワカ
[(Figure 14.77)参照]
　　　如此ケン筆ヲ書ニ心ニ観念シテ立ノ棒ヲ引時犬ヲ撞[51]ト
　　　思テ棒ヲ引時ヲンマリシエイ
　　　右之通リ奉書上ヲタトウ紙ヲ四角ニキリ夫ニテ封シテ持ヘシ
　　　是ヲ枕ニシテ伏事也旅宿等常ニモ無心許時ハ心用ル事

　　　　亦懐中ニ無之時ハ間之内ニ四方ト[52]書事口傳

一　戸尻錐モミ仕タルカヨシ其錐拵様口傳

　　　　戸障子ヲカタメタル所ヱ忍入ニモヨシ

　　　　火事ノ時ヤ子ヱノホル[53]ニモヨシ

一　家屋舗ノ内ヱ大勢夜盗来ル時先火ヲトモノ[54]事悪シ

　　　　人スクナクシテシセカン[55]ト思フ時ハ

　　　　時々囁声抔シテ聞セ切ラント思ハ

　　　　夜盗此所ヨリ忍ヘキト思フロニ細引ヲ高サ四五寸斗張

　　　　手頃成物ヲ楯ニ持打物ヲシヤニ[56]持テ拂切ニスヘシ

　　　　火持事第一也口傳

　　　　夜打ヒシマクト云習道具等口傳有リ

一　敵忍来ル時不知シテモ必我心ニ覚有物也

　　　　其時ハ心得テ気遣可仕

　　　　其時忍物心得テ畜類ノ来ル様ニスル事有リ

　　　　畜類ト不可思忍ト云ハ色々方便ノ有事也

　　　　縁ノ下抔ニ畜類の物ヲカシル音ス

　　　　遠キ所カスカニセキ抔スル事アラハ必近キ所ニ人有ト可知

　　　　近キ所ニテスルセキヲ遠キ所ノヤウニ聞ユル習有

一　敵忍入時ハ近所ニ堀川池抔有レハ

　　　　其ヱンテニ能程ノ石ヲ置テ内ニ入物也

　　　　是ハ起合追出る時右ノ石を

　　　　彼ノ水ノ中ヘ打込ニクヘキタクミ也

　　　　是等之事心得ナケレハ氣ヲトラル事

一　忍入タル敵屋サカシスルニハ刀ヲ抜キカケ

　　　　切先二三寸程鞘に残シ下緒ヲ延シ其先ヲ我帯ニツケ

　　　　左ノ手ニ能程ノ物ヲ楯ニ持身ヲカコイサカスヘシ

一　又弓ニテ尋ヌル事モ有甲矢ヲ存ルノ儘ニ引込

　　　　能勝手ニ納メテ乙矢ヲ押手ク[57]人指ヲキツクヒ[58]ヲハサミ

　　　　其矢尻にてサカスヘシ

　　　　サレ共弓ニテハ爰カシコツカヘテ思フ程尋事難成者也

一　忍タル者我ヲ尋ルト思ハ、能心納テ囲炉裏ノ内立入リ臥シテ

　　　　此方ノ緩ヲ窺ヒ見テハスヽ事有ヘシ

　　　　此外口傳トハ起合候程常ニ見置タル故ニ

　　　　彼イロリヲ人皆ヨケテ通ル者也

　　　　是ヲ心得ナク火抔燈ニ近寄ヲ窺ヒ切ルヽ事有リ

一　忍入タル敵ヲ追掛出申時心得品々有

　　　　口傳トハ諸事ニ心ヲ付ル事肝要也

　　　　彼物大事思フ忍入時ハ入口ト縄ヲ張リノフレン[59]抔有所ハ

341

上ヨリ下ヱ簾ノコトク切サキ四五寸残シ置申事

又縄簾抔ハ左右ヱ端ヲ取結ヒ置事モ有リ

扨次ノ間ニ檀抔有レハ臥テ身ヲソハメ

彼檀ヨリ下リ申所ヲ切事有

此手立心得ヘシ

急ニ追カケラルヽ時其道ニ菱ト云物ヲマク事モ有リ

是足ニ踏立テハ一足も行事不可成

又門ヲ出申時ハ後ロノ手ニ尻戸ヲ引立行者也

追出ル者アケントスル間五間ツヽ行過ル者也

扨追カクルニモニケ出ルニモ習有

是ハ何モ業也口傳

一 忍仕時ハ鳥類抔ノマ子ヲ仕習フヘシ忍ノ時入事多シ

昔唐士漢国ノ関[60]ヲ鶏ノ空音ニ謀ラレテ通シタル例有也

就中庚申之夜忍入ニハ鶏ノマ子仕事有之也

或人ノ云庚申ノ夜仕タル事必アラワルヽ物ト云傳

是ハ盗人ノ申出シタル事也

常ノ夜ヨリアラワルハ亦必アラワレス亦是如何口傳

一 忍ノ時塀ヲ越ルニハ刀等塀ニ立掛テ下ケ緒ノ先ヲ取テ結ヒ

足首ニ掛テ鍔ヲ踏テ棟木ニ取附其侭刀ナヽ取テ腰ニ指テ可越

若シ其塀高時ハ棟木ニ取付事難成ハ

口傳ト云事ハ習ノ錐ヲ取出シ打立テ越ヘシ

又所カキ[61]ヲ掛テ越タルモヨシ

トカク塀高クシテ難越時ハ

越ヘキ以前ニ取カキヨリ弐尺斗ニ縄ヲ残シ

我後ロノ帯ヨリ引通シ其侭後ロヨリ肩ヲ越ヘシ

ウテ木ニ取付候ハ彼カキヲウテ木ニ掛テ

我身心易ツカフヘシ

一 塀ヲ下リ申時ハ如常々申

能心納テ下モニ重ミヲ付テ能所カギヲ掛

右ノ縄ヲタグリテ下カルモヨシ

又ハ彼ノ錐ヲモミ立是ニ刀ヲ取付

フラリト下カリ片手ヲ放シ足斗心ヲ付テ

地際三尺斗上レ思所ニテ飛可申

又高キ所ヨリ飛事悪キ也

但飛ト思ハ所[62]ノホリテ上シスリニナツテ

下モ軽ク成ル故身ヲ強ク打事有リ

就中心得タル人ハ身ヲ討ル事少シモナシ

尤トモ稽古右ノ仕様色々有口傳

　　　外ニ高キ所ヨリ飛習有リ二丈三丈飛術口傳
一　夜中大勢出座有之テ不計口論ニ及ニ
　　　其座ノ人数皆一手成リテ
　　　我一人別ニ成誰ヲ相手ニ可取様モナケレハ不叶
　　　去共武士ノ道ニハツルゝ事モ難成
　　　如何セント思時ハ我身心ヲ納テ死ヲ易仕テ
　　　骸ヲ陰ニシテ陽ヲ含其座ノ勝手之様子ヲ能見置テ
　　　術ヲ以可討其方便ト云ハ心静ニ人之ノ気ヲ不付様ニシテ
　　　燈ノ方ヨリ時分ヲ窺テ討ント思時
　　　口傳ト云儀ハ時分ヲ能窺テ立上リ打モノ也
　　　小手ヲカケント思フ時足にて燈ヲフミ返シ申カ
　　　又蝋燭ナラハシンヲ取ル様ニモテナシ
　　　火ヲ消シ其燭臺ヲ楯ニシテ身ヲカコイ
　　　兼て其勝手ヲ見置タル所ニ身ヲソハメ
　　　節ニ當リ分別シ沈カ臥申カ又クハツシテ切リタルモヨシ
　　　トカク太刀ヲシヤニトリナクリタル太刀ニテ直⁶³シ拂ヘシ
　　　四方の口々ニ心ヲ付ケ申ヘシ
　　　此手立ニ逢テハ大剛ノ者大勢有ト云共
　　　誠ヲ失ヒコトコトク周章騒キ昏キ故ニ同士討有者也
　　　此時却て敵ノ誠ヲ大奪トリ我カセイト成事有リ口傳
一　夜中三人居テ咄申内不討⁶⁴人論及ニテ切結フ時
　　　我壱人シテサエント思ハ先脇指ヲ抜
　　　両人ノ思切ト見ユル方ニ脇指ヲ持刃ノマハラサル様ニ能之見定
　　　左ノ手に鞘ヲ持両人切合申中墨ヨリ弐尺斗脇ニ居テ
　　　両人切出人動キノカシラヲ能左右ニ眼ヲクハリハ子返スヘシ
　　　夫ニて不分ハ能断手首ら臂ノ間ヲ打落ヘシ
　　　先我脇指ヲ抜サル以前ニサエ人ト能シラスル事肝要也
　　　但口傳ト云儀ハ脇指ヲ不抜シテサユル事肝要也
　　　畳ヲコシテ間ヱハ子カケ亦戸障子ヲ隔ニ入ルカ
　　　間ノ戸ヲ立切タルモヨシ
　　　前ノ云分ノ理非ノ批判必無用ニ候
　　　善悪ノ批判ニヨリサエント思テ脇指ヲ抜候ヘハ
　　　助太刀ト心得必切ラルゝ事有リ可成事ニ候
　　　無刀ニテ業ヲ以てサエ申カ能候
　　　是等之心得何ニ不寄取合サユヘシ
一　乗タル馬舟ニ不乗時ニ習有ト云ハ
　　　馬ヨリ下リテ轡ノハミニ月ト云字書テ
　　　馬ノヒタイ辻ノ上ニ賦ト云字ヲ書テ

左ノ手ニテ馬ノ口ヲ取テ賦ト云字ニ口傳

一　船ノアヤマチ有ル無キヲ知ヘキ事は

先乗ヘキ前ニ伏此字ヲ足ノ大指ニテ地ニ書テンヲ打

フマエテ船頭ノ面ヲ見レハ

大事有レハ首ナシ亦大事無時ハ首見ユル者也

一　舟ニ不酔習事ハ日本武観念シテ

舟ノ内エ賦ノ字ヲ書テテンヲ其人ノヒタイへ打也

亦菅笠ヲキテ乗モヨシ

懐中ニハンケ[65]ヲ持事是モ所持ナキ時ハカベヲヲコイテ持事

イ黄ヲ懐中スルモヨシ亦小ヨリヲヨリ鼻ヲヒテ乗モヨシ

鉄砲ヲ打者ハ舟ニ酔ヌ者也

小刀ニクリ伽羅不動ヲホリタルヲ持ハ舟ニヨハヌ

小刀小柄ニテモ破波ヲノカル事

乗物必シモ此品同事ニ宜敷也

一　常ノ如ク行時後ヨリ声ヲ掛討時刀抜様之習有

又不抜シテ留様ノ業有口傳

一　山立ニ逢ヒタル時心得ト云儀先我心ヲ能納テ臆不立品々可通

子細ハ口傳

扨又弐三里カ間前後左右ヨリ来ル人心ヲ不可免

先定リタル山立ト云中間六人斗リ之物也其中ヨ

リ壱人出テ残五人ハ能所ノ草ニ臥シ居ル物也

口傳ト云儀ハ

山立ハ左ノ耳ヲ地ニ當強弱ヲ知ル又音声ニテモ聞事

心ニケツタン有ル物ハ必タヽシキ事

声鏡ノ如クヒヽタル有ハ心強キ事

夫故山野ニテハ必腹ヲハル事ヲソロシキトモ

腹ハレス声足上にヒヽクニヨリ奥ハヲカミ腹ヲハレハ

地ヒヽキ有ル事

又山野ニてヲソロシキ時ハ不動のシクノ咒[66]ヲクル事

心ツヨク成事

一　足音強クヒヾクハ剛強成者弱キ者ハ

足ヲトカロシ足ヲ知テ山立ハ勝負ヲスルトソ

亦道先ニ縄ヲ張リヲク事アリ此時ハ口傳

一　道端ニ無心許病人有テ苦シケナル声ニテ薬抔所望スル者アラハ

心得テ近付クヘカラ[67]亦昼中共ニ不知者道連レ無心許候口傳

一　或ハ右ノ手ヲ懐ノ内ニ入テ

討物ヲカタ子如何ニモスカリタル躰ニモテナシ来ル者アラハ

昼夜トモニ心ヲユルスヘカラス

子細ハ色々方便多有物也

去共爰ヲ云時ハ心得五ツ可有

口傳ト云儀ハ夜ハ黒反古ヲ鞘ノ様ニ袋ニシテ

白刃ヲ包肩ヨリ直ニ打事有

サ昼ハ折金ヲ我カ髪ノワケニ懸テ右ノ手斗ニテ抜打ニ

左手懐中シナカラ打事有リ

扨其所四十四五丁モ行過候得ハ必心ユルミ

前後左右ヨリ来ル人ヲ我同道ノ様ニ思ヒ

互ニ物語抔仕懸シ心ニ成物也

其時彼ハ時分ヲ窺反古ニ包タル刀打ニハスルヽ事ナシ

可心得事也

一　案内ヲ不知川ヲ越ス時ハ上ヱ筋違ヒ越申者也

一　盗賊可入方ヲ知事

子午酉巳亥寅日ハ　　　　其日支ヨリ八ツ目ゟ入ル

丑未戌卯申辰日ハ　　　　其日支ヨリ四ツ目ゟ入ル

右十二支ヲ方ニ當テ知ル

甲乙日ハ戌ノ時ニ入　　丙庚　　子寅戌亥時ニ入

戌辛日ハ子戌時ニ入　　巳壬ハ　午亥時ニ入

癸丁ハ子時ニ入

一　旅平宅等ニテ目覚ニ気付ル事鼡サハキ蚊シキリニチル事

庭ノ虫鳴ニモ気付ノ事平宅ニてハ外等見廻リノ事口傳

一　勤番心得之事若我家来等乱心候トモ懐中内縮ニテ病人ニシテ出ス

懐中ニテ（カ）シハリ足ノ間壱尺ニテシハリ出ス事

一　馬ニ咬候事舛にても馬ヒシヤクニテモ二刀ノ印ニて離火消水ト書

咬レ候者ニ少シ宛三口呑也残ノ水ヲ疵ニ懸ル事

又生粟ヲカミ付ルモヨシ

一　蜂ニサヽレシ時イモノ葉ヲスリテ付ルモヨシ

又サヽレシウエニ南無赤不動明王ト書モヨシ口傳

一　早付木ノ事両方イヲヽ付置事

厚キ紙ニ硫黄トシヤウノフ當分ニ合煮付て置事

一　息合不切事

是ハ平世其心得持事也手掛ノ色ニヘニ浅黄ニシテ置事

又ワラノフシヲ手一足ニ切初メ横ニクハヘル事

一　夜中妖怪ノ事

是ハ軍中抔ニテ忍ノ者ノ術ニテ座中女之姿ナル事

別テアヤシキ事てもナク術有之事口傳

其時松ノ木ノヤニ又ハ松ノ木ノヤニヲ焼ハ

コトゴトク此術キエル事

一　或ハ又悪敷所ニテケシカラン者ニ手合シトモ石ヲ取リ
　　　我守リ本尊カ又ユン佛ユン神ヲ唱
　　　石ニツハキ懸アヤシキ者ニ打事
　　　マホウナトニテ木像抔アラハレル事
　　　此時打事伊賀甲斐長門此傳ヲスル也
一　間ノ内ヱ蚊不入事
　　　風煙此二字紙ニ書テ窓ノ下押ス
　　　赤カウモリヲ取テ足ヲクヽリ東ノ方ニサカサマニツリヲキ
　　　血ヲ取縄ニシメテ寝タル高ニ張ル也
　　　此傳ハ義経寝ヤノ大事ト云
一　瘧[68]不震事
　　　是ハ春三ツ月ノ内ニ浅の出花ヲスリテ鼻ニカミ
　　　浅ノ葉ノシホリシルヲ茶碗ニ水入テ交朝日ヲウツシ呑ハ
　　　其年一年瘧不震事
一　赤子夜鳴留様
　　　是ハアシケ[69]馬ノ血ヲ取タル縄ヲヤ子[70]ニハル事
　　　亦守左ノ通リ

[(Figure 14.89)参照]

一　右ノ守青紙抔ニ書テ先ヲ剣形ニスル也
　　　此札ヲカマトノ中取立ル也
一　門出ノ習是ハ門出ニ義経ノ御哥ニ
　　　門出ニスハリシ食ニモミアラハ仕合ノヨキスイソウトシレ
　　　門出ニカラスノ声ノスルトモハ半ナルハヨシ丁ハツヽシメ
　　　亦畜類ノ道ヲヨコキルモ悪シ門出ニハ必陽ノ足ヲ先ヱ出ス事
一　湿来物調様ハ硯墨ヲスルトモ耳ノアカヲ取テ交ル事
　　　夫枚陣中ニてハ硯箱ノ間ヘハ耳カキヲ入ル事
　　　是本シキ之大事ニ掛テ書物ハ其間ヱトコロ[71]ヲ交テスレハ
　　　妖怪ヲ除ル者也又書タル物上ヲトコロニテスレハハケン物也
一　凡道ヲ行ニマカリ角ニテ左右ヲ能見テ心ヲツケテ通
　　　ルヘシ急ニ曲事悪キ也
一　鳥類ノ大事云事戦国ニ時々鳥ノ行時帰時ヲ見ル事
　　　鳥ノ我ニ向鳴ハ吉シフンカケル事悪キ事
　　　鳥ノ間ヱ入ルニ庵ニテモ悪敷鶴ノス懸ル事モアシ丶
　　　鳥聚ル事キラヲ夜中鳥サハク事悪シ
　　　宵鳴ニ忍ノ法抔ニテ鳴ス事色々口傳

　　　右七拾五ケ條爲一巻内之忍之事
　　　常ニ心得之儀書抜記ト云共

余之常ニ是ヲ専トスルニハ不有
若不討不叶強敵有テ我壱人トシテ夜討ニセント思時
此術ヲ以テ可討
儀ニ當テ死ヲ易シテ此術以テ討ニイカ成強敵ト云トモ
必不叶ト云事不可有
無道事ニ右之習御取出無之様ニ
前誓紙ヲ以堅ク戒候ヘハ今更改申ニ不及無候□事
御用ニ候得ハ誓紙神罰可難逃者也

右一巻者雖爲家傳之秘書深依御執心令相傳候
死他見他言有之間鋪者也依如件

廣化二年巳正月

1. AN INTRODUCTION TO THE LOST SCHOOL: MUBY SHI RY AT A GLANCE

1. For a full explanation on the division between military and civilian skills, see Antony Cummins, *Samurai and Ninja: The Real Story behind the Japanese Warrior Myth that Shatters the Bushido Mystique* (Clarendon, VT: Tuttle, 2015).
2. Uematsu Sensei only claims his lineage from Kaneko Kichibei, but with careful research, Mieko Koizumi has managed to redefine the correct lineage. This could increase to the 16th if Niki Shinjūrō is entered into the lineage. However, this count was started at Hagiwara Jūzō.

7. THE ORIGINS OF THE SCHOOL

1. There are no personal pronouns in this document; they have been added in translation for grammatical ease. This additional information was probably written by Hagiwara Jūzō's students or by him, and *he* is not used in the original text.
2. The concept here is that the skills were not invented by those using them, and while those using them may not understand their origins, it does not hamper their effectiveness.
3. The two versions of this scroll state different meanings for the word: *torii* (gateway to a shrine) and *tori* (a bird). Here it has been transcribed as *bird*. In the Kinseishiryōkan version of the Bishamonden it is 無極鳥居之構 *(mukyoku torii no kamae)*; in the Kensei Kusabuka Jinshirō book version Bishamonden, 無極鳥之構 *(mukyoku tori no kamae)*.
4. This skill can be seen in the scrolls *Mizukagami Kuden no Oboe* and *Bishamonden Kenjutsu*. It is also the name of a martial skill.
5. A skill with a similar name can be seen in the scroll *Mizukagami Kuden no Oboe*.
6. Yuikarigane, a design of a family crest that contains a bird with simplified crossed wings in a circle form.
7. The implication here is a form of smoke screen and a shinobi-bullet or shinobi-ball.

8. THE MARTIAL ARTS OF MUBY SHI RY

1. Kusari-dama is an alternative for 鎖分銅 *(kusari-fundō)*.

2. Unknown. Literal translation. No transcription has the full information on this tool.

3. This title is also used in other places to indicate throwing an appropriate tool at the enemy to help capture him.

9. THE SIXTEEN POEMS OF MUBYŌSHI RYŪ

1. Meaning that the farther afield you search, the less you will find.

2. The original manual is worm-bitten, and sections are missing. The Japanese has been compiled from a modern transcription from another version. Therefore the meaning may differ.

3. Meaning that trying too hard to control the mind is not mastery over the mind.

4. The second half loses some of its essence in translation, and its correct interpretation may be lost.

10. THE SCROLL OF THE MIND

1. The character used in the title of the scroll, 鑑, can be translated various ways, including "paragon," "model," "criteria," and "reflection," and in this scroll it has been translated differently to better convey the original message. For example, in the title, the term *reflecting* has been used to show that the information within the scroll is information used to advance the mind, while *criteria* and *model* have been used later to show that it is a list of states or ideals to be reached for.

2. 請 *(uke)* in this context means "to receive from outside," and while less detailed and more ambiguous in the original text, it has been rendered here as "perception."

3. The original text states "do not touch anything" because if you do, the cart will run downhill, meaning keep your mind on the "cart."

13. THE ART OF SEPPUKU

1. Meaning that compliments should be subtle and reserved.

2. A person observing whether the ritual is performed (後見の人, kōken no hito).

3. *Kaishaku.*

4. 咄者.

5. This is described in the scroll *Mizukagami* and implies where the rhythm and feel are correct.

6. One horizontal cut and one vertical cut in the abdomen.

7. 検使 *(kenshi).*

8. かんなかけ *(kanna kake).*

9. たとう紙 *(tatōshi).*

14. Deep Secrets and the Arts of the Shinobi

1. Meaning that the victim will pick up the white item, and the killer will identify his position in the harsh conditions.

2. 中間 *(chūgen)*, servants to samurai.

3. Meaning that fallen blood will not give away your path, and they will not know if you went to higher or lower ground.

4. It will appear that you have walked out of the river, not into it.

5. 邯鄲の枕 *(kantan no makura)*, found in Chinese literature under the title *Chinchūki* (枕中記) by Zheg-Zhong-Ji (沈既済). In the story, the man borrows a pillow from a monk and falls asleep. In his dream the man is shown a vision of his future full of promotion and glory, but wakes up to realize that only a few moments have passed. The term *kantan* (邯鄲) in the name of this pillow is a city in China, and in Chinese this means "the pillow of Kantan City" (Japanese reading). As described in the scroll *Mizukagami Shinsatsu* and the *Mizukagami Kuden no Oboe*, this pillow foretells an intruder. Two terms, 邯鄲師 *(kantan-shi)* and 枕探し *(makura sagashi)*, appear In Japanese customs and are associated with thieves stealing belongings from the beds of travelers. Therefore, here kantan is to avoid theft.

6. Iga and Koka traditions state that when under a net like this, a samurai should have his swords partially drawn and the scabbard jutting out under the netting. This way if a thief takes a sword, he will only grip the scabbard, and the sword will remain with the sleeping man. See Antony Cummins and Yoshie Minami, *Iga and Koka Ninja Skills: The Secret Shinobi Scrolls of Chikamatsu Shigenori* (Stroud, UK: Spellmount, 2013).

7. About three feet behind and to the left of the samurai.

8. Literally, "it is wrapped."

9. Extra information inserted from the scroll *Mizukagami Shinsatsu*.

10. おりかね *(orikane)*, a hook on a scabbard that hooks under the samurai's belt. This gives the scabbard a fixed position and allows a better draw. In this situation, the sword is not in the belt, and the attacker does not need to hold the scabbard in place with his left hand when he draws it. In this case, the attacker has his sword on his shoulder, moves it upward, hooks this fitting onto his topknot, and draws one-handed. From this position it appears that he cannot draw.

11. The last sentence has been inserted from the *Mizukagami Shinsatsu* scroll. The two articles are almost identical, so it has been omitted from the latter and the extra information inserted here.

12. "Enemy" has been inserted from the same article in the *Mizukagami Shinsatsu* scroll. This article has been deleted from the latter.

13. 忍ひ人, "shinobi person." Each version differs in the characters used for

shinobi. The version here is taken from the Tamagawa Library. This should not be mistaken for忍び入 *(shinobi-iru)*.

14. 甲矢乙矢 *(kōya* and *otsuya)*, two arrows held together when performing archery.

15. のうれん *(nouren)*.

16. 縄簾 *(nawasudare)*.

17. 尻戸 *(shirido)*.

18. Gateways and checkpoints were closed at night. A cockerel's cry meant it was morning, and the gate was opened for them to pass.

19. 庚申 *(kōshin)*, one of a sixty-day cycle used in the traditional Japanese calendar, where the day of the Monkey and Kanoe meet, both of which are days of the metal element. The association with metal implies that the hearts of people are cold and cruelty abounds. Also, there is a Japanese traditional gathering called Kōshinmachi (庚申待) on this day, and people did not sleep that night. The origin of this is from China, where it is said that a "worm" that took on human shape, animal shape, or a mixture of human legs and a bull's head, and measured two sun (2 inches) in height, would leave the body and visit the King of Heaven to divulge all the sins of its host. People would therefore stay awake to stop the worms leaving their bodies and reporting their faults. After eighteen festivals over a three-year period, people would erect monuments.

20. とりかき *(torikagi)*.

21. For this skill, see Cummins and Minami, *Iga and Koka Ninja Skills*. However, the original can be taken a second way, to mean "estimate the distance."

22. This last sentence is taken from the *Mizukagami Shinsatsu* scroll. This article has been deleted from that scroll due to the repetition.

23. This first sentence has been moved from the *Mizukagami Shinsatsu* scroll.

24. 武士の道 *(bushi no michi)*.

25. The concept is found in Cummins and Minami, *Iga and Koka Ninja Skills*, 129. The concept is that the body should be set to die and be "solid," meaning brave and formidable, while the mind should remain tactical, giving a samurai a strong and formidable presence while having the ability to find a way out of the situation.

26. 蝋燭 *(rōsoku)*, most likely a form of oil lamp and not a candle in the modern sense of the word.

27. Meaning that as the samurai turns to observe the other man, he must make sure that the blade does not turn away with him.

28. A flicking action to strike the underside of their blades with the hard back edge of the sword.

29. The text has the intention that the strike should be made when the feeling of the correct time and rhythm is apparent, and not to be too analytical on the matter.

30. Some transcriptions only have points 1 and 3.
31. Used to tie the hair back.
32. おかミ討 (*ogamiuchi*).
33. The implication here is that they are not full-time professional shinobi but that they have acquired the skills of the shinobi in their school. It is clear that these articles are concerned with revenge.
34. The title of the article suggests how to deal with bandits, but the text implies that the samurai reading this instruction should be a bandit. The original manual is not clear about whether this is an instruction in the art of thieving, but it may have purposely been made vague. The words *you should* do not appear in the text, but the instructions show that these are actions to be done.
35. Meaning to work as a mountain bandit.
36. *Tsuba.*
37. Unknown point.
38. See note 5, above.
39. This tradition is expanded upon in the *Mizukagami Shinsatsu* scroll.
40. 寝長ケのけむもむ.
41. Meaning move to the left of the ally or opponent and use the sheathed katana to stop the enemy strike.
42. The original text is unclear. This could mean place a hand behind your own back, pull your own scabbard, and break the seal between the sword and scabbard. However, it could also mean that you hold your friend's scabbard to break the seal of the sword in secret to allow him a faster draw.
43. Again, an unclear meaning. It can be interpreted a few ways: maybe to grab the opponent's scabbard and twist the sword in the belt. However, the original is too vague to fully understand. An alternative version is that the sword, which is at your side when sitting, is turned blade inward. This will prepare the blade for drawing when standing to fight. Furthermore, it could refer to the sword being bound with a silk seal in a person's house and bringing about advantage for allies and disadvantage for opponents.
44. Unknown samurai.
45. Literally; "sword in the space between kimonos."
46. Alternative reading: *futokorogatana no daiji.*
47. Tsuba.
48. In Hyōgo province, a remote mountain area.
49. 八重菊 (*yaegiku*).
50. 本尊 (*honzon*). This could indicate a statue.
51. The front and back of a sword changes depending on the type and position it is worn. Here it is a tachi; the correct side can be seen in figure 14.55.
52. *Shinogi.*
53. Ibid.

54. Japanese folklore holds that a fox, upon reaching the age of one thousand years, becomes highly magical and has nine tails.

55. The methods of the shinobi.

56. Documents that carry multiple signatures, letters of promise, and so on.

57. 佛割の志のひ.

58. 沈切, a small flexible saw.

59. Either gold paper or gold leaf.

60. Do not show surprise at such occurrences.

61. A similar poem also appears in Yoshimori's poems, poem number 49 in *The Secret Traditions of the Shinobi*. See Antony Cummins and Yoshie Minami, *The Secret Traditions of the Shinobi: Hattori Hanzo's Shinobi Hiden and Other Ninja Scrolls* (Berkeley, CA: Blue Snake Books, 2012).

62. 勢 *(sei)*.

63. Shave the head into the hairline of a samurai.

64. Tsuba.

65. *Bakemono*.

66. Meaning a supernatural creature.

67. 化生之者 *(keshō no mono)*.

68. *Hon'nin*.

69. 悪物 *(ashiki mono)*.

70. Bakemono.

71. Extremely tentative translation. 前トル馬 is an unknown term.

72. 10 p.m.

73. Walking in the chi of yō is a positive aspect, but the middle of the road turns to chi of in after this time, which is negative.

74. The scabbard opening that the sword fits into. The newly chopped end protrudes out of the water.

75. This differs from the *Mizukagami* scroll. Here it says to use a branch and not a walking cane. This is done to leave a false trail.

76. When the samurai has killed someone, this chant must be spoken.

77. Meaning when the nights get longer. Traditionally the Japanese New Year is around February.

78. 大福掛物 *(daifuku kakemono)*.

79. The second floor; in British English called the first floor.

80. ケン筆 *(kenpitsu)*.

81. This could be a stabbing or a hitting motion, or may also be shooting with a bow.

82. Possibly the cardinal points.

83. The stone is to be thrown into the water to make the pursuer think that the shinobi has jumped into the water.

84. Literally "inside the ship."

85. The text does not say so, but it is likely that this mean small blades with the image of Kurikara Fudō engraved on them.

86. *Chūgen,* servants to samurai.

87. Meaning count eight and four places around the traditional compass directions (fig. 14.85) in a clockwise direction. Those are the directions thieves will come from.

88. Most likely the hands clasped together with the index and middle finger extended.

89. Possibly a skill for a horse but may also be used for humans.

90. It is unknown whether burning pine resin is a magical element or if it is to induce coughing to be able to distinguish a male cough from female.

91. *Keshikaran-mono.*

92. Possibly エン佛 *(en butsu)* rather than ユン佛 *(yun hotoke).*

93. Modern-day Yamaguchi Prefecture.

94. Literally "red bat."

95. A version of this poem is also found in Yoshimori's one hundred shinobi poems, number 42 in Cummins and Minami, *The Secret Traditions of the Shinobi.*

96. Ear wax is mixed into the ink and an ear pick is put in the writing set so that the samurai can get ear wax when out on campaign or traveling.

97. The syntax sounds as if the shinobi are making the birds chirp as a part of their strategy and plans.

98. Many of those that replicate early scrolls have been omitted from this list but are still found in this book.

15. Ritual Magic

1. Images in this scroll are courtesy of the Amagasaki Municipal Archives (尼崎市立地域研究史料館蔵石田太郎氏文書をもとに加工).

2. For example, for the author, honmyō is the Horse, and eight places along the zodiac is the Ox, the author's ganshin. This way, a person can find the points that affect his or her horoscope.

3. Serge Mol, *Invisible Armor: An Introduction to the Esoteric Dimension of Japan's Classical Warrior Arts* (Mol, Belgium: Eibusha, 2008).

16. Kuden — Oral Traditions

1. *Hae,* in modern Japanese.

18. Bonus Material

1. Different sources have variations on this date.

Appendix E. Japanese Transcriptions

1. 戦国時代に活躍した剣豪で、塚原卜伝と互角に戦い引き分けとなったという逸話がある。13歳で郷里を離れ、剣の修行をつみ、29歳のとき郷里に戻り、深甚流を編み出したと伝えられている。甚四郎についての記録は後世のものだけで、彼自身の書いたものや、生存していた頃の史料はなく、彼の生没年すら不明である。しかしながら、深甚流は江戸時代、加賀藩の武学校経武館に伝授され、多くの子弟を養育した。

2. 慶尊院とする伝書もあるが、二木新十郎政長と思われる。

3. 深甚流では、「みずかがみ」と読む。萩原重蔵の伝書も「みずかがみ」と読むが、現在、伝わる無拍子流柔術の技名は「すいきょう」と読む。

4. 他書では「岩井」となっているものもあるが、上松先生の伝書には「岸井」と書かれている。

5. 近年では利家を藩祖、初代藩主を利長とし、綱紀を四代目藩主とする解釈もある。

6. 「吉平」と書かれているものもある。

7. 近年では十二代目藩主とする解釈もある。

8. 「宗助」と書かれているものもある。

9. 奥書の「興」の文字は「與」にも見える。『加賀藩経武館武藝小伝』[示野喜三郎, 1975]では「与三兵衛」。

10. 近年では十代目藩主とする解釈もある。

11. 安政の頃(1854年頃)に加えられた。

12. 文政11年(1828)11月には、石丸弥太郎は経武館で無拍子流と一相流を教授していた。金子吉兵衛の弟子・石丸太郎政より無拍子流を学ぶ。(『加賀藩経武館武藝小伝』[示野喜三郎, 1975])

13. 大田清蔵は、一惣無躰流を編んで、安政頃(1854〜)、山岸流居合と共に一惣無躰流を経武館で教授した。(『加賀藩経武館武藝小伝』[示野喜三郎, 1975])

14. ここでは、大田鍋次郎を一相無躰流としているが、『加賀藩経武館武藝小伝』[示野喜三郎, 1975]では、大田鍋次郎の弟子・大田清蔵が一惣無躰流を編み出したとある。また、大田鍋次郎は、無拍子流を金子吉兵衛の弟子・下村冬蔵から、一相流を松本是太夫に学び、二流を折衷し一相無拍子流と称し、安政年頃(1854〜)無拍子流と共に経武館で教授していたという。

15. 近年では十二代目とする解釈もある。

16. 山立ち。山賊のこと。

17. ノリ(血)

18. 邯鄲の枕。唐の沈既済の小説『枕中記』の故事のひとつ。また、古くは、宿泊して目が覚めたら就寝中に盗難の被害にあっていたという状況を邯鄲といった。

19. 方人(かたうど)。味方、仲間のこと。

20. 甲矢(はや)と思われる。2本持って射る矢のうち、初めに射る矢。

21. 乙矢(おとや)。2番目に射る矢。

22. 函谷関(かんこくかん)。中国河南省にあった関所。

23. 「敗軍」か?

24. 傾くの意か。

25. 泥み

26. 髻(たぶさ、もとどり)。日本で行われた昔の結髪法のひとつで、髪を頭上に束ねたもの、またはその部分をいう。

27. 検脈

28. (Figure 14.77) 参照

29. 鱗(ウロコ)

30. 不明

31. 空手水(からちょうず)。柄杓で手に水をかけるまねをして、手を清めたことにすること。

32. 不明

33. かわらけ(土器)

34. ケサヌ(消さぬ)と思われる。

35. アラハル(現る)か?

36. 唾(つばき)

37. タカイ(違い)

38. コト成(異なる)

39. 足を切られた化物は、前足を取られた(失った)馬のようである、の意か?

40. 「拾う」の書き間違いか。

41. 「拾ハ子ハ(拾わねば)」の書き間違いか。

42. 意味不明

43. 者き物(はきもの、履物)

44. あとさき(後先)

45. 弓手(ゆんで)。左手のこと。

46. 馬手(めて)。右手のこと。

47. 七曜の星(しちようのほし)。北斗七星のこと。

48. 柔らかなるところ

49. 寝さすべし

50. もし二階などは

51. 撞く(つく)。つきさす。

52. 「四方に」か?

53. 屋根へ上る

54. トモス(灯す)か?

55. フセカン(ふせがん)か?

56. 斜に

57. 押手ノ(右手の)」か。

58. 「ヒ」は「此」の書き間違いか?

59. のふれん(暖簾)

60. 函谷関(かんこくかん)

61. とり鍵

62. 「取」か?

63. 「置」か?

64. 「計」か?

65. 半夏(はんげ)。カラスビシャクの根茎を、外皮を取り除いて乾燥したもの。漢方で去痰・鎮嘔(ちんおう)・鎮吐薬などに用いる。

66. 不動のじく(慈救)の咒(呪)。不動明王の慈救呪。

67. ヘカラス(べからず)

68. 瘧(おこり)。一定の周期で発熱し、悪寒やふるえのおこる病気。マラリヤ性の熱病の昔の名称。

69. 芦毛

70. 屋根

71. トコロ(野老)。ヤマイモ科の蔓性多年草。根茎は正月の飾り物とされ、また苦味を抜けば食用となり、煎(せん)じて消炎・利尿薬とし、腰やひざの痛みに用いる。

BIBLIOGRAPHY

Cummins, Antony. *Samurai and Ninja: The Real Story behind the Japanese Warrior Myth that Shatters the Bushido Mystique*. Clarendon, VT: Tuttle, 2015.

Cummins, Antony, and Yoshie Minami. *Iga and Koka Ninja Skills: The Secret Shinobi Scrolls of Chikamatsu Shigenori*. Stroud, UK: Spellmount, 2013.

Cummins, Antony, and Yoshie Minami. *The Secret Traditions of the Shinobi: Hattori Hanzo's Shinobi Hiden and Other Ninja Scrolls*. Berkeley, CA: Blue Snake Books, 2012.

Mol, Serge. *Invisible Armor: An Introduction to the Esoteric Dimension of Japan's Classical Warrior Arts*. Mol, Belgium: Eibusha, 2008.

伊賀上野観光協会『忍秘展』伊賀上野観光協会、2007年

池田諭『沢庵不動智神妙録』徳間書店、1970年

剣聖草深甚四郎編纂委員会『剣聖草深甚四郎』川北町役場、1990年

示野喜三郎編『加賀武術の遺蹤』金沢工業大学古武道部、1992年

示野喜三郎編『加賀藩経武舘武藝小伝』金沢工業大学且月会郷土史古武術調査部、1975年

戸部新十郎『兵法秘伝考』新人物往来社、1995年

野々市町立図書館『野々市町のいしぶみ』野々市町教育委員会、1992年

日置謙編『加能強度辞彙』金沢文化協会、1942年

綿谷雪・山田忠志編『武芸流派大事典』新人物往来社、1969年

その他、Appendix Dの表にある伝書類（Antony Cummins所蔵、尼崎市立地域研究史料館石田太郎文書所蔵、上松義幸氏所蔵、金沢市立玉川図書館近世史料館所蔵、小松市立図書館所蔵。川北町立図書館所蔵・鏑木悠紀夫家文書所蔵・畑俊六家文書所蔵の伝書については『剣聖草深人四郎』掲載の翻刻を参考）

INDEX

ABOUT THE AUTHOR

For more information about the work of ANTONY CUMMINS and his team, see current social media sites and his website www.natori.co.uk. Cummins also leads the resurrection of the samurai school of war Natori Ryū; information can be found at the website. He is the author of multiple books on the samurai and the shinobi, including *True Path of the Ninja*, *The Book of Ninja*, *The Book of Samurai*, *Samurai War Stories*, *Iga and Koka Ninja Skills*, *In Search of the Ninja*, *The Secret Traditions of the Shinobi*, and *Samurai and Ninja*. He has also published *The Illustrated Guide to Viking Martial Arts*.

TITLES BY ANTONY CUMMINS

available from Blue Snake Books

The Secret Traditions of the Shinobi
978-1-58394-435-6

Secrets of the Ninja
978-1-58394-864-4

BLUE SNAKE BOOKS
WWW.BLUESNAKEBOOKS.COM

Blue Snake Books, inaugurated in 2005, is one of the largest publishers of internal and historical martial arts books in the world.

About North Atlantic Books

North Atlantic Books (NAB) is a 501(c)(3) nonprofit publisher committed to a bold exploration of the relationships between mind, body, spirit, culture, and nature. Founded in 1974, NAB aims to nurture a holistic view of the arts, sciences, humanities, and healing. To make a donation or to learn more about our books, authors, events, and newsletter, please visit www.northatlanticbooks.com.